CENSUS OF INDIA 1891

CENSUS OF INDIA, 1891

BOOK-41: VOLUME XXVI

RAJPUTANA

PART II.—THE PROVINCIAL
TABLES AND REMARKS

LIEUT -COL H. B. ABBOTT

GYAN

Published by

Gyan Publishing House
5, Ansari Road
Daryaganj, New Delhi-110002
Phone: 011-47034999, 9811692060
E-mail: books@gyanbooks.com

Distribution Network
gyanbooks.com
India, USA, Canada, UK, Australia

ISBN: 978-81-212-7129-5 (Set) 28 Vols. In 49 Bindings
978-81-212-6911-7 (PB) Book-41, Vol. XXVI, Pt. II

First Published, 1892

2nd Impression 2024

Printed at: Gyan Press, Delhi.

CENSUS OF INDIA 1891

CENSUS OF INDIA, 1891.

VOLUME XXVI.

RAJPUTANA.

PART II.

THE PROVINCIAL TABLES AND REMARKS.

BY

LIEUT.-COL. H. B. ABBOTT, *of the Indian Staff Corps,*
IN CHARGE CENSUS OPERATIONS.

CALCUTTA:
OFFICE OF THE SUPERINTENDENT OF GOVERNMENT PRINTING, INDIA.
1892.

PART II.

CONTENTS.

ERRATA.—Vol. XXVI—Part II.

	Page.	Column.	Line.	Read	For
Provincial Tables.	I	1	14	Pirawa . . .	Purawa.
	II	7	18	2,823,966	2,823,965
	XI	1	7	Jhoonjhnu . . .	Jhoonjhun.
	XX	Foot-note	3	Marwar . . .	Meywar.
	XXVII	1	58	Detached . . .	Attached.
	XXXI	20	42	229,839	220,839
	XLI	17	6	399	400
	XLI	17	7	118	117
	XLI	18	6	203	204
	XLI	18	7	71	70
	LXI	1	38	Bansur . . .	Boosur.
	LXXVI	270	14	7	70

CENSUS OF INDIA, 1891.

VOLUME XXVI.

RAJPUTANA.

PART II.

THE PROVINCIAL TABLES AND REMARKS.

Remarks on Provincial Tables.

1. Such Provincial tables only have been taken in hand as it was found possible to prepare within the time at the disposal of the Rajputana Agency Office; they are the following:—

No. of Tables.	Tables.
I.—	General statement of area, houses and population, by pargannahs or other administrative divisions.
II.—	Variation in the population since the Census of 1881, by pargannahs or other administrative divisions.
III.—	Statement shewing the distribution of the population according to religion, by pargannahs or other administrative divisions.
IV.—	Statement of population for towns with more than 500 inhabitants, by political charges.
V.—	Statement shewing Mussalmans, by sects and by pargannahs or other administrative divisions.
VI.—	Statement shewing the sub-divisions of Rajputs, by territorial units.
VII.—	Statement shewing the number of eunuchs, by caste and age, in two Parts and for territorial units.
VIII.—	Statement shewing the distribution of Christians in Rajputana, by race and for territorial units.

2. The time now left admits of but the briefest remarks being made on these useful tables.

Provincial Table I.

3. The different Political charges stand in the following order as regards their total areas:—

Political Charge.	Area in square miles.
1. Western Rajputana States Residency	52,989
2. Bikanir Agency	23,173
3. Meywar Residency	17,032
4. Jeypore Residency	16,456
5. Haraoti and Tonk Agency*	5,177
6. Eastern States Agency	4,378
7. Kotah Agency	3,784
8. Alwar Agency	3,144
9. Jhalawar Agency	2,722

* Inclusive of Central India area of Tonk = 1,438·93 square miles.

and in the following order of the greatest number of subjects belonging to the States embraced in them:—

	Political Charge.	Population.	Remarks.
1.	Jeypore Residency	2,952,842	
2.	Western Rajputana States Residency	2,834,715	
3.	Meywar Residency*	2,310,024	*Excluding the detached areas of Central India.
4.	Eastern States Agency	1,076,780	
5.	Bikanir Agency	831,955	
6.	Alwar Agency	767,786	
7.	Haraoti and Tonk Agency†	739,390	†Including the Central India portion of Tonk.
8.	Kotah Agency	526,267	
9.	Jhalawar Agency	343,601	
	Total	12,383,360	

4. The statements below shew the densities of the different districts in Jeypore, Alwar, Tonk, Jhalawar, and some of the Marwar districts. Other States have not furnished this information.

Density of Sub-Divisions of States.

Density of Population—Jeypore.

	Sub-Division.	Area in square miles.	Population.	Density.	Remarks.
1	Jeypore (*a*)	2,395	726,253	303·23	(*a*) Including Jeypore City.
2	Dausa (*b*)	1,088	326,279	299·90	(*b*) Including population of Bandikui.
3	Gangapur	277	81,216	293·19	
4	Hindown	674	186,905	277·30	
5	Kot Kasim	6,275	17,054	271·77	
6	Torawatti (*c*)	1,504	315,239	209·60	(*c*) Including ½ Khetri population.
7	Madhopore (*d*)	1,774	264,526	149·11	(*d*) Including ½ population of Ooniara.
8	Shekhawatti (*e*)	3,696	515,331	139·42	(*e*) Including ½ population of Khetri and whole Sikar.
9	Malpura (*f*)	1,460	200,898	137·60	(*f*) Including ½ population of Ooniara.
10	Sambhar	1,597	191,935	120·18	

Density of Population—Alwar.

	Sub-Division.	Area in square miles.	Population.	Density.	Remarks.
1	Govindgarh	52	21,694	417·19	
2	Ramgarh	146	47,912	328·16	
3	Kathumbar	122	38,964	319·38	
4	Alwar	496	141,157	284·59	Including Alwar Town.
5	Mandawar	229	56,886	284·41	
6	Kishengarh	217	61,671	284·19	
7	Luchmangarh	221	60,479	273·66	
8	Behror	264	69,419	262·95	
9	Nimrana	30	7,340	244·66	
10	Rajgarh	373	88,901	238·34	
11	Tijara	257	52,570	204·55	
12	Bansur	330	65,203	197·58	
13	Thana Ghazi	287	54,561	190·10	

Density of Population—Tonk.

	Sub-Divisions.	Area.	Population.	Density.	Remarks.
1	Nimbahera . . .	374·73	65,013	173·11	Rajputana.
2	Tonk	578·59	114,298	197·5	
3	Aligarh	160·09	19,623	122·5	
	Total .	1,113·41	198,934	178·6	
1	Chabra	307·71	46,473	151	Central India (*a*) Males . 96,345 Females . 84,790
2	Parawa	262·18	40,806	155·6	
3	Sironj	869·04	93,856	108	
	Total .	1,438·93	181,135*a*	125·9	
	GRAND TOTAL TONK STATE . . .	2,552·34	379,944	148·9	

Density of Population—Jhalawar.

	Sub-Divisions.	Area.	Population.	Density.	Remarks.
1	Patun	171	51,640	302	Including the Town and Chasni of Jhalra Patun.
2	Awar	80	15,755	196·93	
3	Gungdhar	187	30,821	187·81	
4	Chechat	156	25,066	160·68	
5	Suket	103	16,424	159·44	
6	Iklera	107	16,763	156·66	
7	Dag	168	26,206	156	
8	Pachpahar	131	18,173	138·72	
9	Ghatoli	129	16,007	124·08	
10	Manohar Thana . .	232	27,796	119·81	
11	Bakani	253	28,195	111·10	
12	Chipa Barode . . .	318	34,225	107·62	
13	Asnawar	95	9,600	101·05	
14	Talaiti	243	13,551	55·76	
15	Uprehti	321	13,361	41·62	
1	Chowmehla	566	90,955	160·69	
2	Central Jhalawar . .	1,564	225,716	144·30	
3	Shahabad	564	26,912	47·71	

Density of Population—Marwar.

	Sub-Divisions.	Area.	Population.	Density.	Remarks.
1	Marote	468	56,806	121·38	
2	Nawa	260	31,538	121·30	
3	Bilara	756	84,952	112·37	
4	Sojat	1,277	141,782	111·02	
5	Jaswantpura	1,030	111,550	108·30	
6	Pali	577	58,463	101·32	
7	Jodhpore	3,408	327,367	96·07	Including Jodhpore itself.
8	Jalore	1,800	170,428	94·67	
9	Siwana	1,092	64,747	59·29	
10	Pachbadra	936	52,904	56·52	
11	Sanchore	1,876	95,890	51·11	
12	Malani	6,432	221,184	34·38	
13	Sheo	2,492	30,291	12·15	

Provincial Table No. V.

5. The Mussalman subjects of the Rajputana States, that is to say Mussalmans inclusive of those living in the Central India portions of Tonk, and exclusive of those inhabiting the detached areas of Central India in Meywar, amount in all to 1,005,757. Of these 980,398 are Sunnis, 20,143 are Sihas, and 5,216 are unspecified: in other words, out of every 1,000 Mussalmans, 974·8 are Sunnis, 20 are Sihas, and 5·2 are unspecified. The greatest number of Mussalmans are found in the following Political charges :—

(i)	Western Rajputana States Residency	215,238
(ii)	Jeypore Residency	208,330
(iii)	Alwar Agency	180,426

Sihas are found in the greatest numbers in the Meywar Residency, where they number 10,267, of whom 7,300 are in Meywar itself; the Eastern States Agency comes next with 3,770, Bhartpur containing 3,078 of them.

6. It may here be mentioned that the proportion of Mussalman subjects of Tonk to the total population of that State, which for the Rajputana portion alone is 15 per. cent., falls, with the Central India portion included, to 12 per cent. Abstract No. 1 shews the distribution of the Sihas and Sunnis among the several units and Census divisions, also the female ratio for each sect.

The Sihas shew a higher female ratio than the Sunnis, namely 975 to 885, the proportion being specially high in Alwar 1,367, Bharatpur 1,248, Sirohi 1,063, Dungarpur 1,054, and Karauli 1,000.

7. The highest female ratios among the Sunnis are 970 in Tonk and 964 in Banswara. The figures in this abstract do not take into account the Central India portion of Tonk, but include the small Central India areas in Meywar.

Abstract No. 1.

Statement shewing the distribution of the Sihas and Sunnis among the several units and Census Divisions, also the female ratio for each sect.

	Census units.	Sihas.					Sunnis.					Proportion per 1,000 of each sect in every unit. Distribution.	
		Total number.	Ratio per 1,000 Mussulmans.	Males.	Females.	Female ratio per 1,000 Males.	Total number.	Ratio per 1,000 Mussulmans.	Males.	Females.	Female ratio per 1,000 Males.	Ratio per 1,000 Sihas.	Ratio per 1,000 Sunnis.
1	Marwar	1,056	1	575	481	836	179,097	181	95,617	83,479	873	53	184
2	Jesalmir	130	...	84	46	548	29,313	30	16,677	12,636	758	7	30
3	Bikanir	30	...	17	13	765	79,999	81	43,090	36,909	857	1	83
	Western Division	1,216	1	676	540	798	288,409	292	155,384	133,024	856	61	298
4	Jeypore	1,545	2	799	746	946	195,495	197	102,824	92,672	901	78	202
5	Kishangarh	...	...	...	...	...	9,411	9	4,929	4,482	909	...	10
6	Lawa	...	...	...	...	...	160	...	91	69	758	...	...
7	Bharatpur	3,078	3	1,369	1,709	1,248	104,057	105	56,150	47,907	853	156	107
8	Karauli	28	...	14	14	1,000	8,905	9	4,584	4,321	943	1	9
9	Dholpur	664	1	354	310	876	16,725	17	8,704	8,021	922	34	17
10	Alwar	1,207	1	510	697	1,367	178,982	181	93,733	85,249	909	61	185
11	Tonk (Rajputana)	56	...	38	18	474	29,410	30	14,029	14,481	970	3	30
12	Bundi	118	...	63	55	873	11,488	116	6,076	5,412	891	6	12
13	Shahpura	...	...	...	...	...	3,136	30	1,638	1,498	915	...	3
14	Kotah	392	...	202	190	941	33,529	33	17,248	16,281	944	20	35
15	Jhallawar	1,104	1	606	498	822	20,603	21	10,832	9,771	902	56	21
	Eastern Division	8,192	8	3,955	4,237	1,069	611,901	617	321,738	290,164	902	414	631
16	Meywar	7,300	7	3,787	3,513	928	51,598	52	27,549	24,049	800	369	53
17	Banswara	774	1	444	330	743	4,021	4	2,047	1,974	964	39	4
18	Partabgarh	687	1	372	315	847	4,250	4	2,443	1,807	740	35	4
19	Dungarpur	1,506	2	733	773	1,054	2,808	3	1,496	1,312	877	76	3
20	Sirohi	106	...	49	57	1,063	2,743	3	1,690	1,053	623	6	3
	Southern Division	10,373	10	5,385	4,988	926	65,420	66	35,225	30,195	857	525	67
	RAJPUTANA	19,781	20	10,016	9,765	975	965,730	974	512,347	453,383	885	1,000	1,000

Provincial Table No. VI.

8. Putting aside Banswara and Partabgarh, the total number of Rajputs is 748,868. Of these 79,211 or 106 in a thousand have not had their clans or sub-divisions recorded, and are therefore returned as unspecified. Twenty-five thousand three hundred and fifty-five others have been returned by sub-divisions with doubtful or untraceable names, and as time for further reference and enquiry is wanting, they have collectively been termed "Miscellaneous." Of the remainder the figures for 643,208 or 858 in a thousand Rajputs will be found in Abstract No. 2. The numbers for 2 in the thousand are too small to shew in the Abstract.

Abstract No. 2.

Shewing the proportion of Rajput clans to the total number of Rajputs.

	Clans.	Race.	Total number of Rajputs.	Ratio per 1,000 Rajputs.	Males.	Females.	Female ratio per 1,000 Males.
1	Rahtore	Solar	173,909	232	102,534	71,375	696
2	Kuchhawah	Do.	106,705	142	68,677	38,028	554
3	Chohan, Hara, Deora	Agnicula	101,820	136	54,817	47,003	857
4	Jadon, Bhati, Tuar	Lunar	94,445	126	53,987	40,458	750
5	Ghelote, Sisodia	Solar	76,853	102	41,494	35,359	852
6	Parmar, Panwar	Agnicula	42,553	57	24,021	18,532	771
7	Chalook, Solanki	Do.	13,555	18	7,348	6,207	845
8	Prithihara, Parihar	Do.	11,694	16	5,926	5,768	973
9	Gor	Doubtful	6,259	8	3,511	2,748	783
10	Jhalla, Macwana	Do.	4,800	6	2,915	1,885	647
11	Bir-Goojar	Solar	4,267	6	2,214	2,053	927
12	Sikarwal	Not known	4,045	5	1,930	2,115	1,096
13	Beis or Byce	Solar	805	1	474	331	698
14	Sengar	Not known	768	1	373	395	1,058
15	Doda	Do.	730	1	308	422	1,370
	Total	...	643,208	858	370,529	272,679	736

Note 1.—Excluding Banswara, Partabgarh and Tonk in Central India, but including 396 Males and 322 Females of detached tracts of Central India in Meywar, the total number of Rajputs under the Rajputana Agency is 748,868, *viz.* :—

(1) Clans (1-15) noted above	643,208
(2) Bundela	236
(3) Dabi	226
(4) Dahia	183
(5) Gohel	150
(6) Tak (Takshac)	101
(7) Katti	94
(8) Chaora	74
(9) Dahima	30
(10) Miscellaneous and unspecified	104,566
Total	748,868

2. There are 6,375 Males and 5,561 Females residing in detached tracts of Tonk in Central India.

9. Of all the Rajput clans the Rahtore is the most numerous, bearing the proportion of 232 to 1,000 of all Rajputs; the other principal clans are in the following order of proportion to 1,000 of all Rajputs:—

Kuchhawaha	142
Chohan-Hara-Deora	136
Jadu-Bhati	126
Sisodia	102
Parmar (Pramara)	57
Solanki	18
Jhala Macwana	6

10. In the next Abstract, No. 3, is shewn the distribution of each of these 15 clans among the several Census divisions and territorial units.

Abstract No. 3.

Distribution of Rajput clans throughout Rajputana shewing the proportion per 1,000 of each clan in every unit.

		1.—Rahtore.					2.—Kachhawah.					3.—Chohan.				
		Total number.	Ratio per 1,000 Rahtores.	Males.	Females.	Female ratio per 1,000 Males.	Total number.	Ratio per 1,000 Kachawah.	Males.	Females.	Female ratio per 1,000 Males.	Total number.	Ratio per 1,000 Chohans.	Males.	Females.	Female ratio per 1,000 Males.
1	Marwar	86,858	499	56,654	30,204	533	13,944	131	5,501	8,443	1,535	25,803	253	13,866	11,937	861
2	Jesalmir	4,463	26	1,938	2,525	1,303	7	...	7	...	...	1,010	9	490	520	1,061
3	Bikanir	27,754	160	18,638	9,116	489	7,479	70	4,155	3,324	800	5,851	57	3,104	2,747	885
	Western Division	119,075	685	77,230	41,845	542	21,430	201	9,663	11,767	1,218	32,664	320	17,460	15,204	871
4	Jeypore	19,135	110	5,355	13,780	2,573	66,873	627	48,590	18,283	376	16,583	163	8,098	8,485	1,048
5	Kishengarh	3,919	23	2,406	1,513	629	1,393	13	553	840	1,519	216	2	126	90	714
6	Lawa	38	...	17	21	1,285	54	...	31	23	742	1	...	...	1	...
7	Bharatpur	501	3	273	228	835	1,593	15	955	638	668	1,832	18	993	839	845
8	Karauli	192	1	97	95	979	809	8	232	577	2,487	513	5	212	301	1,420
9	Dholpur	351	2	65	286	4,400	303	3	110	193	1,755	1,934	10	462	1,472	3,186
10	Tonk	533	3	371	162	437	905	9	481	424	881	651	6	376	275	731
11	Bundi	388	2	177	211	1,192	739	7	271	468	1,727	3,073	30	1,996	1,077	540
12	Shahpura	370	2	216	154	713	240	2	131	109	832	73	...	39	34	872
13	Alwar	1,307	8	653	654	1,001	10,159	98	6,691	3,768	563	8,718	86	5,200	3,518	677
14	Jhalawar	1,150	7	675	475	704	587	6	367	220	599	1,848	18	886	962	1,086
15	Kota	775	4	452	323	715	1,242	12	551	691	1,254	8,063	79	4,569	3,494	765
	Eastern Division	28,659	165	10,757	17,902	1,664	85,197	798	58,963	26,234	445	43,505	427	22,957	20,548	895
16	Meywar	21,349	123	12,068	9,281	769	11	...	8	3	375	18,793	185	10,195	8,598	843
17	Banswara	...					Details not furnished by the Durbar.									
18	Partabgarh	...					Details not furnished by the Durbar.									
19	Dungarpur	3,385	14	1,786	1,599	895	53	...	29	24	828	3,507	34	1,912	1,595	834
20	Sirohi	1,430	8	682	748	1,097	...	...	...	...	...	3,316	33	2,264	1,052	469
21	Cantonments	11	...	11	...	...	14	...	14	...	...	35	...	29	6	207
	Southern Division	26,175	150	14,547	11,628	799	78	1	51	27	529	25,651	252	14,400	11,251	781
	RAJPUTANA	173,909	1,000	102,534	71,375	696	106,705	1,000	68,677	38,028	554	101,820	1,000	54,817	47,003	857

		4.—Sesodia.					5.—Jadon.					6.—Jhalla.				
		Total Number.	Ratio per 1,000 Sesodias.	Males.	Females.	Female ratio per 1,000 Males.	Total Number.	Ratio per 1,000 Jadons.	Males.	Females.	Female ratio per 1,000 Males.	Total Number.	Ratio per 1,000 Jhallas.	Males.	Females.	Female ratio per 1,000 Males.
1	Marwar	13,622	177	4,866	8,756	1,799	29,173	309	16,295	12,873	790	207	43	118	89	754
2	Jesalmir	428	5	176	252	1,432	13,711	145	8,712	4,999	574	...	...	...	...	...
3	Bikanir	1,313	17	690	623	903	13,850	147	7,136	6,714	940	37	8	23	14	609
	Western Division	15,363	200	5,732	9,631	1,680	56,734	601	32,143	24,591	765	244	51	141	103	730
4	Jeypore	1,309	17	654	646	988	15,194	161	9,425	5,769	612	...	...	...	...	...
5	Kishengarh	155	2	55	100	1,818	267	3	158	109	670	...	...	...	...	...
6	Lawa	3	...	...	3	...	1	...	...	1	...	...	...	...	...	...
7	Bharatpur	77	1	32	45	1,406	2,878	30	1,672	1,206	721	...	...	...	...	...
8	Karauli	101	1	48	53	1,104	4,905	52	3,334	1,571	471	...	...	...	...	...
9	Dholpur	335	4	118	217	1,839	3,879	41	2,283	1,596	699	...	...	...	...	...
10	Tonk	616	8	370	246	665	127	1	72	55	764	...	...	...	...	...
11	Bundi	392	5	112	280	2,500	170	2	84	86	1,024	77	16	9	68	7,556
12	Shahpura	1,027	13	588	439	747	232	2	129	103	798	1	...	...	1	...
13	Alwar	186	2	104	82	788	2,926	31	1,189	1,737	1,461	...	...	...	...	...
14	Jhalawar	993	13	525	468	891	644	7	413	231	559	1,385	289	970	415	428
15	Kota	843	11	355	488	1,375	2,051	22	1,207	844	699	205	42	98	107	1,092
	Eastern Division	6,028	78	2,961	3,067	1,036	33,274	352	19,966	13,308	667	1,668	347	1,077	591	549
16	Meywar	53,528	696	31,737	21,791	687	4,143	44	1,717	2,426	1,413	2,861	596	1,684	1,177	699
17	Banswara						Details not furnished.									
18	Partabgarh						Details not furnished.									
19	Dungarpur	1,802	23	971	831	856	272	3	142	130	915	27	6	13	14	1,077
20	Sirohi	103	1	67	36	537	...	...	...	...	...	...	...	...	...	...
21	Cantonments	29	...	26	3	115	22	...	19	3	198	...	...	...	...	...
	Southern Division	55,462	722	32,801	22,661	691	4,437	47	1,878	2,559	1,363	2,888	602	1,697	1,191	702
	RAJPUTANA	76,853	1,000	41,494	35,359	852	94,445	1,000	53,987	40,458	750	4,800	1,000	2,915	1,885	647

Abstract No. 3—*contd.*

Distribution on Rajput clans throughout Rajputana shewing the proportion per 1000 of each clan in every unit—contd.

		7.—Gor.					8.—Bir-Goojar.					9.—Sikerwal.				
		Total number.	Ratio per 1,000 Gors.	Males.	Females.	Female ratio per 1,000 Males.	Total number.	Ratio per 1,000 Bir-Goojars.	Males.	Females.	Female ratio per 1,000 Males.	Total number.	Ratio per 1,000 Sikerwals.	Males.	Females.	Female ratio per 1,000 Males.
1	Marwar	...	...	...	...	...	...	...	...	...	...	...	...	...	...	...
2	Jesalmir	...	...	...	...	...	...	...	...	...	...	...	...	...	...	...
3	Bikanir	...	...	...	...	...	...	...	...	...	...	...	...	...	...	...
	Western Division	...	...	...	...	...	...	...	...	...	...	...	...	...	...	...
4	Jeypore	2,057	329	1,189	868	730	1,555	364	832	723	869	405	100	214	191	893
5	Kishengarh	94	15	47	17	362	308	72	162	146	901	...	...	...	...	...
6	Lawa	3	...	1	2	2,000	1	...	...	1	...	...	...	...	...	...
7	Bharatpur	493	79	307	186	606	146	34	78	68	872	386	95	218	168	771
8	Karauli	189	30	83	106	1,205	277	65	117	160	1,365	...	...	...	...	...
9	Dholpur	663	106	391	272	696	104	24	59	45	763	2,660	658	1,284	1,376	1,072
10	Tonk	...	...	...	...	...	...	...	...	...	...	34	8	20	14	700
11	Bundi	158	25	73	85	1,164	2	...	...	2	...	61	15	38	23	605
12	Shahpura	112	18	68	44	647	...	...	...	...	...	...	...	...	...	...
13	Alwar	352	56	205	147	717	1,702	399	900	802	809	180	44	54	126	2,333
14	Jhallawar	141	22	75	66	880	95	22	45	50	1,111	166	41	102	64	627
15	Kota	590	94	353	237	671	11	3	8	3	375	153	38	...	153	...
	Eastern Division	4,852	775	2,792	2,060	774	4,201	983	2,201	2,000	909	4,045	1,000	1,930	2,115	1,096
16	Meywar	1,407	225	719	688	957	66	15	13	53	4,077	...	...	...	...	...
17	Banswara						Details not furnished by the Durbar.									
18	Partabgarh						Details not furnished by the Durbar.									
19	Dungarpur	...	...	...	...	...	...	...	...	...	...	...	...	...	...	...
20	Sirohi	...	...	...	...	...	...	...	...	...	...	...	...	...	...	...
21	Cantonments	...	...	...	...	...	...	...	...	...	...	...	...	...	...	...
	Southern Division	1,407	225	719	688	957	66	15	13	53	4,077	...	...	...	...	...
	RAJPUTANA	6,259	1,000	3,511	2,748	783	4,267	1,000	2,214	2,053	927	4,045	1,000	1,930	2,115	1,096

No.	State	10.—Beis or Byce. Total number.	Ratio per 1,000 Beis.	Males.	Females.	Female ratio per 1,000 Males.	11.—Sengar. Total number.	Ratio per 1,000 Senyas.	Males.	Females.	Female ratio per 1,000 Males.	12.—Doda. Total number.	Ratio per 1,000 Dodas.	Males.	Females.	Female ratio per 1,000 Males.
1	Marwar	...	...	...	...	...	...	...	...	...	...	...	...	...	...	...
2	Jesalmir	...	...	...	...	...	...	...	...	...	...	...	...	...	...	...
3	Bikanir	...	...	...	...	...	...	...	...	...	...	...	...	...	...	...
	Western Division	...	...	...	...	...	...	...	...	...	...	...	...	...	...	...
4	Jeypore	309	384	184	125	679	...	...	...	...	...	...	...	...	...	...
5	Kishengarh	...	...	...	...	...	...	...	...	...	...	...	...	...	...	...
6	Lawa	...	...	...	...	...	...	...	...	...	...	...	...	...	...	...
7	Bharatpur	3	4	3	...	...	...	...	...	...	...	...	...	...	...	...
8	Karauli	164	204	76	88	1,158	426	555	209	217	1,038	...	...	...	...	...
9	Dholpur	31	38	9	22	2,444	19	25	7	12	1,714	...	...	...	...	...
10	Tonk	25	31	16	9	562	300	390	147	153	1,041	...	...	...	...	...
11	Bundi	15	19	9	6	666	...	...	...	...	...	...	...	...	...	...
12	Shahpura	...	...	...	...	...	...	...	...	...	...	...	...	...	...	...
13	Alwar	105	130	65	40	615	...	...	...	...	...	...	...	...	...	...
14	Jhallawar	150	186	109	41	376	17	22	10	7	700	...	...	...	...	...
15	Kota	...	...	...	...	...	6	8	...	6	...	...	...	...	...	...
	Eastern Division	802	996	471	331	698	768	1,000	373	395	1,059	...	...	...	...	...
16	Meywar	...	...	...	...	...	...	...	...	...	...	700	459	289	411	1,422
17	Banswara							Details not furnished.								
18	Partabgarh							Details not furnished.								
19	Dungarpur	...	...	...	...	...	...	...	...	...	...	30	41	19	11	579
20	Sirohi	...	...	...	...	...	...	...	...	...	...	...	...	...	...	...
21	Cantonments	3	4	3	...	...	...	...	...	...	...	...	...	...	...	...
	Southern Division	3	4	3	...	...	...	...	...	...	...	730	1,000	308	422	1,370
	RAJPUTANA	805	1,000	474	331	698	768	1,000	373	395	1,059	730	1,000	308	422	1,370

11. Noting the more important clans, it will be found that out of every thousand Rahtores, 685 are in the Western Division of whom 499 are in Marwar alone; the Eastern Division has 165 of whom 110 were found in Jeypore; the Southern Division has the remaining 150 of whom 123 are in Meywar.

The Kachhawah ratios are for the divisions—

Eastern	798	Western	201
Southern	1		

Among the units, their highest ratios are—

Jeypore	627	Alwar	98
Marwar	131	Bikanir	70

For Chohans, the divisional ratios are—

Eastern	427	Western	320
Southern	252		

Their highest ratios in the units are—

Marwar	253	Jeypore	163
Meywar	185	Alwar	86
Kotah	79		

The ratios for Jadons are, in the divisions—

Western	601	Eastern	352
Southern	47		

In the units their highest ratios, are—

Marwar	309	Bikanir	147
Jeypore	161	Jesalmir	145
Karauli	52		

The Sisodias have the following ratios for the divisions—

Southern	722	Western	200
Eastern	78		

Their highest in the units are—

Meywar	696	Dungarpur	23
Marwar	177	Bikanir	17
Jeypore	17		

The Jhala Ratios are—

For Divisions.		For Units.	
Southern	602	Jhalawar	289
Eastern	347	Marwar	43
Western	51	Kota	42
Meywar	596		

12. In the more important Rajput clans, the ratio of females to 1,000 males, as ascertained from the provincial tables, is as follows:—

Chohan	857	Rahtore	696
Sesodia	852	Jhala	647
Jadon	750	Kachhawah	554

In the Doda, Sikarwal and Sengar clans, now of little note and insignificant in numbers, the females are in excess of the males.

13. In considering the female ratios in the Census divisions and Territorial units it has to be borne in mind that in accordance with Rajput custom wives have been entered in the enumerators' schedules by their fathers' and not their husbands' clans, and therefore, speaking generally, where the female ratios of a clan are the lowest and highest there the daughters of the clan have been given and received in marriage, respectively.

Abstract No. 4.

Female ratios among Rajputs.

Rahtore.		Kachhawah.		Chohan.		Jadon.		Sesodia.		Parmar.		Solankhi.		Jhala.	
Eastern Division . . 1,664		Western Division . 1,218		Eastern Division . 895		Southern Division . 1,363		Western Division . 1,680		......		......		Western Division . 730	
Southern " . . 799		*Rajputana* . . . 554		Western " . 871		Western " . 765		Eastern " . 1,036		......		......		Southern " . 702	
Rajputana . . . 696		Southern Division . 539		*Rajputana* . . . 857		*Rajputana* . . 750		*Rajputana* . . . 852		......		......		*Rajputana* . . . 647	
Western Division . . 542		Eastern " . . 445		Southern Division . 781		Eastern Division . 667		Southern Division . 691		......		......		Eastern Division . . 549	
Highest.	Lowest.	Highest.	Lowest.	Highest.	Lowest.	Highest.	Lowest.	Highest.	Lowest.	Highest.	Lowest.	Highest.	Lowest.	Highest.	Lowest.
Jeypore , 2,573	Bikanir . 489	Karauli 2,487	Jeypore . 376	Dholpur 3,186	Sirohi . 469	Alwar . 1,461	Karauli 471	Marwar 1,799	Meywar 687	...	...	...	...	Bundi . 7,556	Jhalawar 428
Jesalmir 1,303	Marwar . 533	Bundi . 1,737	Alwar . 554 563	Jhalawar 1,086	Bundi . 540	Meywar 1,413	Jesalmir 574	Dholpur 1,839	Tonk . 665	...	...	...	...	Kota . 1,092	Bikanir . 609
Sirohi . 1,097	Kishengarh 629	Marwar 1,535	...	Jesalmir 1,061	Alwar . 677	Bikanir 940	Jhalawar 559	Bundi . 2,500	Shahpura 747	...	...	...	...	Dungarpur 1,077	Meywar . 647 699
Dungarpur 895	696	Kishngarh 1,519	...	Jeypore 1,048	Tonk . 731	Marwar 790 750	Jeypore 612	Kota . 1,375	Alwar . 788	...	...	...	...	Marwar 754	...
Meywar . 769	...	Kota . 1,354	...	Karauli 1,420	Kota . 765 857	...	...	Jesalmir 1,432	852	...	...	...	...	...	...

14. In this way, it will be seen from the figures in Abstract No. 4 that the Chohan girls of Sirohi, Bundi, Alwar, Tonk and Kota, whose ratios range from 469 to 765, have been given in marriage to other clans in Karauli, Jeypore, Jesalmir, Jhallawar and Dholpur in which States the ratio of Chohan females range from 1,048 to 3,186.

The Sesodia girls of Meywar, Tonk, Shahpura and Alwar, where the ratios are from 687 to 788, have been married into other clans residing in Kota, Bundi, Dholpur, Jesalmir and Marwar where the Sesodia female ratio is from 1,375 to 2,500.

The girls of the Jadon clan in Karauli, Jesalmir, Jhallawar and Jeypore, where their ratios vary from 471 to 612, have been mated with other clans in Marwar, Bikanir, Meywar and Alwar where their ratios are from 790 to 1,461.

The daughters of the Rahtore in Bikanir, Marwar and Kishengargh, in which States the female ratio ranges from 489 to 629, have been mostly given in marriage to the other principal clans living in Meywar, Sirohi, Jesalmir and Jeypore as in these States the Rahtore female ratio ranges from 769 to 2,573.

The Jhala girls of Jhallawar, Bikanir and Meywar (ratios 428 to 699) have found mates in other clans living in Marwar, Dungarpur, Kota and Bundi where the Jhala female ratio is from 754 to 7,556. Lastly, the Kacháwah girls of Jeypore and Alwar, where the female ratio of the clan is 376 and 563, have been given in marriage to other clans, mostly Rahtore, residing in Kota, Kishengarh, Marwar, Bundi and Karauli, where the Kachawah female ratio stands at, from 1,254 to 2,487.

15. As rulers over the greatest number of subjects, the Rajput clans stand in the order below:—

Clan.	Number of subjects.
Kachawah	3,600,063
Rahtore	3,477,339
Sesodia	2,030,477
Chohan	1,010,827
Jhala	343,601
Jadon	272,288

Jat. 920, 93.

16. Abstract No. 5, from which the above figures are taken, shews also the ratio these clans bear to the total population of the States they are ruling races in. The Jadon has the highest ratio of 61 in a thousand and the Jhala the lowest with only 4 in a thousand. By way of comparison it will be noted that Jats and Mussalmans as ruling races have ratios of 110 and 40 to the total population.

Abstract No. 5.

Ruling Races and States in the order of highest ratios of the Ruling Race to total Population.

	Ruling Race.	Total Population.	Number of the Ruling Race.	Ratio of the Ruling Race to 1,000 of the Total Population.	Remarks.
1	Jat	920,193	10,102	110	
2	Rajput—Jadon	272,288	18,616	61	
3	Mussalman—Pathan	198,934	7,929	40	
4	Rajput—Rahtore	3,477,339	118,531	34	
5	Rajput—Sesodia	2,030,477	55,359	22	
6	Rajput—Kachawah	3,600,063	77,332	21	
7	Rajput—Chohan	1,010,827	14,452	14	
8	Rajput—Jhala	343,601	1,385	4	

Abstract No. 5 —contd.

Ruling Races and States in the order of highest ratios of the Ruling Race to total Population—contd.

	Ruling Race.	Total Population.	Number of the Ruling Race.	Ratio of the Ruling Race to 1,000 of the Total Population.	Remarks.
	State.				
1	Bharatpur (Jat)	640 303	98,277	154	
2	Jesalmir (Rajput—Jadon)	115,701	13,711	119	
3	Tonk in Rajputana (Mussalman—Pathan*)	198,934	7,929	40	* The figures for Central India population are :— Total Population 379,944 Mussalman—Pathans 10,738 Ratio of the Ruling Race . . 28
4	Marwar (Rajput—Rahtore)	2,519,868	86,858	34	
5	Bikanir (Rajput—Rahtore)	831,955	27,754	33	
6	Kishengarh (Rajput—Rahtore)	125,516	3,919	31	
7	Karauli (Rajput—Jadon)	156,587	4,905	31	
8	Meywar (Rajput—Sesodia)	1,862,328	53,528	29	
9	Jeypore (Rajput—Kachawah)	2,832,276	66,873	24	
10	Sirohi (Rajput—Chohan)	188,885	3,316	18	
11	Kota (Rajput—Chohan)	526,267	8,063	15	
12	Alwar (Rajput—Kachawah)	767,786	10,459	14	
13	Dungarpur (Rajput—Sesodia)	165,400	1,802	11	
14	Bundi (Rajput—Chohan)	295,675	3,073	10	
15	Dholpur (Jat)	279,890	2,825	10	
16	Jhalawar (Rajput—Jhala)	343,601	1,385	4	

17. In the same abstract the ratios of the ruling races to the total population of each State are also given. Bharatpur heads the list with a ratio of 154, followed by Jesalmir with 119, while Dholpur and Jhalawar are last with ratios of 10 and 4.

Owing to the absence of figures from Banswara and Partabgarh, the ratio for the Sesodia clan is not altogether correct, and the ratios for the States are incomplete.

Provincial Table No. VII.

18. The eunuchs number altogether 356. Their highest numbers in the different States are as follows :—

Marwar	125	Bharatpur	20
Jeypore	68	Tonk	16
Kota	30	Kishengarh	13
Meywar	22	Dholpur and Alwar	12 each.

By religions, their numbers are—

Hindu and Jain	186	Animistic (Bhil)	3
Mussalman	167		

For castes, the highest figures are—

Brahmin and Rajput	20 each.	Mahajans	9 (The few Jains are among them.)
Mali	14		
Jat	13	Kumhar	8

Forty-eight have been returned without caste and been grouped as, "Others."

Of the total Mussalman eunuchs no less than 103 are Sheikhs.

Taken by age, only 5 eunuchs were found under 4 years of age, their numbers rise up to 9 for the period 15 to 19. At 20 to 24 there is a sudden rise to 24, and at 30 to 34 the number reaches 57 ; at this age period and at 60 and over when the number is even more, *i.e.*, 73, the most eunuchs were found alive. Between these last two periods the numbers fluctuate and fall at times to 17.

Provincial Table VIII.

19. The 1,855 Christians in Rajputana are distributed by race as follows :—

	Males.	Females.	TOTAL.
Foreign	414	351	765
Eurasians	237	207	444
Native Converts	387	259	646

Among the Foreigners the numbers below shew the races chiefly represented in the order of greatest magnitude :—

	Males.	Females.	TOTAL.
1 English	281	223	504
2 Irish	67	54	121
3 Scotch	49	50	99
4 American	5	9	14
5 German	3	8	11

H. B. ABBOTT, *Lieut.-Colonel.*

ABU;
Dated 2nd June, 1892.

RAJPUTANA AGENCY.

CENSUS OF 1891.

PROVINCIAL TABLE I.

General Statement of Area, Houses and Population by Pergunnahs, Tehsils or other administrative divisions.

This Table includes the following details :—

DETAILS.	NUMBER OF		OCCUPIED HOUSES.			POPULATION.									AREA.
						TOTAL.			MALES.			FEMALES.			
	Town.	Village.	TOTAL.	Town.	Village.	TOTAL.	Town.	Village.	TOTAL.	Town.	Village.	TOTAL.	Town.	Village.	
1	2	3	4	5	6	7	8	9	10	11	12	13	14	15	16
(i).—Persons enumerated in Native States in Rajputana . . .	123	30,278	2,169,971	289,194	1,880,777	11,955,670	1,509,405	10,446,265	6,319,651	778,821	5,540,830	5,636,019	730,584	4,905,435	* Total area = 129,065 square miles including 210 square miles of disputed lands.
(ii).—Persons enumerated in Railway limits and Europeans and Eurasians in Rajputana .	...	...	3,710	3,710	...	13,967	13,921	46	9,004	8,972	32	4,963	4,949	14	
(iii).—Persons enumerated in cantonments of Erinpura, Kherwara, Kotra and Abu (Sanitarium)	...	4	993	...	993	2,749	...	2,749	2,077	...	2,077	672	...	672	
(iv).—Detached tract of Tonk in Central India, i. e., Chabra, Purawa and Sironj . . .	3	698	40,218	6,059	34,159	181,135	24,790	156,345	96,345	13,225	83,120	84,790	11,565	73,225	
(v).—Unenumerated population—Bhils and Grassias	...	...	...	...	...	229,839	...	229,839	115,165	...	115,165	114,674	...	114,674	
TOTAL RAJPUTANA AGENCY.	126	30,980	2,214,892	298,963	1,915,929	12,383,360	1,548,116	10,835,244	6,542,242	801,018	5,741,224	5,841,118	747,098	5,094,020	
(vi).—Detached tracts of Central India situated in Meywar (Nundwas and Gangapur) . .	1	43	2,751	902	1,849	18,118	6,761	11,357	9,711	3,721	5,990	8,407	3,040	5,367	
GRAND TOTAL .	127	31,023	2,217,643	299,865	1,917,778	12,401,478	1,554,877	10,846,601	6,551,953	804,739	5,747,214	5,849,525	750,138	5,099,387	

* DETAIL OF DISPUTED LANDS.

		Sqr. miles.
1.	Between Jodhpore and Bikanir	8·20
2.	,, ,, and Jesalmir	39·88
3.	,, Oodeypur and Serohi	16·64
4.	,, ,, and Guzerat	1·83
5.	,, ,, and Tonk	4·07
6.	,, ,, and Partabgarh	15·40
7.	,, ,, and Gwalior	3·25
8.	,, ,, and Jhallawar	1·11
9.	,, ,, and Holkar	105·80
10.	,, ,, and Kota	4·96
11.	,, Jeypore and Bikanir	4·95
12.	,, ,, and Karauli	0·30
13.	,, Alwar and Nabha	1·33
14.	,, Tonk and Kota	2·18
	TOTAL	209·90

Table I.—Area, Houses and Population—Rajputana Agency.

Summary of Provincial Table No. I.

Names of Agency and States.	Number of — Town.	Number of — Village.	Occupied Houses. — Total.	Occupied Houses. — Town.	Occupied Houses. — Village.	Population. Total. — Total.	Population. Total. — Town.	Population. Total. — Village.	Population. Males. — Total.	Population. Males. — Town.	Population. Males. — Village.	Population. Females. — Total.	Population. Females. — Town.	Population. Females. — Village.	Area in square miles.
1	2	3	4	5	6	7	8	9	10	11	12	13	14	15	16
(i) MEYWAR RESIDENCY—															
Meywar	13	5,810	372,454	32,484	339,970	1,844,210	131,302	1,712,908	961,056	68,451	892,605	883,154	62,851	820,303	12,753
Banswara	1	1,344	47,602	2,043	45,559	211,641	8,234	203,407	108,505	3,998	104,507	103,136	4,236	98,900	1,946
Dungarpur	1	506	22,685	1,526	21,159	165,400	6,431	158,969	82,920	3,003	79,917	82,480	3,428	79,052	1,447
Pertabgarh	1	615	21,174	3,560	17,614	87,975	14,819	73,156	45,842	7,906	37,936	42,133	6,913	35,220	886
Kherwara Cantonment	...	1	154	...	154	648	...	648	588	...	588	60	...	60	...
Kotra Cantonment	...	1	7	...	7	150	...	150	147	...	147	3	...	3	...
Total Meywar Residency	16	8,277	464,076	39,613	424,463	2,310,024	160,786	2,149,238	1,199,058	83,358	1,115,700	1,110,966	77,428	1,033,538	17,032
(ii) WESTERN RAJPUTANA STATES RESIDENCY—															
Marwar	26	4,199	501,659⅓	59,902⅓	441,757	2,519,892	268,951	2,250,941	1,324,946	134,952	1,189,994	1,194,945	133,998	1,060,947	34,963
⅓ Sambhar Joint Jurisdiction	⅓	6	1,592	1,250⅓	341⅓	8,286	6,181	2,105	4,531	3,401	1,130	3,755	2,780	975	...
Total Marwar	26⅓	4,205	503,251⅓	61,153	442,098⅓	2,528,178	275,132	2,253,046	1,329,477	138,353	1,191,124	1,198,700	136,778	1,061,922	34,963
Serohi	1	396	42,317	2,281	40,036	188,885	8,782	180,103	98,710	4,667	94,043	90,175	4,115	86,060	1,964
Jesalmir	1	396	25,273	3,023	22,250	115,701	10,509	105,192	62,699	5,015	57,684	53,002	5,494	47,508	16,062
Erinpura Cantonment	...	...	802	...	862	1,859	...	1,859	1,286	...	1,286	573	...	573	...
Abu Sanitarium	...	...	30	...	30	92	...	92	56	...	56	36	...	36	...
Total Western Rajputana States Residency	28⅓	4,997	571,673⅓	66,457	505,216⅓	2,834,715	294,423	2,540,292	1,492,228	148,035	1,344,193	1,342,486	146,387	1,196,099	52,989
(iii) JEYPORE RESIDENCY—															
Jeypore	86	5,735	385,842⅓	67,419⅓	318,423	2,815,679	461,480	2,354,199	1,501,235	241,805	1,259,430	1,314,445	219,676	1,094,769	15,579
⅓ Sambhar Joint Jurisdiction	⅓	6	1,592	1,250⅓	341⅓	8,286	6,181	2,106	4,531	3,401	1,130	3,756	2,780	976	...
Total Jeypore	86⅓	5,741	387,434⅓	68,670	318,764⅓	2,823,965	467,661	2,356,305	1,505,766	245,206	1,260,560	1,318,201	222,456	1,095,745	15,579

Names of Agency and States.	Number of		Occupied Houses.			Population.									Area in square miles.
						Total.			Males.			Females.			
	Town.	Village.	Total.	Town.	Village.	Total.	Town.	Village.	Total.	Town.	Village.	Total.	Town.	Village.	
1	2	3	4	5	6	7	8	9	10	11	12	13	14	15	16
(iii) JEYPORE RESIDENCY—*contd.*															
Kishengarh	3	227	19,079	4,985	14,094	125,516	26,372	99,144	65,038	13,537	51,501	60,478	12,835	47,643	858
Lawa	...	8	493	...	493	3,360	...	3,360	1,728	...	1,728	1,632	...	1,632	19
Total Jeypore Residency	39½	5,976	407,006⅓	73,655	333,351⅓	2,952,842	494,033	2,458,809	1,572,532	258,743	1,313,789	1,380,311	235,291	1,145,020	16,456
(iv) HAROWTI AND TONK AGENCY—															
Tonk	2	526	43,958	12,204	31,754	198,934	51,426	147,508	103,752	26,021	77,731	95,182	25,405	69,777	1,113
Detached tracts of Tonk under Central India	3	698	40,218	6,059	34,159	181,135	24,790	156,345	96,345	13,225	83,120	84,790	11,565	73,225	1,439
Total Tonk	5	1,224	84,176	18,263	65,913	380,069	76,216	303,853	200,097	39,246	160,851	179,972	36,970	143,002	2,552
Bundi	2	882	52,137	5,126	47,011	295,675	28,637	267,038	156,033	15,128	140,905	139,642	13,509	126,133	2,220
Shahpura Estate	1	134	13,653	2,920	10,733	63,646	11,718	51,928	33,243	5,930	27,313	30,403	5,788	24,615	405
Total Harowti and Tonk Agency	8	2,240	149,966	26,309	123,657	739,390	116,571	622,819	389,373	60,304	329,069	350,017	56,267	293,750	5,177
(v) EASTERN STATES AGENCY—															
Bharatpur	7	1,352	87,452	22,167	65,285	640,303	123,605	516,698	347,830	66,752	281,078	292,473	56,853	235,620	1,982
Karauli	1	840	34,852	4,623	30,229	156,587	23,124	133,463	84,555	11,769	72,786	72,032	11,355	60,677	1,242
Dholpur	4	518	60,290	8,434	51,856	279,890	34,821	245,069	157,123	18,259	138,864	122,767	16,562	106,205	1,154
Total Eastern States Agency	12	2,710	182,594	35,224	147,370	1,076,780	181,550	895,230	589,508	96,780	492,728	487,272	84,770	402,502	4,378
(vi) Bikanir Agency	9	1,959	135,694	22,180	113,514	831,955	119,323	712,632	440,046	59,158	380,888	391,909	60,165	331,744	23,173
(vii) Alwar "	7	1,740	136,270	18,745	117,525	767,786	90,815	676,971	403,898	47,836	356,062	363,888	42,979	320,909	3,144
(viii) Kotah "	4	1,626	106,611	10,836	95,775	526,267	56,451	469,816	273,121	28,992	244,129	253,146	27,459	225,687	3,784
(ix) Jhalawar "	2	1,455	61,001	5,944	55,057	343,601	34,164	309,437	182,478	17,812	164,666	161,123	16,352	144,771	2,722
Total Rajputana Agency	126	30,980	2,214,892	298,963	1,915,929	12,383,360	1,548,116	10,835,244	5,542,242	801,018	5,741,224	5,841,118	747,098	5,094,020	129,065
Detached Tracts of Gungapur and Nundwas in Meywar	1	43	2,751	902	1,849	18,118	6,761	11,357	9,711	3,721	5,990	8,407	3,040	5,367	Not available.
GRAND TOTAL	**127**	**31,023**	**2,217,643**	**299,865**	**1,917,778**	**12,401,478**	**1,554,877**	**10,846,601**	**6,551,953**	**804,739**	**5,747,214**	**5,849,525**	**750,138**	**5,099,387**	***129,065**

* Inclusive of 210 square miles in dispute.

PROVINCIAL TABLE.

TABLE I.—Area, Houses and Population.

Names of Agency and States.	Area in Square Miles.	Number of		Occupied Houses.			Population.									
							Total.			Males.			Females.		
		Town.	Villages.	Total.	Town.	Village.	Total.	Town.	Village.	Total.	Town.	Village.	Total.	Town.	Village.
1	2	3	4	5	6	7	8	9	10	11	12	13	14	15	16
I.—MEYWAR RESIDENCY—															
1.—Meywar—															
1. Oodeypore	Separate area of each subdivision not available.	1	79	18,211	11,722	6,489	73,439	46,658	26,781	38,795	24,855	13,940	34,644	21,803	12,841
2. Meja			17	1,136	...	1,136	5,099	...	5,099	2,663	...	2,663	2,436	...	2,436
3. Parsoli			46	1,735	...	1,735	8,477	...	8,477	4,502	...	4,502	3 975	...	3,975
4 Sirdargarh			22	1,384	...	1,384	6,583	...	6,583	3,433	...	3,433	3,150	...	3,150
5. Kankroli			19	1,851	...	1,851	8,294	...	8,294	4,258	...	4,258	4,036	...	4,036
6. Kelwara			126	9,654	...	9,654	44,662	...	44,662	23,686	...	23,686	20,976	...	20,976
7. Bansi			16	968	...	968	4,617	...	4,617	2,378	...	2,378	2,239	...	2,239
8. Amet			63	3,440	...	3,440	16,506	...	16,506	8,623	...	8,623	7,883	...	7,883
9. Jharol			45	1,864	...	1,864	8,110	...	8,110	4,259	...	4,259	3,851	...	3,851
10. Kanor			78	3,291	...	3,291	15,786	...	15,786	8 173	...	8,173	7,613	...	7,613
11. Dilwara			81	6,739	...	6,739	30,099	...	30,099	15,704	...	15,704	14,395	...	14,395
12. Shivrati			18	2,049	...	2,049	9,487	...	9,487	4,945	...	4,945	4,542	...	4,542
13. Bijaypur			79	2,314	...	2,314	10,030	...	10,030	5,234	...	5,234	4,796	...	4,796
14. Banera		1	112	7,242	1,253	5,989	36,804	5,760	31,044	19,136	2,886	16,250	17,668	2,874	14,794
15. Khamnor			51	7,789	...	7,789	34,249	...	34,249	17,994	...	17,994	16,255	..	16,255
16. Gogunda			88	3,278	...	3,278	13,972	...	13,972	7,275	...	7,275	6,697	...	6,697
17. Bidnor			156	5,694	...	5,694	27,519	...	27,519	14,713	...	14,713	12,806	...	12,806
18. Kurabar			65	5,725	...	5,725	25,452	...	25,452	13,260	...	13,260	12,192	...	12,192
19. Kotharia		...	74	3 045	...	3,045	15,364	...	15,364	7,994	...	7,994	7,370	...	7,370
20. Karjali		...	22	1,212	...	1,212	5,282	...	5,282	2,675	...	2,675	2,607	...	2,607
21. Nathdwara		1	30	5,273	2,466	2,807	21,661	9,331	12,330	11,301	4,877	6,424	10,360	4,454	5,906
22. Devasthan		...	107	9,229	...	9,229	41,696	...	41,696	21,628	...	21,628	20,068	...	20,068
23. Fatehgarh		...	5	266	...	266	1,303	...	1,303	695	...	695	608	...	608
24. Asind		...	76	4,466	...	4,466	21,416	...	21,416	11,130	...	11,130	10,286	...	10,286
25. Hurra and Shinbhugarh		...	101	10,650	...	10,650	53,986	...	53,986	28,509	...	28,509	25,477	...	25,477
26. Kapasin		1	150	11,093	1,272	9,821	52,355	5,514	46,841	27,178	2,909	24,269	25,177	2,605	22,572
27. Bagor		...	28	2,648	...	2,648	12,568	...	12,568	6,556	...	6,556	6,012	...	6,012
28. Bijolia		...	88	3,159	...	3,159	14,949	...	14,949	7,719	...	7,719	7,230	...	7,230
29. Kanera		...	25	2,093	...	2,093	8 289	...	8,289	4,219	...	4,219	4.070	...	4,070
30. Deogarh		1	223	12,133	1,793	10,340	56,531	7,400	49,131	29,828	3.635	26,193	26,703	3,765	22,938
31. Bari Sadri		...	89	3,489	...	3,489	16,499	...	16,499	8,641	...	8,641	7,858	...	7,858
32. Begun		1	170	6,901	1,523	5,378	30,835	5,882	24,953	15,966	2,988	12,978	14,869	2,894	11,975
33. Magra Sarara		...	182	12,354	...	12,354	54,715	...	54,715	28,852	...	28,852	25,863	...	25,863
34. Dhariavad		...	54	1,439	...	1,439	6,162	...	6,162	3,090	...	3,090	3,072	...	3,072
35. Sayra		...	59	5,629	...	5,629	23,543	...	23.543	12,326	...	12,326	11,217	...	11,217
36. Choti Sadri		1	238	10,839	1,321	9,518	48,060	5,368	42,692	24.788	2.709	22,079	23,272	2,659	20,613
37. Salumbar		1	176	12,966	1,598	11,368	55,009	6,029	48,980	28,022	2,952	25,070	26,987	3,077	23,910
38. Kotra Bhumat		...	94	1,754	...	1,754	7,648	...	7,648	4,189	...	4,189	3,459	...	3,459
39. Kherwara Bhumat		...	85	2,512	...	2,512	13,346	...	13,346	6,782	...	6,782	6,564	...	6,564

Table I.—Area, Houses and Population—Rajputana Agency.

Names of Agency and States.	Area in Square Miles.	Number of		Occupied Houses.			Population. Total.			Males.			Females.		
		Town.	Village.	Total.	Town.	Village.	Total.	Town.	Village.	Total.	Town.	Village.	Total.	Town.	Village.
1	2	3	4	5	6	7	8	9	10	11	12	13	14	15	16
I.—MEYWAR RESIDENCY—*contd.*															
I.—Meywar—*contd.*															
40. Rincher	Not available.	...	13	1,561	...	1,561	7,103	...	7,103	3,761	...	3,761	3,342	...	3,342
41. Bhindar		1	118	5,360	1,529	3,831	24,899	6,790	18,109	12,774	3,434	9,340	12,125	3,356	8,769
42. Chitorgarh		1	331	25,582	2,434	23,148	116,348	9,354	106,994	60,534	4,955	55,579	55,814	4,399	51,415
43. Bhainsrorgarh		...	119	6,045	...	6,045	23,500	...	23,500	12,261	...	12,261	11,239	...	11,239
44. Bhilwara		2	253	20,529	4,009	16,520	96,443	17,143	79,300	50,313	8,935	41,378	46,130	8,208	37,922
45. Girwa		...	275	19,608	...	19,608	93,316	...	93,316	48,142	...	48,142	45,174	...	45,174
46. Mandalgarh		...	316	16,476	...	16,476	84,472	...	84,472	44,651	...	44,651	39,821	...	39,821
47. Bedla		...	121	5,149	...	5,149	23,923	...	23,923	12,452	...	12,452	11,471	...	11,471
48. Rasmi		...	92	10,032	...	10,032	46,757	...	46,757	24,368	...	24,368	22,389	...	22,389
49. Rajnagar		...	117	8,645	...	8,645	39,858	...	39,858	20,857	...	20,857	19,001	...	19,001
50. Sahran		...	289	21,021	...	21,021	99,929	...	99,929	52,228	...	52,228	47,701	...	47,701
51. Jahazpur		1	381	18,600	1,245	17,355	85,637	5,106	80,531	45,899	2,665	43,234	39,738	2,441	37,297
52. Kachola Shahpura		...	88	6,013	...	6,013	26,227	...	26,227	13,832	...	13,832	12,395	...	12,395
Total Meywar Districts		13	5,810	372,135	32,165	339,970	1,708,814	130,335	1,578,479	893,191	67,800	825,391	815,623	62,535	753,088
Meywar Residency—Military Cantonments in Meywar.															
53. Total Kherwara Cantonment		...	1	154	...	154	648	...	648	588	...	588	60	...	60
54. Kotra Cantonment		...	1	7	...	7	150	...	150	147	...	147	3	...	3
Total Cantonments		...	2	161	...	161	798	...	798	735	...	735	63	...	63
55. Railway Population in Meywar	Not available.	...	...	308	308	...	932	932	...	633	633	...	299	299	...
56. Europeans, etc., in Meywar		...	...	11	11	...	35	35	...	18	18	...	17	17	...
Detached tracts of Central India in Meywar.															
57. *Nandwas Pargana of Indore State*		...	31	1,239	...	1,239	5,840	...	5,840	3,122	...	3,122	2,718	...	2,718
58. *Gangapur Pargana of Gwalior State*		1	12	1,512	902	610	12,278	6,761	5,517	6,589	3,721	2,868	5,689	3,040	2,649
Total Detached Tracts (57&58)		1	43	2,751	902	1,849	18,118	6,761	11,357	9,711	3,721	5,990	8,407	3,040	5,367
Total Enumerated Population of Meywar		14	5,855	375,366	33,386	341,980	1,728,697	138,063	1,590,634	904,288	72,172	832,116	824,409	65,891	758,518
59. Unenumerated—Unenumerated Bhils of Meywar—															
Oodeypore		...	...	...	...	...	2,883	...	2,883	1,442	...	1,442	1,441	...	1,441
Girva		...	...	...	...	...	12,393	...	12,393	6,196	...	6,196	6,197	...	6,197
Magra Sarara		...	...	...	...	...	24,332	...	24,332	12,166	...	12,166	12,166	...	12,166

TABLE I.—Area, Houses and Population—*contd.*

Names of Agency and States.	Area in Square Miles.	Number of		Occupied Houses.			Population.								
							Total.			Mails.			Females.		
		Town.	Village.	Total.	Town.	Village.	Total.	Town.	Village.	Total.	Town.	Village.	Total.	Town.	Village.
1	2	3	4	5	6	7	8	9	10	11	12	13	14	15	16
I.—MEYWAR RESIDENCY—*contd.*															
I.—Meywar—*contd.*															
59. Unenumerated—*contd.*															
Salumbar	Not available.	...	...	...	...	...	8,253	...	8,253	4,126	...	4,126	4,127	...	4,127
Kanor		...	...	...	...	...	4,166	...	4,166	2,083	...	2,083	2,083	...	2,083
Bansi		...	...	...	...	...	4,204	...	4,204	2,102	...	2,102	2,102	...	2,102
Jharol		...	...	...	...	...	6,381	...	6,381	3,191	...	3,191	3,190	...	3,190
Dhariawad		...	...	...	...	...	23,815	...	23,815	11,907	...	11,907	11,908	...	11,908
Kherwara Bhumat		...	...	...	...	...	34,169	...	34,169	17,085	...	17,085	17,084	...	17,084
Kotra Bhumat		...	...	...	...	...	13,833	...	13,833	6,916	...	6,916	6,917	...	6,917
Total (59) Unenumerated Population		...	...	...	...	...	134,429	...	134,429	67,214	...	67,214	67,215	...	67,215
Total Population, etc., of Meywar, excluding detached tracts of Central India		13	5,812	372,615	32,484	340,131	1,845,008	131,302	1,713,706	961,791	68,451	893,340	883,217	62,851	820,366
Detached tracts of Central India in Meywar		1	43	2,751	902	1,849	18,118	6,761	11,357	9,711	3,721	5,990	8,407	3,040	5,367
GRAND TOTAL MEYWAR STATE	**12,758**	**14**	**5,855**	**375,366**	**33,386**	**341,980**	**1,863,126**	**138,063**	**1,725,063**	**971,502**	**72,172**	**899,330**	**891,624**	**65,891**	**825,733**
II.—Banswara—															
1. Banswara	1,607	1	1,031	41,262	2,043	39,219	180,268	8,234	172,034	92,540	3,998	88,542	87,728	4,236	83,492
2. Chiefship of Kushalgarh	339	...	313	6,340	...	6,340	5,775	...	5,775	2,920	...	2,920	2,855	...	2,855
3. Unenumerated Population		...	...	...	...	...	25,598	...	25,598	13,045	...	13,045	12,553	...	12,553
Total		...	313	6,340	...	6,340	31,373	...	31,373	15,965	...	15,965	15,408	...	15,408
Total Banswara State	1,946	1	1,344	47,602	2,043	45,559	211,641	8,234	203,407	108,505	3,998	104,507	103,136	4,236	98,900
III.—Total Pertabgarh State	886	1	615	21,174	3,560	17,614	87,975	14,819	73,156	45,842	7,906	37,936	42,133	6,913	35,220
IV.—Dungarpur—															
1. Dungarpur	Separate area of each sub-division not available.	1	58	2,730	1,526	1,204	11,401	6,431	4,970	5,496	3,003	2,493	5,905	3,428	2,477
2. Kunba		...	73	2,289	...	2,289	10,158	...	10,158	5,208	...	5,208	4,950	...	4,950
3. Guneshpore		...	50	1,881	...	1,881	8,694	...	8,694	4,447	...	4,447	4,247	...	4,247
4. Aspur		...	35	2,149	...	2,149	9,360	...	9,360	4,799	...	4,799	4,561	...	4,561
5. Pujpore		...	32	1,748	...	1,748	7,773	...	7,773	3,903	...	3,903	3,870	...	3,870
6. Nithava		...	61	2,496	...	2,496	10,790	...	10,790	5,440	...	5,440	5,350	...	5,350
7. Sagwara		...	23	2,584	...	2,584	10,663	...	10,663	5,293	...	5,293	5,370	...	5,370

Table I.—Area, Houses and Population—Rajputana Agency.

Names of Agency and States.	Area in Square Miles.	Number of		Houses Occupied.			Population.								
							Total.			Males.			Females.		
		Town.	Village.	Total.	Town.	Village.	Total.	Town.	Village.	Total.	Town.	Village.	Total.	Town.	Village.
	2	3	4	5	6	7	8	9	10	11	12	13	14	15	16
I.—MEYWAR RESIDENCY—*contd.*	Separate area of each sub-division not available.														
IV.—Dungarpur—*contd.*															
8. Padva		...	48	2,761	...	2,761	11,991	...	11,991	5,933	...	5,933	6,058	...	6,058
9. Gulliakote		...	50	1,940	...	1,940	8,227	...	8,227	4,009	...	4,009	4,218	...	4,218
10. Dhumbora		...	76	2,107	...	2,107	9,391	...	9,391	4,916	...	4,916	4,475	...	4,475
Total		1	506	22,685	1,526	21,159	98,448	6,431	92,017	49,444	3,003	46,441	49,004	3,428	45,576
II. Unenumerated Bhils of Dungarpur taken from the Census of 1881		...	...	...	...	...	66,952	...	66,952	33,476	...	33,476	33,476	...	33,476
GRAND TOTAL DUNGARPUR STATE	1,447	1	506	22,685	1,526	21,159	165,400	6,481	158,969	82,920	3,003	79,917	82,480	3,428	79,052
Total Meywar Residency	17,082	16	8,277	464,076	39,613	424,463	2,310,024	160,786	2,149,238	1,199,058	83,358	1,115 700	1,110,966	77,428	1,033,538
Detached Tracts of Central India in Meywar		1	43	2,751	902	1,849	18,118	6,761	11,357	9 711	3,721	5,990	8 407	3,040	5,367
GRAND TOTAL, MEYWAR RESIDENCY	17,032	17	8,320	466,827	40,515	426,312	2,328,142	167,547	2,160,595	1,208,769	87,079	1,121,690	1,119,373	80,468	1,038,905
II.—WESTERN RAJPUTANA STATES RESIDENCY—															
V.—Marwar and Malani—															
1. Jodhpore City		1	...	13,513	13,513	...	61,759	61,759	...	31,663	31,663	...	30,096	30,096	...
2 Do. Kasba		...	23	3,953	...	3,953	18,646	...	18,646	11,664	...	11,664	6,982	...	6,982
3. Do. Pargana		1	433	45,793	1,726	44,067	246,962	7,895	239,067	131,134	3,893	127,241	115,828	4,002	111,826
Total	3,408	2	456	63,259	15,239	48,020	327,367	69,654	257,713	174,461	35,556	138,905	152,906	34,098	118,808
4. Nagore	...	4	428	50,099	7,065	43,034	252,257	34,830	217,427	130,640	16,812	113,828	121,617	18,018	103,599
5. Bali	...	2	352	45,782	3,074	42,708	212,479	12,950	199,529	109,179	6,273	102,906	103,300	6,677	96,623
6. Merta	...	3	390	42,284	4,185	38,099	205,704	17,834	187,870	107,089	9,155	97,934	98,615	8,679	89,936
7. Jalore	1,800	1	247	35,567	2,341	33,226	170,428	9,656	160,772	88,069	4,768	83,301	82,359	4,888	77,471
8. Sojat	1,277	1	230	30,136	3,075	27,061	141,782	12,624	129,158	73,597	6,060	67,537	68,185	6,564	61,621
9. Jaswantpura	1,030	1	212	22,333	1,277	21,056	111,550	5,736	105,814	58,517	2,906	55,611	53,033	2,830	50,203
10. Parbatsar	...	...	162	20,452	...	20,452	104,962	...	104,962	55,926	...	55,926	49,036	...	49,036
11. Sanchore	1,876	...	259	16,374	...	16,374	95,890	...	95,890	51,530	...	51,530	44,360	...	44,360
12. Jaitaran	...	1	118	18,655	1,203	17,452	87,635	5,744	81,891	45,720	2,928	42,792	41,915	2,816	39,099
13. Bilara	756	2	91	17,304	4,147	13,157	84,952	19,537	65,415	44,338	9,920	34,418	40,614	9,617	30,997

TABLE I.—Area, Houses and Population—*contd.*

Names of Agency and States.	Area in Square Miles.	Number of Town.	Number of Village.	Occupied Houses. Total.	Occupied Houses. Town.	Occupied Houses. Village.	Population. Total. Total.	Population. Total. Town.	Population. Total. Village.	Population. Males. Total.	Population. Males. Town.	Population. Males. Village.	Population. Females. Total.	Population. Females. Town.	Population. Females. Village.
1	2	3	4	5	6	7	8	9	10	11	12	13	14	15	16
II. WESTERN RAJPUTANA STATES RESIDENCY—*contd.*															
V.—Marwar and Malani—*contd.*															
14. Phalodi	...	2	77	12,836	3,271	9,565	71,803	15,863	55,940	37,341	7,613	29,728	34,462	8,250	26,212
15. Shergarh	...	...	111	11,973	...	11,973	70,919	...	70,919	39,048	...	39,048	31,871	...	31,871
16. Siwana	1,092	...	120	13,472	...	13,472	64,747	...	64,747	33,425	...	33,425	31,322	...	31,122
17. Pali	577	1	78	12,864	4,623	8,241	58,463	17,150	41,313	29,949	8,535	21,414	28,514	8,615	19,899
18. Marote	468	...	102	11,596	...	11,596	56,806	...	56,806	30,710	...	30,710	26,096	...	26,096
19. Didwana	...	1	112	10,852	2,421	8,431	54,272	11,376	42,896	28,435	5,768	22,667	25,837	5,608	20,229
20. Pachbhadra	936	2	100	11,226	2,603	8,623	52,904	10,560	42,344	27,944	5,418	22,526	24,960	5,142	19,818
21. Nawa	260	2	16	6,355	3,551	2,804	31,538	17,942	13,596	16,721	9,269	7,452	14,817	8,673	6,144
22. Sheo	2,492	...	65	6,073	...	6,073	30,291	...	30,291	16,426	...	16,426	13,865	...	13,865
23. Shankra	...	...	25	1,853	...	1,853	10,074	...	10,074	5,675	...	5,675	4,399	...	4,399
Total (1-23)	...	25	3,751	461,345	58,075	403,270	2,296,823	261,456	2,035,367	1,204,740	130,981	1,073,759	1,092,083	130,475	961,608
24. Malani	6,432	1	448	39,770	1,283	38,487	221,184	5,610	215,574	119,036	2,801	116,235	102,148	2,809	99,339
Total Marwar and Malani		26	4,199	501,115	59,358	441,757	2,518,007	267,066	2,250,941	1,323,776	133,782	1,189,994	1,194,231	133,284	106,947
25. ½ Sambhar Jeypore Jodhpore joint jurisdiction		½	6	1,592	1,250½	341½	8,286	6,181	2,105	4,531	3,401	1,130	3,755	2,780	975
½ Sambhar Railway		...	...	2½	2½	...	24	24	...	12	12	...	11	11	...
Total Sambhar (25)		½	6	1,594½	1,253	341½	8,310	6,205	2,105	4,543	3,413	1,130	3,767	2,791	975
26. Total Rajputana Malwa Railway Population in Marwar		...	...	542	542	...	1,771	1,771	...	1,115	115	...	656	656	...
27. Europeans, etc., Jodhpore		...	...	...	...	...	32	32	...	16	16	...	16	16	...
Do. Nawa		...	...	...	...	...	23	23	...	11	11	...	12	12	...
Do. Didwana		...	...	...	...	...	12	12	...	6	6	...	6	6	...
Do. Puchbadra		...	...	...	...	...	15	15	...	7	7	...	8	8	...
Do. Phalodi		...	...	...	...	...	8	8	...	3	3	...	5	5	...
Total R. M. Railway and European, etc., Population in Marwar		...	...	542	542	...	1,861	1,861	...	1,158	1,158	...	703	703	...
GRAND TOTAL MARWAR STATE	**34,963**	**26½**	**4,205**	**503,251½**	**61,153**	**442,098½**	**2,528,178**	**275,182**	**2,253,046**	**1,329,477**	**138,353**	**1,191,124**	**1,198,701**	**136,778**	**1,061,922½**

Table I.—Area, Houses and Population—Rajputana Agency.

Names of Agency and States.	Area in Square Miles.	Number of Town.	Number of Village.	Occupied Houses. Total.	Occupied Houses. Town.	Occupied Houses. Village.	Population. Total. Total.	Population. Total. Town.	Population. Total. Village.	Population. Males. Total.	Population. Males. Town.	Population. Males. Village.	Population. Females. Total.	Population. Females. Town.	Population. Females. Village.
1	2	3	4	5	6	7	8	9	10	11	12	13	14	15	16
II.—WESTERN RAJPUTANA STATES RESIDENCY—*contd.*															
VI.—Sirohi—	Separate area of each sub-division not available.	Details not furnished.	Details not furnished.	Details not furnished.	Details not furnished.	Details not furnished.									
1. Sirohi Tehsil		1					7,136	6,207	929	3,525	3,075	450	3,611	3,132	479
2. Khooni "							25,456	...	25,456	13,181	...	13,181	12,275	...	12,275
3. Magra							23,610	...	23,610	12,187	...	12,187	11,423	...	11,423
4. Jara Kharel Tehsil							20,304	...	20,304	10,428	...	10,428	9,876	...	9,876
5. Pamera "							19,235	...	19,235	9,893	...	9,893	9,342	...	9,342
6. Madar "							18,777	...	18,777	9,853	...	9,853	8,924	...	8,924
7. Anadra "							7,874	...	7,874	4,150	...	4,150	3,724	...	3,724
8. Santpura "							11,424	...	11,424	6,173	...	6,173	5,251	...	5,251
9. Rohera "							18,259	...	18,259	9,290	...	9,290	8,969	...	8,969
10. Pindwara "							20,670	...	20,670	10,964	...	10,964	9,706	...	9,706
11. Abu Road							4,438	...	4,438	2,465	...	2,465	1,973	...	1,973
12. *Mount Abu*— (Villages on Abu)—															
Mount Abu. Villages. 1 Delwara							357	...	357	219	...	219	138	...	138
2 Guha							65	...	65	39	...	39	26	...	26
3 Torna							100	...	100	46	...	46	54	...	54
4 Sâl							136	...	136	79	...	79	57	...	57
5 Hetamjee							84	...	84	37	...	37	47	...	47
6 Dhundai							99	...	99	52	...	52	47	...	47
7 Mach							74	...	74	34	...	34	40	...	40
8 Sani							143	...	143	90	...	90	53	...	53
9 Javai							121	...	121	68	...	68	53	...	53
10 Achalgarh							161	...	161	81	...	81	80	...	80
11 Uria							299	...	299	150	...	150	149	...	149
12 Utraj							334	...	334	171	...	171	163	...	163
13 Akhi							9	...	9	6	...	6	3	...	3
14 Sher							234	...	234	129	...	129	105	...	105
15 Arna							43	...	43	28	...	28	15	...	15
Total Villages on Abu							2,259	...	2,259	1,229	...	1,229	1,030	...	1,030
Mount Abu. Abu Station. Chowkis							73	...	73	47	...	47	26	...	26
Abu Bazar							1,280	...	1,280	768	...	768	512	...	512
Abu Civil Station							1,048	...	1,048	723	...	723	325	...	325
Abu Sanitarium Population		...	...	30	...	30	92	...	92	56	...	56	36	...	36
Europeans, etc., on Abu		...	...	21	21	...	165	165	...	98	98	...	67	67	...
Total Mount Abu		...	...	51	21	30	4,917	165	4,752	2,921	98	2,823	1,596	67	1,929
13. Sirohi Railway		...	...	682	682	...	2,410	2,410	...	1,494	1,494	—	916	916	...
14. Erinpura Bazar		...	...	...	...	...	1,607	...	1,607	812	...	812	795	...	795
15. Erinpura Cantonment		...	...	802	...	802	1,859	...	1,859	1,286	...	1,286	573	...	573
Total Enumerated Population in Sirohi		...	...	...	...	...	187,976	8,782	179,194	98,622	4,667	93,955	89,354	4,115	85,239
16. Total Unenumerated Population (Grassias)		...	...	...	...	...	2,860	...	2,860	1,430	...	1,430	1,430	...	1,430
GRAND TOTAL SIROHI STATE	**1,964**	**1**	**396**	**43,149**	**2,281**	**40,868**	**190,836**	**8,782**	**182,054**	**100,052**	**4,667**	**95,385**	**90,784**	**4,115**	**86,669**

TABLE I.—Area, Houses and Population —*contd.*

Names of Agency and States.	Area in Square Miles.	Number of		Occupied House.			Population. Total.			Population. Males.			Population. Females.		
		Town.	Village.	Total.	Town.	Village.	Total.	Town.	Village.	Total.	Town.	Village.	Total.	Town.	Village.
1	2	3	4	5	6	7	8	9	10	11	12	13	14	15	16
II.—WESTERN RAJPUTANA STATES RESIDENCY—*concld.*															
VII.—Jesalmir—															
1. Total Jesalmir State	16,062	1	396	25,273	3,023	22,250	115,701	10,509	105,192	62,699	5,015	57,684	53,002	5,494	47,508
Total Western Rajputana States Residency	**52,989**	**28½**	**4,997**	**571,673½**	**66,457**	**505,216**	**2,884,715**	**294,428**	**2,540,292**	**1,492,228**	**148,035**	**1,344,193**	**1,342,487**	**146,387**	**1,196,099**
III.—BIKANIR AGENCY—															
VIII.—Bikanir—															
1. Anupgarh	Separate area of each Tehsil not available.	...	59	1,462	...	1,462	8,507	...	8,507	4,631	...	4,631	3,876	...	3,876
2. Bahaderan		...	95	5,623	...	5,623	38,026	...	38,026	20,612	...	20,612	17,414	...	17,414
3. Bikanir City		1	...	10,330	10,330	...	50,037	50,037	...	24,705	24,705	...	25,332	25,332	...
3. " Suburb		...	...	1,187	1,187	...	6,203	6,203	...	3,184	3,184	...	3,019	3,019	...
3. " Tehsil		...	314	21,614	...	21,614	149,053	...	149,053	78,638	...	78,638	70,415	...	70,415
Total		1	314	33,131	11,517	21,614	205,293	56,240	149,053	106,527	27,889	78,638	98,766	28,351	70,415
4. Churu		2	160	14,097	3,526	10,571	82,889	20,567	62,332	44,032	10,159	33,873	38,867	10,408	28,459
5. Doongargarh		...	90	6,739	...	6,739	44,007	...	44,007	22,603	...	22,603	21,404	...	21,404
6. Hanumangarh		...	158	6,562	...	6,562	37,459	...	37,459	20,405	...	20,405	17,054	...	17,054
7. Luakaransar		...	182	9,554	...	9,554	65,224	...	65,224	35,010	...	35,010	30,214	...	30,214
8. Mirzawala		...	96	1,814	...	1,814	10,375	...	10,375	5,711	...	5,711	4,664	...	4,664
9. Nuhar		1	192	12,632	986	11,646	80,311	5,655	74,656	43,002	2,894	40,108	37,309	2,761	34,548
10. Rajgarh		1	181	10,172	898	9,274	61,277	4,677	56,600	33,249	2,346	30,903	28,028	2,331	25,697
11. Ratangarh		1	112	10,246	1,685	8,561	60,267	10,536	49,731	31,666	5,123	26,543	28,601	5,413	23,188
12. Sardarshehr		1	104	7,741	1,438	6,303	44,911	9,196	35,715	23,313	4,463	18,850	21,598	4,733	16,865
13. Sujangarh		1	138	13,104	1,637	11,467	77,031	9,781	67,250	40,490	4,824	35,666	36,541	4,957	31,584
14. Suratgarh		1	78	2,817	493	2,324	16,356	2,659	13,697	8,788	1,453	7,335	7,568	1,206	6,362
Total		9	1,959	135,694	22,180	113,514	831,943	119,311	712,632	440,039	59,151	380,888	391,904	60,160	331,744
Total European, etc., Bikanir		...	...	...	...	...	12	12	...	7	7	...	5	5	...
GRAND TOTAL BIKANIR AGENCY	**28,173**	**9**	**1,959**	**135,694**	**22,180**	**113,514**	**831,955**	**119,323**	**712,632**	**440,046**	**59,158**	**380,888**	**391,909**	**60,165**	**331,744**

Table I.—Area, Houses and Population—Rajputana Agency.

Names of Agency and States.	Area in Square Miles.	Number of Town.	Number of Village.	Occupied Houses Total.	Occupied Houses Town.	Occupied Houses Village.	Population Total Total.	Population Total Town.	Population Total Village.	Males Total.	Males Town.	Males Village.	Females Total.	Females Town.	Females Village.
1	2	3	4	5	6	7	8	9	10	11	12	13	14	15	16
IV.—JEYPORE RESIDENCY—															
IX.—Jeypore—															
1. Jeypore City	3	1	...	23,964	23,964	...	158,787	158,787	...	84,024	84,024	...	74,763	74,763	...
Total	3	1	...	23,964	23,964	...	158,787	158,787	...	84,024	84,024	...	74,763	74,763	...
2. { Jeypore Tehsil		2	588	30,368	2,097	28,271	195,101	15,152	179,949	103,838	7,737	96,101	91,263	7,415	83,848
Jamua Ramgarh		1	371	21,417	944	20,473	153,055	5,326	147,729	80,786	2,686	78,100	72,269	2,640	69,629
Chaksu		1	347	15,710	1,621	14,089	112,488	7,870	104,618	59,783	4,589	55,194	52,705	3,281	49,424
Kalegh }		...	249	13,920	...	13,920	106,822	...	106,822	56,749	...	56,749	50,073	...	50,073
Total	2,392	4	1,555	81,415	4,662	76,753	567,466	28,348	539,118	301,156	15,012	286,144	266,310	13,336	252,974
3. Dausa Tehsil		1	303	17,575	1,189	16,386	124,203	8,416	115,787	65,776	4,518	61,258	58,427	3,898	54,529
4. Lalsote		1	242	14,675	881	13,794	102,360	8,163	94,197	54,050	4,021	50,029	48,310	4,142	44,168
5. Sikrai		...	66	3,840	...	3,840	26,103	...	26,103	13,905	...	13,905	12,198	...	12,198
6. Baswa		2	166	9,737	2,035	7,702	69,334	11,590	57,744	36,453	5,983	30,470	32,881	5,607	27,274
Total	1,088	4	777	45,827	4,105	41,722	322,000	28,169	293,831	170,184	14,522	155,662	151,816	13,647	138,169
Shekhawatti. { 7. Jhoonjhun Pargana		5	363	23,693	5,174	18,519	207,538	44,337	163,201	111,718	22,232	89,486	95,820	22,105	73,715
8. Udeypore }		1	69	6,380	1,014	5,366	62,768	10,343	52,425	35,385	6,562	28,823	27,383	3,781	23,602
Total	3,696	6	432	30,073	6,188	23,885	270,306	54,680	215,626	147,103	28,794	118,309	123,203	25,886	97,317
Torawatti. { 9. Sawai Ramgarh		1	164	14,491	492	13,999	127,269	5,733	121,536	70,001	3,323	66,678	57,268	2,410	54,858
10. Khandela		1	132	7,976	1,178	6,798	68,832	10,067	58,765	36,586	4,980	31,606	32,246	5,087	27,159
11. Bairath Tehsil }		1	65	7,156	797	6,359	53,450	5,748	47,702	28,456	2,912	25,544	24,994	2,836	22,158
Total	1,504	3	361	29,623	2,467	27,156	249,551	21,548	228,003	135,043	11,215	123,828	114,508	10,333	104,175
12. Madhopore Tehsil		1	128	10,887	2,956	7,931	60,631	13,972	46,659	31,659	7,143	24,516	28,972	6,829	22,143
13. Bauli Tehsil		...	147	10,822	...	10,822	69,463	...	69,463	36,762	...	36,762	32,701	...	32,701
14. Malarna		...	138	9,081	...	9,081	53,497	...	53,497	28,105	...	28,105	25,392	...	25,392
15. Khandar		...	88	6,137	...	6,137	33,499	...	33,499	17,790	...	17,790	15,709	...	15,709
16. Isarda		...	39	2,360	...	2,360	13,481	...	13,481	7,090	...	7,090	6,391	...	6,391
17. Barwara		...	25	2,076	...	2,076	12,264	...	12,264	6,448	...	6,448	5,816	...	5,816
Total	1,774	1	565	41,363	2,956	38,407	242,835	13,972	228,863	127,854	7,143	120,711	114,981	6,829	108,152

TABLE I.—Area, Houses and Population—*contd.*

Names of Agency and States.	Area in Square Miles.	Number of Town.	Number of Village.	Occupied Houses. Total.	Occupied Houses. Town.	Occupied Houses. Village.	Population. Total. Total.	Population. Total. Town.	Population. Total. Village.	Population. Males. Total.	Population. Males. Town.	Population. Males. Village.	Population. Females. Total.	Population. Females. Town.	Population. Females. Village.
1	2	3	4	5	6	7	8	9	10	11	12	13	14	15	16
IV.—JEYPORE RESIDENCY—*contd.*															
IX.—JEYPORE—*contd.*															
18. Hindown Tehsil		1	83	6,360	1,932	4,428	50,737	12,996	37,741	27,212	6,780	20,432	23,525	6,216	17,309
19. Toda Bhim do.		1	101	6,043	980	5,063	43,991	7,053	36,938	23,225	3,682	19,543	20,766	3,371	17,395
20. Mahwa		...	91	4,994	...	4,994	37,188	...	37,188	19,668	...	19,668	17,520	...	17,520
21. Walghat		...	65	3,245	...	3,245	25,269	...	25,269	13,951	...	13,951	11,318	...	11,318
22. Ghonsla		...	39	1,821	...	1,821	14,862	...	14,862	8,208	...	8,208	6,654	...	6,654
23. Ratanzilla		...	30	1,774	...	1,774	14,858	...	14,858	8,095	...	8,095	6,763	...	6,763
TOTAL	674	2	409	24,237	2,912	21,325	186,905	20,049	166,856	100,359	10,462	89,897	86,546	9,587	76,959
24½. Sambhar (Joint jurisdiction, Jeypore and Marwar)		½	6	1,592	1,250½	341½	8,287	6,181	2,106	4,531	3,401	1,130	3,756	2,780	976
25½. Sambhar Railway		...	...	2½	2½	...	24	24	...	13	13	...	12	12	...
TOTAL		½	6	1,594½	1,253	341½	8,311	6,205	2,106	4,544	3,414	1,130	3,768	2,792	976
26. Naraina Tehsil		1	81	5,345	902	4,443	33,147	5,071	28,076	17,565	2,668	14,897	15,582	2,403	13,179
27. Danta Ramgarh		1	98	9,935	799	9,136	82,522	6,130	76,392	41,719	3,094	41,625	37,803	3,036	34,767
28. Mauzamabad		...	114	8,182	...	8,182	59,693	...	59,693	31,481	...	31,481	28,212	...	28,212
TOTAL	1,597	2	293	23,462	1,701	21,761	175,362	11,201	164,161	93,765	5,762	88,003	81,597	5,439	76,158
29. Malpura Tehsil		1	130	11,662	1,553	10,109	76,643	8,345	68,298	40,180	4,336	35,844	36,463	4,009	32,454
30. Toda Rai Singh		1	118	8,911	655	8,256	62,904	5,649	57,255	33,145	2,927	30,218	29,759	2,722	27,037
31. Newai		1	80	4,893	854	4,039	39,660	5,832	33,828	21,171	3,569	17,602	18,489	2,263	16,226
TOTAL	1,460	3	328	25,466	3,062	22,404	179,207	19,826	159,381	94,496	10,832	83,664	84,711	8,994	75,717
32. Gungapore Tehsil		1	95	7,000	1,162	5,838	44,687	5,880	38,807	23,558	3,108	20,450	21,129	2,772	18,357
33. Wazirpore		...	30	3,109	...	3,109	22,718	...	22,718	11,844	...	11,844	10,874	...	10,874
34. Bamaniawas		1	27	2,751	1,151	1,600	13,811	5,806	8,005	7,200	3,014	4,186	6,611	2,792	3,819
TOTAL	277	2	152	12,860	2,313	10,547	81,216	11,686	69,530	42,602	6,122	36,480	38,614	5,564	33,050
35. Kote Kasim		...	52	2,238	...	2,238	17,054	...	17,054	8,939	...	8,939	8,115	...	8,115
TOTAL	6,275	...	52	2,238	...	2,238	17,054	...	17,054	8,939	...	8,939	8,115	...	8,115

Name of Agency and States.	Area in Square Miles.	Number of		Occupied Houses.			Population.								
							Total.			Males.			Females.		
		Town.	Village.	Total.	Town.	Village.	Total.	Town.	Village.	Total.	Town.	Village.	Total.	Town.	Village.
1	2	3	4	5	6	7	8	9	10	11	12	13	14	15	16
IV.—JEYPORE RESIDENCY—*contd.*															
IX.—Jeypore—*contd.*															
36. Bandikui	Included in Dawsa.	...	7	698	...	698	4,297	...	4,297	2,303	...	2,303	1,994	...	1,994
Total		...	7	698	...	698	4,297	...	4,297	2,303	...	2,303	1,994	...	1,994
37. Sikar	Included in (Shekhawati)	4	422	20,860	7,141	13,719	179,337	58,181	121,156	95,431	29,192	66,239	83,906	28,989	54,917
38. Khetri	(Ditto and Torawati.)	3	257	15,068	3,181	11,887	131,377	22,708	108,669	70,578	11,598	58,980	60,799	11,110	49,689
39. Uniara	(Malpura and Madhopur.)	1	125	7,013	1,092	5,921	43,382	5,728	37,654	23,191	2,920	20,271	20,191	2,808	17,383
Total		8	804	42,941	11,414	31,527	354,096	86,617	267,479	189,200	43,710	145,490	164,896	42,907	121,989
Total		3,672	5,741	385,761½	66,997	318,764½	2,817,393	461,088	2,356,305	1,501,572	241,012	1,260,560	1,315,822	220,077	1,095,745
Total Jeypore Railway		...	...	1,673	1,673	...	6,455	6,455	...	4,123	4,123	...	2,332	2,332	...
Total Europeans, etc.		...	...	...	...	...	118	118	...	71	71	...	47	47	...
GRAND TOTAL JEYPORE STATE	15,579	36½	5,741	387,434½	68,670	318,764½	2,823,966	467,661	2,356,305	1,505,766	245,206	1,260,560	1,318,201	222,456	1,095,745
X.—Kishengarh—															
1. Kishengarh City	Not available.	1	...	2,862	2,862	...	15,363	15,363	...	7,954	7,954	...	7,409	7,409	...
2. District of Kishengarh		...	82	4,521	...	4,521	32,266	...	32,266	16,861	...	16,861	15,405	...	15,405
3. Do. Roopnagar		1	37	3,947	1,037	2,910	24,656	5,011	19,645	12,724	2,486	10,238	11,932	2,525	9,407
4. Do. Araeen		...	50	3,291	...	3,291	24,277	...	24,277	12,589	...	12,589	11,688	...	11,688
5. Do. Surwar		1	58	4,428	1,056	3,372	28,860	5,904	22,956	14,842	3,029	11,813	14,018	2,875	11,143
Total		3	227	19,049	4,955	14,094	125,422	26,278	99,144	64,970	13,469	51,501	60,452	12,809	47,643
Total Kishengarh Railway		...	...	30	30	...	94	94	...	68	68	...	26	26	...
GRAND TOTAL KISHENGARH STATE	858	3	227	19,079	4,985	14,094	125,516	25,672	99,144	65,038	13,537	51,501	60,478	12,835	47,643
XI.—Lawa—															
1. Lawa (Thakurate)		...	8	493	...	493	3,360	...	3,360	1,728	...	1,728	1,632	...	1,632
TOTAL JEYPORE RESIDENCY	16,456	39½	5,976	407,006½	73,655	333,351½	2,952,842	494,033	2,458,809	1,572,532	258,743	1,313,789	1,380,311	235,291	11,450,110

TABLE I.—Area, Houses and Population—*contd.*

Names of Agency and States.	Area in Square Miles.	Number of Town.	Number of Village.	Occupied Houses Total.	Occupied Houses Town.	Occupied Houses Village.	Population Total Total.	Population Total Town.	Population Total Village.	Males Total.	Males Town.	Males Village.	Females Total.	Females Town.	Females Village.
1	2	3	4	5	6	7	8	9	10	11	12	13	14	15	16
V.—EASTERN STATES AGENCY—															
XII.—Bhartpur—															
1. Bhartpur City	Separate Area not available.	1	...	12,251	12,251	...	67,553	67,553	...	37,337	37,337	...	30,216	30,216	...
2. Bhartpur Tehsil		...	177	5,665	...	5,665	40,431	...	40,431	21,929	...	21,929	18,502	...	18,502
3. Uchain		...	97	6,302	...	6,302	47,735	...	47,735	25,585	...	25,585	22,150	...	22,150
4. Akhaigarh		...	99	4,541	...	4,541	45,695	...	45,695	25,635	...	25,635	20,060	...	20,060
5. Bayana		1	159	8,277	1,176	7,101	75,126	8,085	67,041	40,646	4,154	36,492	34,480	3,931	30,549
6. Bhosawar		2	141	11,322	2,654	8,668	82,663	14,243	68,420	44,134	7,287	36,847	38,529	6,956	31,573
7. Pahari		...	84	4,414	...	4,414	27,737	...	27,737	15,038	...	15,038	12,699	...	12,699
8. Deeg		1	115	9,291	2,733	6,558	62,725	15,166	47,559	34,315	8,223	26,092	28,410	6,943	21,467
9. Rupbas		...	71	3,150	...	3,150	30,186	...	30,186	16,351	...	16,351	13,835	...	13,835
10. Kama		1	105	5,526	1,866	3,660	44,058	11,417	32,641	23,444	5,951	17,493	20,614	5,466	15,148
11. Kumheir		1	105	7,345	1,352	5,993	51,180	6,661	44,519	27,478	3,443	24,035	23,702	3,218	20,484
12. Gopalgarh		...	122	6,449	...	6,449	40,791	...	40,791	21,595	...	21,595	19,196	...	19,196
13. Nagpur		...	77	2,784	...	2,784	23,943	...	23,943	13,986	...	13,986	9,957	...	9,957
Total		7	1,352	87,317	22,032	65,285	639,823	123,125	516,698	347,473	66,395	281,078	292,350	56,730	235,620
Bhartpur Railway		...	...	135	135	...	478	478	...	355	355	...	123	123	...
Europeans, etc., in Bhartpur		...	...	...	...	...	2	2	...	2	2	...	...	...	...
GRAND TOTAL BHARTPUR STATE	**1,982**	**7**	**1,352**	**87,452**	**22,167**	**65,285**	**640,303**	**123,605**	**516,698**	**347,830**	**66,752**	**281,078**	**292,473**	**56,853**	**235,620**
XIII.—Karauli—															
1. Karauli City	Not available.	1	...	4,623	4,623	...	23,110	23,110	...	11,761	11,761	...	11,349	11,349	...
2. Hazur Tehsil		...	229	8,590	...	8,590	37,821	...	37,821	20,832	...	20,832	16,989	...	16,989
3. Jirota		...	182	7,350	...	7,350	31,611	...	31,611	17,035	...	17,035	14,576	...	14,576
4. Machilpura		...	139	6,036	...	6,036	24,981	...	24,981	13,670	...	13,670	11,311	...	11,311
5. Mandrail		...	174	4,599	...	4,599	23,139	...	23,139	12,404	...	12,404	10,735	...	10,735
6 Utgir		...	116	3,654	...	3,654	15,911	...	15,911	8,845	...	8,845	7,066	...	7,066
Total		1	840	34,852	4,623	30,229	156,573	23,110	133,463	84,547	11,761	72,786	72,026	11,349	60,677
Europeans, etc., in Karauli		...	...	...	...	...	14	14	...	8	8	...	6	6	...
GRAND TOTAL KARAULI STATE	**1,242**	**1**	**840**	**34,852**	**4,623**	**30,229**	**156,587**	**23,124**	**133,463**	**84,555**	**11,769**	**72,786**	**72,032**	**11,355**	**60,677**

Table I.—Area, Houses and Population—Rajputana Agency.

Names of Agency and States.	Area in Square Miles.	Number of Town.	Number of Village.	Occupied Houses Total.	Occupied Houses Town.	Occupied Houses Village.	Population Total Total.	Population Total Town.	Population Total Village.	Males Total.	Males Town.	Males Village.	Females Total.	Females Town.	Females Village.
1	2	3	4	5	6	7	8	9	10	11	12	13	14	15	16
V.—EASTERN STATES AGENCY —*contd.*															
XIV.—Dholpur—															
1. Gird Tehsil	Separate Area not available.	2	148	15,004	3,588	11,416	76,607	15,825	60,782	45,512	8,170	37,342	31,095	7,655	23,440
2. Bari		1	109	12,414	3,307	9,107	54,564	12,090	42,474	29,989	6,271	23,718	24,575	5,819	18,756
3. Basehri		...	79	11,668	...	11,668	48,732	...	48,732	26,902	...	26,902	21,830	...	21,830
4. Kolari		...	75	10,654	...	10,654	46,831	...	46,831	24,955	...	24,955	21,876	...	21,876
5. Rajakhera		1	76	5,868	1,539	4,329	34,532	6,786	27,746	19,366	3,731	15,635	15,166	3,055	12,111
6. Sir Muthra		...	31	4,682	...	4,682	18,458	...	18,458	10,280	...	10,280	8,178	..	8,178
Total		4	518	60,290	8,434	51,856	279,724	34,701	245,023	157,004	18,172	138,832	122,720	16,529	106,191
Europeans, etc.		...	...	...	...	...	5	5	...	4	4	...	1	1	...
Indian Midland Railway—															
Dholpur		...	...	...	...	...	115	115	...	83	83	...	32	32	...
Mania Station		...	...	...	...	...	46	...	46	32	...	32	14	...	14
GRAND TOTAL, DHOLPUR	**1,154**	**4**	**518**	**60,290**	**8,484**	**51,856**	**279,890**	**34,821**	**245,069**	**157,123**	**18,259**	**138,864**	**122,767**	**16,562**	**106,205**
TOTAL EASTERN STATES AGENCY	...	**12**	**2,710**	**182,594**	**35,224**	**147,370**	**1,076,780**	**181,550**	**895,230**	**589,508**	**96,780**	**492,728**	**487,272**	**84,770**	**402,502**
VI.—ALWAR AGENCY—															
XV.—Alwar—															
1. Alwar	496	1	223	27,304	10,530	16,774	141,157	51,369	89,788	74,703	27,734	46,969	66,454	23,635	42,819
2. Bansur	330	1	137	10,459	1,062	9,397	65,203	5,005	60,198	34,866	2,598	32,268	30,337	2,407	27,930
3. Bahrore	264	1	130	9,038	889	8,149	69,419	5,719	63,700	35,898	2,810	33,088	33,521	2,909	30,612
4. Govindgarh	52	1	50	3,130	1,016	2,114	21,694	5,243	16,451	11,310	2,688	8,622	10,384	2,555	7,829
5. Kathumbar	122	...	77	5,415	...	5,415	38,964	...	38,964	20,783	...	20,783	18,181	...	18,181
6. Kishengarh	217	...	162	13,277	...	13,277	61,671	...	61,671	32,033	...	32,033	29,638	...	29,638
7. Luchmangarh	221	...	176	12,758	...	12,758	60,479	...	60,479	31,516	...	31,516	28,963	...	28,963
8. Mundawar	229	...	129	8,415	...	8,415	56,886	...	56,886	29,870	...	29,870	27,016	...	27,016
9. Rajgarh	373	1	201	13,511	2,037	11,474	88,901	10,302	78,599	46,536	5,084	41,452	42,365	5,218	37,147
10. Ramgarh	146	1	117	11,390	1,323	10,067	47,912	5,099	42,813	25,155	2,649	22,506	22,757	2,450	20,307
11. Thanaghazi	287	...	139	9,675	...	9,675	54,561	...	54,561	28,674	...	28,674	25,887	...	25,887
12. Tijara	257	1	186	10,652	1,636	9,016	52,570	7,049	45,521	27,930	3,543	24,387	24,640	3,506	21,134
13. Nimrana State	30	...	13	994	...	994	7,340	...	7,340	3,894	...	3,894	3,446	...	3,446
Total	3,144	7	1,740	136,018	18,493	117,525	766,757	89,786	676,971	403,168	47,106	356,062	363,589	42,680	320,909
Total Railway	...	...	...	252	252	...	971	971	...	700	700	...	271	271	...
Total Europeans, etc.	...	...	...	...	...	...	58	58	..	30	30	...	28	28	...
GRAND TOTAL ALWAR AGENCY	**3,144**	**7**	**1,740**	**136,270**	**18,745**	**117,525**	**767,786**	**90,815**	**676,971**	**403,898**	**47,836**	**356,062**	**363,888**	**42,979**	**320,909**

TABLE I.—Area, Houses and Population—*contd.*

Names of Agency and States.	Area in Square Miles.	Number of Town.	Number of Village.	Occupied Houses Total.	Occupied Houses Town.	Occupied Houses Village.	Population Total Total.	Population Total Town.	Population Total Village.	Males Total.	Males Town.	Males Village.	Females Total.	Females Town.	Females Village.
1	2	3	4	5	6	7	8	9	10	11	12	13	14	15	16
VII.—HAROWTI AND TONK AGENCY—															
XVI.—Tonk (Rajputana)—															
1. Tonk	578·59	1	249	24,662	10,759	13,903	114,298	45,944	68,354	59,591	23,203	36,388	54,707	22,741	31,966
2. Aligarh	160·09	...	79	4,300	...	4,300	19,623	...	19,623	10,466	...	10,466	9,157	...	9,157
3. Nimbahera	374·73	1	198	14,945	1,394	13,551	64,888	5,957	59,531	33,609	2,732	30,877	31,279	2,625	28,654
Total	1,113·41	2	526	43,907	12,153	31,754	198,809	51,301	147,508	103,666	25,935	77,731	95,143	25,366	69,777
Total Railway	...	...	...	50	50	...	122	122	...	84	84	...	38	38	...
Europeans, etc.	...	...	...	1	1	...	3	3	...	2	2	...	1	1	...
Total Rajputana, Tonk	1,113·41	2	526	43,958	12,204	31,754	198,934	51,426	147,508	103,752	26,021	77,731	95,182	25,405	69,777
Detached Tracts of Tonk under Central India—															
1. Chabra	807·71	1	187	10,657	1,878	8,779	46,473	7,426	39,047	24,290	3,730	20,560	22,183	3,696	18,487
2. Parwa	62·18	1	121	9,129	1,481	7,648	40,806	5,627	35,179	21,567	2,819	18,748	19,239	2,808	16,431
3. Sironj	569·04	1	390	20,432	2,700	17,732	93,856	11,737	82,119	50,488	6,676	43,812	43,368	5,061	38,307
Total	1,438·93	3	698	40,218	6,059	34,159	181,135	24,790	156,345	96,345	13,225	83,120	84,790	11,565	73,225
TOTAL TONK STATE	2,552·84	5	1,224	84,176	18,263	65,913	380,069	76,216	303,853	200,097	39,246	160,851	179,972	36,970	143,002
XVII.—Bundi—															
1. Bundi	Not available.	1	...	3,955	3,955	...	22,544	22,544	...	11,980	11,980	...	10,564	10,564	...
2. Taragarh		...	13	979	...	979	5,492	...	5,492	2,882	...	2,882	2,610	...	2,610
3. Patan		...	66	5,298	...	5,298	28,252	...	28,252	14,674	...	14,674	13,578	...	13,578
4. Kapran		...	19	1,768	...	1,768	9,235	...	9,235	4,793	...	4,793	4,442	...	4,442
5. Gundowli		...	151	7,087	...	7,087	39,760	...	39,760	20,821	...	20,821	18,939	...	18,939
6. Ajitgarh		...	32	835	...	835	4,634	...	4,634	2,532	...	2,532	2,102	...	2,102
7. Deyi		...	131	7,021	...	7,021	42,940	...	42,940	22,452	...	22,452	20,488	...	20,488
8. Naenwa		1	...	1,171	1,171	...	6,093	6,093	...	3,148	3,148	...	2,945	2,945	...
9. Gotra		...	128	7,102	...	7,102	43,527	...	43,527	23,051	...	23,051	20,476	...	20,476
10. Hindoli		...	129	7,261	...	7,261	41,857	...	41,857	22,420	...	22,420	19,437	...	19,437
11. Selore		...	213	9,660	...	9,660	51,341	...	51,341	27,280	...	27,280	24,061	...	24,061
Total	2,220	2	882	52,137	5,126	47,011	295,675	28,637	267,038	156,033	15,128	140,905	139,642	13,509	126,133

Names of Agency and States.	Area in Square Miles.	Number of		Occupied houses.			Population.								
							Total.			Males.			Females.		
		Town.	Village.	Total.	Town.	Village.	Total.	Town.	Village.	Total.	Town.	Village.	Total.	Towns.	Village.
1	2	3	4	5	6	7	8	9	10	11	12	13	14	15	16
VII.—HARAOWTI AND TONK AGENCY—*contd.*															
XVIII.—SHAHPURA—															
1. Kachola Pargana of Shahpura included under Meywar	...	...	88	6,013	...	6,013	26,227	...	26,227	13,832	...	13,832	12,395	...	12,395
2. Phooliya Pargana (Shahpura)	...	1	134	13,653	2,920	10,733	63,646	11,718	51,928	33,243	5,930	27,313	30,403	5,788	24,615
Total Shahpura Estate	405	1	222	19,666	2,920	16,746	89,873	11,718	78,155	47,075	5,930	41,145	42,798	5,788	37,010
Total Haraowti and Tonk Agency, excluding Kachola.	**5,177**	**8**	**2,240**	**149,966**	**26,309**	**123,657**	**739,390**	**116,571**	**622,819**	**389,373**	**60,304**	**329,069**	**350,017**	**56,267**	**293,750**
VIII.—JHALAWAR—															
1. Jhalrapatan (Chaoni)		1	...	3,746	3,746	...	23,363	23,363	...	12,126	12,126	...	11,237	11,237	...
2. Jhalrapatan (Town)	171	1	...	2,198	2,198	...	10,783	10,783	...	5,680	5,680	...	5,103	5,103	...
3. Patan-(Pargana)		...	99	3,203	...	3,203	17,494	...	17,494	9,219	...	9,219	8,275	...	8,275
4. Chechat	156	...	88	4,644	...	4,644	25,066	...	25,066	13,184	...	13,184	11,882	...	11,882
5. Suket	103	...	56	2,980	...	2,980	16,424	...	16,424	8,610	...	8,610	7,814	...	7,814
6. Asnawar	95	...	73	1,870	...	1,870	9,600	...	9,600	5,170	...	5,170	4,430	...	4,430
7. Bakani	253	...	183	4,997	...	4,997	28,195	...	28,195	14,999	...	14,999	13,196	...	13,196
8. Iklera	107	...	96	2,983	...	2,983	16,763	...	16,763	8,837	...	8,837	7,926	...	7,926
9. Ghatoli	129	...	104	2,564	...	2,564	16,007	...	16,007	8,560	...	8,560	7,447	...	7,447
10. Chipa Barod	318	...	166	6,780	...	6,780	34,225	...	34,225	18,020	...	18,020	16,205	...	16,205
11. Manohar Thana	232	...	173	4,672	...	4,672	27,796	...	27,796	14,563	...	14,563	13,233	...	13,233
Total of Central Jhalawar	1,564	2	1,038	40,637	5,944	34,693	225,716	34,146	191,570	118,968	17,806	101,162	106,748	16,340	90,408
12. Pachpahar	131	...	60	3,051	...	3,051	18,173	...	18,173	9,631	...	9,631	8,542	...	8,542
13. Awar	80	...	40	2,661	...	2,661	15,755	...	15,755	8,475	...	8,475	7,280	...	7,280
14. Dag	168	...	69	4,004	...	4,004	26,206	...	26,206	14,345	...	14,345	11,861	...	11,861
15. Gangdhar	187	...	112	4,972	...	4,972	30,821	...	30,821	16,816	...	16,816	14,005	...	14,005
Total of Chomahla	566	...	281	14,688	...	14,688	90,955	...	90,955	49,267	...	49,267	41,688	...	41,688
16. Uprehti	321	...	69	3,015	...	3,015	13,361	...	13,361	6,993	...	6,993	6,368	...	6,368
17. Taleti	243	...	67	2,661	...	2,661	13,551	...	13,551	7,244	...	7,244	6,307	...	6,307
Total of Shahabad	564	...	136	5,676	...	5,676	26,912	...	26,912	14,237	...	14,237	12,675	...	12,675
Total Jhalawar	2,722	2	1,455	61,001	5,944	55,057	343,583	34,146	309,437	182,472	17,806	164,666	161,111	16,340	144,771
Total Europeans, etc.	...	...	...	...	...	...	18	18	...	6	6	...	12	12	...
GRAND TOTAL, JHALAWAR AGENCY	**2,722**	**2**	**1,455**	**61,001**	**5,944**	**55,057**	**343,601**	**34,164**	**309,437**	**182,478**	**17,812**	**164,666**	**161,123**	**16,352**	**144,771**

TABLE I.—Area, Houses and Population —*concld.*

Names of Agency and States.	Area in Square Miles.	Number of		Occupied Houses.			Population.								
							Total.			Males.			Females.		
		Town.	Village.	Total.	Town.	Village.	Total.	Town.	Village.	Total.	Town.	Village.	Total.	Town.	Village.
1	2	3	4	5	6	7	8	9	10	11	12	13	14	15	16
IX.—KOTAH AGENCY—															
XX.—Kotah—															
1. Kotah City and Suburbs .	Separate area of each sub-division not available.	1	...	6,787	6,787	...	38,620	38,620	...	20,003	20,003	...	18,617	18,617	...
Nizamats—															
2. Anta		...	79	6,361	...	6,361	32,810	...	32,810	16,914	...	16,914	15,896	...	15,896
3. Baran		1	84	8,053	1,679	6,374	37,889	7,067	30,822	19,286	3,503	15,783	18,603	3,564	15,039
4. Barodh		...	75	4,606	...	4,606	23,358	...	23,358	12,134	...	12,134	11,224	...	11,224
5. Digod		...	77	4,210	...	4,210	22,055	...	22,055	11,624	...	11,624	10,431	...	10,431
6. Etawah		...	61	4,683	...	4,683	23,109	...	23,109	11,949	...	11,949	11,160	...	11,060
7. Ghataoli		...	99	3,821	...	3,821	20,069	...	20,069	10,562	...	10,562	9,507	...	9,507
8. Kanwas		...	123	6,021	...	6,021	27,599	...	27,599	14,196	...	14,196	13,403	...	13,403
9. Khanpur		...	85	5,480	...	5,480	26,372	...	26,372	13,798	...	13,798	12,574	...	12,574
10. Kishanganj		...	161	5,848	...	5,848	28,992	...	28,992	15,392	...	15,392	13,600	...	13,600
11. Kunjer		...	61	4,415	...	4,415	21,583	...	21,583	11,146	...	11,146	10,437	...	10,437
12. Ladpura		...	142	8,631	...	8,631	42,290	...	42,290	21,814	...	21,814	20,476	...	20,476
13. Mangrol		1	72	6,609	1,231	5,378	31,984	5,714	26,270	16,451	2,937	13,514	15,533	2,777	12,756
14. Sangod		1	115	7,304	1,139	6,165	32,565	5,046	27,519	16,921	2,547	14,374	15,644	2,499	13,145
15. Shergarh		...	85	5,803	...	5,803	28,313	...	28,313	14,699	...	14,699	13,614	...	13,614
16. Taruj		...	128	6,410	...	6,410	32,928	...	32,928	17,228	...	17,228	15,700	...	15,700
Total Nizamats		3	1,447	88,255	4,049	84,206	431,916	17,827	414,089	224,114	8,987	215,127	207,802	8,840	198,962
Kotah Kotris—															
17. Antarda		...	11	683	...	683	4,219	...	4,219	2,203	...	2,203	2,016	...	2,016
18. Balwan		...	23	544	...	544	2,888	...	2,888	1,562	...	1,562	1,326	...	1,326
19. Gainta		...	6	1,026	...	1,026	4,727	...	4,727	2,425	...	2,425	2,302	...	2,302
20. Indargarh		...	91	5,407	...	5,407	26,208	...	26,208	13,681	...	13,681	12,527	...	12,527
21. Karwar		...	6	595	...	595	2,525	...	2,525	1,285	...	1,285	1,240	...	1,240
22. Khatoli with Farera		...	25	1,798	...	1,798	8,088	...	8,088	4,198	...	4,198	3,890	...	3,890
23. Pipalda with Phusod		...	17	1,516	...	1,516	7,072	...	7,072	3,648	...	3,648	3,424	...	3,424
Total Kotris	...	...	179	11,569	...	11,569	55,727	...	55,727	29,002	...	29,002	26,725	...	26,725
Total Europeans, etc., in Kotah State	...	...	...	...	...	...	4	4	...	2	2	...	2	2	...
GRAND TOTAL, KOTAH AGENCY	**3,784**	**4**	**1,626**	**106,611**	**10,836**	**95,775**	**526,267**	**56,451**	**469,816**	**273,121**	**28,992**	**244,129**	**253,146**	**27,459**	**225,687**
GRAND TOTAL, Rajputana States, including detached Tracts of Tonk in Central India and those of Central India in Meywar	**129,065**	**127**	**31,023**	**2,217,643**	**299,865**	**1,917,778**	**12,401,478**	**1,554,877**	**10,846,601**	**6,551,958**	**804,739**	**5,747,214**	**5,849,525**	**750,138**	**5,099,387**

RAJPUTANA AGENCY.

CENSUS OF 1891.

PROVINCIAL TABLE II.

Variation in the population since the Census of 1881 by Parganas, Tehsils or other administrative divisions.

Statement of the increase or the decrease of the Population.

	According to Imperial Table No. II.			According to Provincial Table No. II.		
	1891.	1881.	Variation.	1891.	1881.	Variation.
Total Population .	11,990,504	9,959,012	+2,031,492	12,200,097	10,149,286	+2,050,811
Males . . .	6,340,443	5,385,175	+ 955,268	6,451,263	5,485,161	+ 966,102
Females . . .	5,650,061	4,573,837	+1,076,224	5,748,834	4,664,125	+1,084,709

In this table the population of the detached tracts of Tonk in Central India, the unenumerated Bhils of Banswara, and Grassias of Sirohi are included, and for this reason the grand totals of 1891 and 1881 will not tally with the total population of Rajputana as given in Imperial Table No. II.

Table II.—Variation in the Population—Rajputana Agency.

Summary of Table No. II.

Name of Agency.	Both Sexes.			Males.			Females.		
	1891.	1881.	Variation.	1891.	1881.	Variation.	1891.	1881.	Variation.
1	2	3	4	5	6	7	8	9	10
I.—MEYWAR RESIDENCY—									
Meywar	1,709,781	1,443,144	+ 266,637	893,842	772,685	+ 121,157	815,939	670,459	+ 145,480
Banswara	211,641	151,902*	+ 59,739	108,505	77,382	+ 31,123	103,136	74,520	+ 28,616
Dungarpur	98,448	86,034†	+ 12,414	49,444	44,308	+ 5,136	49,004	41,726	+ 7,278
Pertabgurh	87,975	79,028‡	+ 8,947	45,842	41,162	+ 4,680	42,133	37,866	+ 4,267
Kherwara Cantonment	648	...	+ 648	588	...	+ 588	60	...	+ 60
Kotra "	150	...	+ 150	147	...	+ 147	3	...	+ 3
Total Meywar Residency	(a) 2,108,643	1,760,108	+ 348,535	10,98,368	935,537	+ 162,831	1,010,275	824,571	+ 185,704
II.—WESTERN RAJPUTANA STATES RESIDENCY—									
Marwar	2,519,892	1,750,403	+ 769,489	1,324,947	969,125	+ 355,822	1,194,945	781,278	+ 413,667
½ Sambhar Joint Jurisdiction	8,286	7,215§	+ 1,071	4,531	3,940	+ 591	3,755	3,275	+ 480
Total Marwar	2,528,178	1,757,618	+ 770,560	1,329,478	973,065	+ 356,413	1,198,700	784,553	+ 414,147
Sirohi	188,885	142,903	+ 45,982	98,710	76,132	+ 22,578	90,175	66,771	+ 23,404
Jesalmir	115,701	108,143	+ 7,558	62,699	61,127	+ 1,572	53,002	47,016	+ 5,986
Erinpura Cantonment	1,859	...	+ 1,859	1,286	...	+ 1,286	573	...	+ 573
Abu Sanitarium	92	...	+ 92	56	...	+ 56	36	...	+ 36
Total Western Rajputana States Residency	2,834,715	2,008,664	+ 826,051	1,492,229	1,110,324	+ 381,905	1,342,486	898,340	+ 444,146
III.—JEYPORE RESIDENCY—									
Jeypore	2,815,679	2,519,926	+ 295,753	1,501,234	1,361,253	+ 139,981	1,314,445	1,158,673	+ 155,772
½ Sambhar Joint Jurisdiction	8,287	7,216§	+ 1,071	4,531	3,941	+ 590	3,756	3,275	+ 481
Total Jeypore	2,823,966	2,527,142	+ 296,824	1,505,765	1,365,194	+ 140,571	1,318,201	1,161,948	+ 156,253
Kishengurh	125,516	112,633	+ 12,883	65,038	59,098	+ 5,940	60,478	53,535	+ 6,943
Lawa Chiefship	3,360	2,682	+ 678	1,728	1,360	+ 368	1,632	1,322	+ 310
Total Jeypore Residency	2,952,842	2,642,457	+ 310,385	1,572,531	1,425,652	+ 146,879	1,380,311	1,216,805	+ 163,506
IV.—HARAOWTI AND TONK AGENCY—									
Tonk	198,934	170,179	+ 28,755	103,752	88,256	+ 15,496	95,182	81,923	+ 13,259
Detached Tracts of Tonk in Central India	181,135	167,850	+ 13,285	96,345	88,613	+ 7,732	84,790	79,237	+ 5,553
Total Tonk	380,069	338,029	+ 42,040	200,097	176,869	+ 23,228	179,972	161,160	+ 18,812
Bundi	295,675	254,701	+ 40,974	156,033	133,103	+ 22,930	139,642	121,598	+ 18,044
Shahpura Estate	63,646	51,750	+ 11,896	33,243	27,217	+ 6,026	30,403	24,533	+ 5,870
Total Haraowti and Tonk Agency	739,390	644,480	+ 94,910	389,373	337,189	+ 52,184	350,017	307,291	+ 42,726
V.—EASTERN STATES AGENCY—									
Bhartpur	640,303	645,540	— 5,237	347,830	350,475	— 2,645	292,473	295,065	— 2,592
Karauli	156,587	148,670	+ 7,917	84,555	80,645	+ 3,910	72,032	68,025	+ 4,007
Dholpur	279,890	249,657	+ 30,233	157,123	138,342	+ 18,781	122,767	111,315	+ 11,452
Total Eastern States Agency	1,076,780	1,043,867	+ 32,913	589,508	569,462	+ 20,046	487,272	474,405	+ 12,867
VI.—BIKANIR AGENCY	831,955	509,021	+ 322,934	440,046	293,650	+ 146,396	391,909	215,371	+ 176,538
VII.—ALWAR "	767,786	682,926	+ 84,860	403,898	360,384	+ 43,514	363,888	322,542	+ 41,346
VIII.—KOTAH "	526,267	517,275	+ 8,992	273,121	269,924	+ 3,197	253,146	247,351	+ 5,795
IX.—JHALAWAR "	343,601	340,488	+ 3,113	182,478	183,039	— 561	161,123	157,449	+ 3,674
Total Rajputana Agency	12,181,979	10,149,286	+ 2,032,693	6,441,552	5,485,161	+ 956,391	5,740,427	4,664,125	+ 1,076,302
Detached Tracts of Gungapur and Nundwas of Central India in Meywar	18,118	(Not available.)	+ 18,118	9,711	...	+ 9,711	8,407	...	+ 8,407
GRAND TOTAL	(a) 12,200,097	10,149,286	+ 2,050,811	6,451,263	5,485,161	+ 966,102	5,748,834	4,664,125	1,084,709

(a) Exclusive of 201,381 unenumerated Bhils of Meywar and Dungarpur.

* Including 47,902 unenumerated Bhils.

† Excluding 395 unenumerated Bhils.

‡ Excluding 270 unenumerated Bhils.

§ Sambhar Joint Jurisdiction villages divided equally between Meywar and Jeypore.

PROVINCIAL TABLE.

TABLE II.—Variation in the population since the Census of 1881.

	Both Sexes.			Males.			Females.		
	1891.	1881.	Variation.	1891.	1881.	Variation.	1891.	1881.	Variation.
1	2	3	4	5	6	7	8	9	10
I.—MEYWAR RESIDENCY—									
Meywar—									
Oodeypore	73,439	61,321	+ 12,118	38,795	32,321	+ 6,474	34,644	29,000	+ 5,644
Meja	5,099	4,530	+ 569	2,663	2,343	+ 320	2,436	2,187	+ 249
Parsoli	8,477	6,380	+ 2,097	4,502	3,466	+ 1,036	3,975	2,914	+ 1,061
Sirdargarh	6,583	5,122	+ 1,461	3,433	2,758	+ 675	3,150	2,364	+ 786
Kankrowli	8,294	6,456	+ 1,838	4,258	3,433	+ 825	4,036	3,023	+ 1,013
Kelwara	44,662	40,863	+ 3,799	23,686	22,981	+ 705	20,976	17,882	+ 3,094
Bansi	4,617	4,169	+ 448	2,378	2,148	+ 230	2,239	2,021	+ 218
Amet	16,506	14,951	+ 1,555	8,623	8,265	+ 358	7,883	6,686	+ 1,197
Jharol	8,110	7,830	+ 280	4,259	4,184	+ 75	3,851	3,646	+ 205
Kanor	15,786	14,196	+ 1,590	8,173	7,391	+ 782	7,613	6,805	+ 808
Delwara	30,099	27,994	+ 2,105	15,704	15,198	+ 506	14,395	12,796	+ 1,599
Shivrati	9,487	7,473	+ 2,014	4,945	3,953	+ 992	4,542	3,520	+ 1,022
Bijaypur	10,030	9,173	+ 857	5,234	4,740	+ 494	4,796	4,433	+ 363
Banera	36,804	31,517	+ 5,287	19,136	17,181	+ 1,955	17,668	14,336	+ 3,332
Khanmor	34,249	31,129	+ 3,120	17,994	17,043	+ 951	16,255	14,086	+ 2,169
Gogunda	13,972	11,906	+ 2,066	7,275	6,340	+ 935	6,697	5,566	+ 1,131
Bidnor	27,519	23,641	+ 3,878	14,713	13,375	+ 1,338	12,806	10,266	+ 2,540
Kurabar	25,452	22,768	+ 2,684	13,260	12,514	+ 746	12,192	10,254	+ 1,938
Kotharia	15,364	12,096	+ 3,268	7,994	6,812	+ 1,182	7,370	5,284	+ 2,086
Karjali	5,282	4,650	+ 632	2,675	2,402	+ 273	2,607	2,248	+ 359
Nathdwara	21,661	18,071	+ 3,590	11,301	9,709	+ 1,592	10,360	8,362	+ 1,998
Devasthan	41,696	34,819	+ 6,877	21,628	18,561	+ 3,067	20,068	16,258	+ 3,810
Fatehgarh	1,303	974	+ 329	695	569	+ 126	608	405	+ 203
Asind	21,416	17,104	+ 4,312	11,130	9,235	+ 1,895	10,286	7,869	+ 2,417
Hurra and Shimbhogarh	53,986	45,003	+ 8,983	28,509	24,507	+ 4,002	25,477	20,496	+ 4,981
Kapasin	52,355	44,443	+ 7,912	27,178	23,555	+ 3,623	25,177	20,888	+ 4,289
Bagor	12,568	10,787	+ 1,781	6,556	5,774	+ 782	6,012	5,013	+ 999
Bijolia	14,949	11,838	+ 3,111	7,719	6,200	+ 1,519	7,230	5,638	+ 1,592
Kanera	8,289	7,566	+ 723	4,219	3,872	+ 347	4,070	3,694	+ 376
Deogarh	56,531	44,669	+ 11,862	29,828	24,886	+ 4,942	26,703	19,783	+ 6,920
Bari Sadri	16,499	13,384	+ 3,115	8,641	7,154	+ 1,487	7,858	6,230	+ 1,628
Begun	30,835	25,162	+ 5,673	15,966	13,342	+ 2,624	14,869	11,820	+ 3,049
Magra Sarara	54,715	42,189	+ 12,526	28,852	22,839	+ 6,013	25,863	19,350	+ 6,513
Dhariavad	6,162	5,272	+ 890	3,090	2,790	+ 300	3,072	2,482	+ 590
Bedla	23,923	19,041	+ 4,882	12,452	9 961	+ 2,491	11,471	9,080	+ 2,391
Sayra	23,543	21,583	+ 1,960	12,326	11,409	+ 917	11,217	10,174	+ 1,043
Choti Sadri	48,060	43,471	+ 4,589	24,788	22,822	+ 1 966	23,272	20,649	+ 2,623
Salumbar	55,009	44,372	+ 10,637	28,022	23,454	+ 4,568	26,987	20,918	+ 6,069
Kotra Bhumat	7,648	2,750	+ 4,898	4,189	1,602	+ 2,587	3,459	1,148	+ 2,311
Khairwara Bhumat	13,346	6,704	+ 6,642	6,782	4,029	+ 2,753	6,564	2,675	+ 3,889
Rincher	7,103	6,595	+ 508	3,761	3,575	+ 186	3,342	3,020	+ 322
Bhindar	24,899	20,707	+ 4,192	12,774	11,556	+ 1,218	12,125	9,151	+ 2,974
Chitorgarh	116,348	89,703	+ 26,645	60,534	48,770	+ 11,764	55,814	40,933	+ 14,881
Bhainsrorgarh	23,500	20,655	+ 2,845	12,261	10,879	+ 1,382	11,239	9,776	+ 1,463
Bhilwara	96,443	85,774	+ 10,669	50,313	45,963	+ 4,350	46,130	39,811	+ 6,319
Girwa	93,316	86,891	+ 6,425	48,142	44,717	+ 3,425	45,174	42,174	+ 3,000
Mandalgarh	84,472	76,466	+ 8,006	44,651	40,858	+ 3,793	39,821	35,608	+ 4,213
Rasmi	46,757	38,673	+ 8,084	24,368	19,909	+ 4,459	22,389	18,764	+ 3,625
Rajnagar	39,858	32,407	+ 7,451	20,857	17,778	+ 3,079	19,001	14,629	+ 4,372
Sahran	99,929	90,336	+ 9,593	52,228	48,806	+ 3,422	47,701	41,530	+ 6,171
Jahazpur	85,637	66,792	+ 18,845	45,899	34,356	+ 11,543	39,738	32,436	+ 7,302
Kachola Shahpura	26,227	20.778	+ 5,449	13,832	10,400	+ 3,432	12,395	10,378	+ 2,017
Total Meywar Districts	1,708,814	1,443,144	+ 265,670	893,191	772,685	+ 120,506	815,623	670,459	+ 145,164
Total Kherwara Cantonment	648	...	+ 648	588	...	+ 588	60	...	+ 60
Total Kotra Cantonment	150	...	+ 150	147	...	+ 147	3	...	+ 3
Total Cantonments	798	...	+ 798	735	...	+ 735	63	...	+ 63
Total Railway	932	...	+ 932	633	...	+ 633	299	...	+ 299
Total Europeans, etc.	35	...	+ 35	18	...	+ 18	17	...	+ 17
Total Meywar	1,710,579	1,443,144	+ 267,435	894,577	772,685	+ 121,892	816,002	670,459	+ 145,543
Nundwas Pargana of Indore State	5,840	No previous Return	5,840	3,122	...	+ 3,122	2,718	...	+ 2,718
Gungapur Pargana of Gowalior State	12,278		+ 12,278	6,589	...	+ 6,589	5,689	...	+ 5,689
Total	18,118	..	+ 18,118	9,711	...	+ 9,711	8,407	...	8,407
GRAND TOTAL	**1,728,697***	**1,443,144**	**+ 285,553**	**904,288**	**772,685**	**+ 131,603**	**824,409**	**670,459**	**153,950**
Banswara—									
Banswara	180,268	128,813	+ 51,455	92,540	65,793	+ 26,747	87,728	63,020	+ 24,708
Chiefship of Kushalgarh	31,373	23,089	+ 8,284	15,965	11,589	+ 4,376	15,408	11,500	+ 3,908
Total Banswara State	211,641	151,902†	+ 59,739	108,505	77,382	+ 31,123	103,136	74,520	+ 28,616

* Exclusive of 134,429 unenumerated Bhils of Meywar.

† Including 47,902 unenumerated Bhils.

TABLE II.—Variation in the population since the Census of 1881—*contd.*

	Both Sexes.			Males.			Females.		
	1891.	1881.	Variation.	1891.	1881.	Variation.	1891.	1881.	Variation.
1	2	3	4	5	6	7	8	9	10
MEYWAR RESIDENCY—*contd.*									
Partabgarh	87,975	79,028†	+ 8,947	45,842	41,162	+ 4,680	42,133	37,866	+ 4,267
DUNGARPUR—									
Dungarpur	11,401	10,989	+ 412	5,496	5,547	— 51	5,905	5,442	+ 463
Kunba	10,158	7,934	+ 2,224	5,208	4,116	+ 1,092	4,950	3,818	+ 1,132
Ganeshpura	8,694	7,430	+ 1,264	4,447	4,068	+ 379	4,247	3,362	+ 885
Aspore	9,360	9,800	— 440	4,799	5,176	— 377	4,561	4,624	— 63
Pujpur	7,773	7,218	+ 555	3,903	3,719	+ 184	3,870	3,499	+ 371
Nithanva	10,790	10,592	+ 198	5,440	5,482	+ 42	5,350	5,110	+ 240
Sagwara	10,663	9,871	+ 792	5,293	4,837	+ 456	5,370	5,034	+ 336
Padwa	11,991	10,691	+ 1,300	5,933	5,544	+ 389	6,058	5,147	+ 911
Galiakot	8,227	6,891	+ 1,336	4,009	3,426	+ 583	4,218	3,465	+ 753
Dhumbhora	9,391	4,618	+ 4,773	4,916	2,393	+ 2,523	4,475	2,225	+ 2,250
TOTAL DUNGARPUR	98,448*	86,034‡	+ 12,414	49,444	44,308	+ 5,136	49,004	41,726	+ 7,278
Total Meywar Residency	2,108,643	1,760,108	+ 348,535	1,098,368	935,537	+ 162,831	1,010,275	824,571	+ 185,704
DETACHED TRACTS OF GUNGAPUR AND NANDWAS OF CENTRAL INDIA IN MEYWAR	18,118	...	18,118	9,711	...	9,711	8,407	...	+ 8,407
GRAND TOTAL	**2,126,761**	**1,760,108**	**+ 366,658**	**1,108,079**	**935,537**	**+ 172,542**	**1,018,682**	**824,571**	**+ 194,111**
II.—WESTERN RAJPUTANA STATES RESIDENCY—									
MARWAR AND MALANI—									
Jodhpore City	61,759	57,211	+ 4,548	31,663	30,205	+ 1,458	30,096	27,006	+ 3,090
" Kasba	18,646	6,118	+ 12,528	11,664	3,160	+ 8,504	6,982	2,958	+ 4,024
" Pargana	246,962	185,409	+ 61,553	131,134	105,812	+ 25,332	115,828	79,597	+ 36,231
TOTAL JODHPORE	327,367	248,738	+ 78,629	174,461	139,177	+ 35,284	152,906	109,561	+ 43,345
Nagore	252,257	167,484	+ 84,773	130,640	93,610	+ 37,030	121,617	73,874	+ 47,743
Bali	212,479	151,622	+ 60,857	109,179	83,522	+ 25,657	103,300	68,100	+ 35,200
Merta	205,704	158,892	+ 46,812	107,089	87,157	+ 19,932	98,615	71,735	+ 26,880
Jalore	170,428	94,067	+ 76,361	88,069	51,902	+ 36,167	82,359	42,165	+ 40,194
Sojat	141,782	102,986	+ 38,796	73,597	55,368	+ 18,229	68,185	47,618	+ 20,567
Jaswantpura	111,550	60,537	+ 51,013	58,517	32,107	+ 26,410	53,033	28,430	+ 24,603
Parbatsar	104,962	75,618	+ 29,344	55,926	42,359	+ 13,567	49,036	33,259	+ 15,777
Sanchore	95,890	49,612	+ 46,278	51,530	28,325	+ 23,205	44,360	21,287	+ 23,073
Jaitaran	87,635	67,336	+ 20,299	45,720	36,180	+ 9,540	41,915	31,156	+ 10,759
Bilara	84,952	60,359	+ 24,593	44,338	32,887	+ 11,451	40,614	27,472	+ 13,142
Phalodi	71,803	32,469	+ 39,334	37,341	19,337	+ 18,004	34,462	13,132	+ 21,330
Shergarh	70,919	40,639	+ 30,280	39,048	24,281	+ 14,767	31,871	16,358	+ 15,513
Siwana	64,747	46,433	+ 18,314	33,425	25,578	+ 7,847	31,322	20,855	+ 10,467
Pali	58,463	42,720	+ 15,743	29,949	22,619	+ 7,330	28,514	20,101	+ 8,413
Marote	56,806	43,763	+ 13,043	30,710	25,020	+ 5,690	26,096	18,743	+ 7,353
Didwana	54,272	38,506	+ 15,766	28,435	20,840	+ 7,595	25,837	17,666	+ 8,171
Pachbhadra	52,904	38,068	+ 14,836	27,944	21,101	+ 6,843	24,960	16,967	+ 7,993
Nawa	31,538	27,872	+ 3,666	16,721	14,801	+ 1,920	14,817	13,071	+ 1,746
Sheo	30,291	18,524	+ 11,767	16,426	11,050	+ 5,376	13,865	7,474	+ 6,391
Sankra	10,074	...	+ 10,074	5,675	...	+ 5,675	4,399	...	+ 4,399
		* 20,400	— 20,400	...	11,200	— 11,200	...	9,200	— 9,200
TOTAL MARWAR	2,296,823	1,586,645	+ 710,178	1,204,740	878,421	+ 326,319	1,092,083	708,224	+ 383,859
Malani	221,184	148,326	+ 72,858	119,036	82,188	+ 36,848	102,148	66,138	+ 36,010
TOTAL MARWAR AND MALANI	2,518,007	1,734,971	+ 783,036	1,323,776	960,609	+ 363,167	1,194,231	774,362	+ 419,869
Population of 1881 cannot be accounted for	...	15,432	— 15,432	...	8,516	— 8,516	...	6,916	— 6,916
‡ Sambhar, Jeypore and Jodhpore Joint Jurisdiction	8,286	7,215	+ 1,071	4,531	3,940	+ 591	3,755	3,275	+ 480
‡ Sambhar Railway	24	...	+ 24	13	...	+ 13	11	...	+ 11
TOTAL	8,310	7,215	+ 1,095	4,544	3,940	+ 604	3,766	3,275	+ 491
TOTAL R. M. RAILWAY	1,771	...	+ 1,771	1,115	...	+ 1,115	656	...	+ 656
Europeans, etc., Jodhpur	32	...	+ 32	16	...	+ 16	16	...	+ 16
Do. Nawa	23	...	+ 23	11	...	+ 11	12	...	+ 12
Do. Didwana	12	...	+ 12	6	...	+ 6	6	...	+ 6
Do. Pachbhadra	15	...	+ 15	7	...	+ 7	8	...	+ 8
Do. Phalodi	8	...	+ 8	3	...	+ 3	5	...	+ 5
TOTAL RAILWAY AND EUROPEAN, etc., POPULATION	1,861	...	+ 1,861	1,158	...	+ 1,158	703	...	+ 703
GRAND TOTAL, MARWAR STATE	**2,528,178**	**1,757,618**	**+ 770,560**	**1,329,478**	**973,065**	**+ 356,413**	**1,198,700**	**784,553**	**+ 414,147**

* Exclusive of 66,952 unenumerated Bhils of Dungarpur. † Excluding 270 unenumerated Bhils. ‡ Excluding 395 unenumerated Bhils.
§ The population of 48 villages was put by guess which were left from being enumerated in the Census of 1881.

TABLE II.—Variation in the population since the Census of 1881—*contd.*

	Both Sexes.			Males.			Females.		
	1891.	1881.	Variation.	1891.	1881.	Variation.	1891.	1881.	Variation.
1	2	3	4	5	6	7	8	9	10
WESTERN RAJPUTANA STATES RESIDENCY—*contd*									
Sirohi—									
Sirohi	186,310*	142,903	+ 43,407	97,118	76,132	+ 20,986	89,192	66,771	+ 22,421
Sirohi Railway	2,410	...	+ 2,410	1,494	...	+ 1,494	916	...	+ 916
European etc., in Abu	165	...	+ 165	98	...	+ 98	67	...	+ 67
Abu Sanitarium Population	92	...	+ 92	56	...	+ 56	36	...	+ 36
Erinpura Cantonment	1,859	...	+ 1,859	1,286	...	+ 1,286	573	...	+ 573
GRAND TOTAL, SIROHI STATE	**190,836**	**142,903**	**+ 47,933**	**100,052**	**76,132**	**+ 23,920**	**90,784**	**66,771**	**+ 24,013**
Jesalmir—									
Jesalmir	115,701	108,143	+ 7,558	62,699	61,127	+ 1,572	53,002	47,016	+ 5,986
GRAND TOTAL, WESTERN RAJPUTANA STATES RESIDENCY	**2,834,715**	**2,008,664**	**+826,051**	**1,492,229**	**1,110,324**	**+381,905**	**1,342,486**	**898,340**	**+444,146**
III.—BIKANIR AGENCY—									
Bikanir—									
Anupgarh	8,507	6,927	+ 1,580	4,631	4,244	+ 387	3,876	2,683	+ 1,193
Bahaderan	38,026	22,183	+ 15,843	20,612	12,660	+ 7,952	17,414	9,523	+ 7,891
Bikanir City	50,037	33,063	+ 16,974	24,705	15,811	+ 8,894	25,332	17,252	+ 8,080
" Suburbs	6,203	1,218	+ 4,985	3,184	623	+ 2,561	3,019	595	+ 2,424
" Tehsil	149,053	65,868	+ 83,185	78,638	40,249	+ 38,389	70,415	25,619	+ 44,796
Total	205,293	100,149	+ 105,144	106,527	56,683	+ 49,844	98,766	43,466	+ 55,300
Churu	82,899	47,003	+ 35,896	44,032	26,406	+ 17,626	38,867	20,597	+ 18,270
Dungargarh	44,007	16,627	+ 27,380	22,603	10,106	+ 12,497	21,404	6,521	+ 14,883
Hanumangarh	37,459	31,781	+ 5,678	20,405	18,124	+ 2,281	17,054	13,657	+ 3,397
Lunkaransar	65,224	36,605	+ 28,619	35,010	20,411	+ 14,599	30,214	16,194	+ 14,020
Mirzawala	10,375	7,925	+ 2,450	5,711	4,712	+ 999	4,664	3,213	+ 1,451
Nuhar	80,311	31,921	+ 48,390	43,002	18,852	+ 24,150	37,309	13,069	+ 24,240
Rajgarh	61,277	38,405	+ 22,872	33,249	23,075	+ 10,174	28,028	15,330	+ 12,698
Ratangarh	60,267	29,634	+ 30,633	31,666	16,500	+ 15,166	28,601	13,134	+ 15,467
Sardarsehr	44,911	21,240	+ 23,671	23,313	11,809	+ 11,504	21,598	9,431	+ 12,167
Sujangarh	77,031	29,150	+ 47,881	40,490	17,517	+ 22,973	36,541	11,633	+ 24,908
Suratgarh	16,356	14,247	+ 2,109	8,788	8,318	+ 470	7,568	5,929	+ 1,639
Population of 1881 cannot be accounted for	...	75,224	— 75,224	...	+ 44,233	— 44,233	...	*30,991	— 30,991
Total	831,943	509,021	+ 322,922	440,039	293,650	+ 146,389	391,904	215,371	176,533
Europeans, etc., in Bikanir	12	...	+ 12	7	...	+ 7	5	...	+ 5
GRAND TOTAL, BIKANIR AGENCY	**831,955**	**509,021**	**+322,934**	**440,046**	**293,650**	**+146,396**	**391,909**	**215,371**	**+176,538**
IV.—JEYPORE RESIDENCY—									
Jeypore—									
Jeypore City	158,787	142,578	+ 16,209	84,024	75,332	+ 8,692	74,763	67,246	+ 7,517
Total	158,787	142,578	+ 16,209	84,024	75,332	+ 8,692	74,763	67,246	+ 7,517
Jeypore Tehsil	195,101	190,021	+ 5,080	103,838	101,744	+ 2,094	91,263	88,277	+ 2,986
Jamua Ramgarh	153,055	144,458	+ 8,597	80,786	76,200	+ 4,586	72,269	68,258	+ 4,011
Chaksu Tehsil	112,488	94,581	+ 17,907	59,783	51,374	+ 8,409	52,705	43,207	+ 9,498
Kalegh "	106,822	95,574	+ 11,248	56,749	51,909	+ 4,840	50,073	43,665	+ 6,408
Total	567,466	524,634	+ 42,832	301,156	281,227	+ 19,929	266,310	243,407	+ 22,903
Dausa Tehsil	124,203	114,754	+ 9,449	65,776	60,526	+ 5,250	58,427	54,228	+ 4,199
Lalsote "	102,360	97,648	+ 4,712	54,050	51,456	+ 2,594	48,310	46,192	+ 2,118
Sikrai "	26,103	26,289	— 186	13,905	13,910	— 5	12,198	12,379	— 181
Baswa	69,334	61,195	+ 8,139	36,453	32,285	+ 4,168	32,881	28,910	+ 3,971
Total	322,000	299,886	+ 22,114	170,184	158,177	+ 12,007	151,816	141,709	+ 10,107
Jhoonjhnu Pargana	207,538	164,807	+ 42,731	111,718	91,098	+ 20,620	95,820	73,709	+ 22,111
Udeypore	62,768	55,792	+ 6,976	35,385	32,052	+ 3,333	27,383	23,740	+ 3,643
Total	270,306	220,599	+ 49,707	147,103	123,150	+ 23,953	123,203	97,449	+ 25,754
Sawai Ramgarh	127,269	116,029	+ 11,240	70,001	64,778	+ 5,223	57,268	51,251	+ 6,017
Khandela	68,832	61,161	+ 7,671	36,586	33,379	+ 3,207	32,246	27,782	+ 4,464
Baraith	53,450	51,407	+ 2,043	28,456	27,630	+ 826	24,994	23,777	+ 1,217
Total	249,551	228,597	+ 20,954	135,043	125,787	+ 9,256	114,508	102,810	+ 11,698

* Including 2,860 Grassias of Sirohi.

TABLE II.—Variation in the population since the Census of 1881 —*contd.*

	Both Sexes.			Males.			Females.		
	1891.	1881.	Variation.	1891.	1881.	Variation.	1891.	1881.	Variation.
1	2	3	4	5	6	7	8	9	10
JEYPORE RESIDENCY— *contd.*									
Jeypore—*contd.*									
Madhopur Tehsil	60,631	59,202	+ 1,429	31,659	31,184	+ 475	28,972	28,018	+ 954
Bauli	69,463	66,063	+ 3,400	36,762	35,573	+ 1,189	32,701	30,490	+ 2,211
Malarnu	53,497	49,650	+ 3,847	28,105	26,529	+ 1,576	25,392	23,121	+ 2,271
Khandar	33,499	28,878	+ 4,621	17,790	15,320	+ 2,470	15,709	13,558	+ 2,151
Isarda	13,481	8,342	+ 5,139	7,090	4,341	+ 2,749	6,391	4,001	+ 2,390
Barwara	12,264	9,116	+ 3,148	6,448	4,788	+ 1,660	5,816	4,328	+ 1,488
Total	242,835	221,251	21,584	127,854	117,735	+ 10,119	114,981	103,516	+ 11,465
Hindown Tehsil	50,737	44,207	+ 6,530	27,212	24,052	+ 3,160	23,525	20,155	+ 3,370
Toda Bhim	43,991	42,942	+ 1,049	23,225	22,850	+ 375	20,766	20,092	+ 674
Mahwa	37,188	33,600	+ 3,588	19,668	17,665	+ 2,003	17,520	15,935	+ 1,585
Walghat	25,269	24,262	+ 1,007	13,951	13,620	+ 331	11,318	10,642	+ 676
Ghonsla	14,862	10,540	+ 4,322	8,208	6,072	+ 2,136	6,654	4,468	+ 2,186
Ratan Zilla	14,858	15,640	— 782	8,095	8,686	— 591	6,763	6,954	— 191
Total	186,905	171,191	+ 15,714	100,359	92,945	+ 7,414	86,546	78,246	+ 8,300
½ Sambhar, Jeypore, and Jodhpore Joint Jurisdiction	8,287	7,216	+ 1,071	4,531	3,941	+ 590	3,756	3,275	+ 481
Naraina Tehsil	33,147	32,204	+ 943	17,565	17,497	+ 68	15,582	14,707	+ 875
Danta Ramgarh	82,522	74,231	+ 8,291	44,719	41,492	+ 3,227	37,803	32,739	+ 5,064
Muazamabad	59,693	51,461	+ 8,232	31,481	27,744	+ 3,737	28,212	23,717	+ 4,495
Total	183,649	165,112	+ 18,537	98,296	90,674	+ 7,622	85,353	74,438	+ 10,915
Malpura Tehsil	16,643	67,942	+ 8,701	40,180	36,819	+ 3,361	36,463	31,123	+ 5,340
Toda Rai Singh	62,904	52,487	+ 10,417	33,145	27,776	+ 5,369	29,759	24,711	+ 5,048
Newai	39,660	35,638	+ 4,022	21,171	19,195	+ 1,976	18,489	16,443	+ 2,046
Total	179,207	156,067	+ 23,140	94,496	83,790	+ 10,706	84,711	72,277	+ 12,434
Gungapur Tehsil	44,687	43,454	+ 1,233	23,558	23,034	+ 524	21,129	20,420	+ 709
Wazirpur	22,718	20,175	+ 2,543	11,844	11,039	+ 805	10,874	9,136	+ 1,738
Bamaniuwas	13,811	14,350	— 539	7,200	7,406	— 206	6,611	6,944	— 333
Total	81,216	77,979	+ 3,237	42,602	41,479	+ 1,123	38,614	36,500	+ 2,114
Kote Kasim	17,054	17,138	— 84	8,939	9,131	— 192	8,115	8,007	+ 108
Total	17.054	17,138	— 84	8,939	9,131	— 192	8,115	8,007	+ 108
Bandikui	4,297	...	+ 4,297	2,303	...	2,303	1,994	...	+ 1,994
Total	4,297	...	+ 4,297	2,303	...	2,303	1,994	...	+ 1,994
Sirkar	179,337	149,709	+ 29,628	95,431	80,661	+ 14,770	83,906	69,048	+ 14,858
Khetri	131,377	108,980	+ 22,397	70,578	60,482	+ 10,096	60,799	48,498	+ 12,301
Uniara	43,382	37,794	+ 5,588	23,191	20,324	+ 2,867	20,191	17,470	+ 2,721
Total	354,096	296,483	+ 57,613	189,200	161,467	+ 27,733	164,896	135,016	+ 29,880
Total	2,817.369	2,521,515	+ 295,854	1,501,559	1,360,894	+ 140,665	1,315,810	1,160,621	+ 155,189
Total ½ Sambhar Railway	24	...	+ 24	12	...	+ 12	12	...	+ 12
Total Jeypore Railway	6,455	...	+ 6,455	4,123	...	+ 4,123	2,332	...	+ 2,332
European, etc.	118	...	+ 118	71	...	+ 71	47	...	+ 47
Population of 1881 cannot be accounted for	...	5,627	— 5,627	...	4,300	— 4,300	...	1,327	— 1,327
GRAND TOTAL OF JEYPORE STATE	**2,823,966**	**2,527,142**	**+ 296,824**	**1,505,765**	**1,365,194**	**+ 140,571**	**1,818,201**	**1,161,948**	**+ 156,253**
Kishengarh—									
Kishengarh City	15,363	14,824	+ 539	7,954	7,513	+ 441	7,409	7,311	+ 98
District Kishengarh	32,266	29,964	+ 2,302	16,861	16,003	+ 858	15,405	13,961	+ 1,444
Do. Roopnagar	24,656	22,793	+ 1,863	12,724	12,141	+ 583	11,932	10,652	+ 1,280
Do. Araeen	24,277	20,547	+ 3,730	12,589	10,650	+ 1,939	11,688	9,897	+ 1,791
Do. Sarwar	28,860	24,505	+ 4,355	14,842	12,791	+ 2,051	14,018	11,714	+ 2,304
Total	125,422	112,633	+ 12,789	64,970	59,098	+ 5,872	60,452	53,535	+ 6,917
Total Kishengarh Railway	94	...	+ 94	68	...	+ 68	26	...	+ 26
GRAND TOTAL, KISHENGARH STATE	**125,516**	**112,633**	**+ 12,883**	**65,088**	**59,098**	**+ 5,940**	**60,478**	**53,535**	**+ 6,943**

TABLE II.—Variation in the population since the Census of 1881—*contd.*

	Both Sexes.			Males.			Females.		
	1891.	1881.	Variation.	1891.	1881.	Variation.	1891.	1881.	Variation.
1	2	3	4	5	6	7	8	9	10
JEYPORE RESIDENCY—*concld.*									
LAWA—									
Lawa	3,360	2,682	+ 678	1,728	1,360	+ 368	1,632	1,322	+ 310
GRAND TOTAL, JEYPORE RESIDENCY	**2,952,842**	**2,642,457**	**+ 310,385**	**1,572,531**	**1,425,652**	**+146,879**	**1,380,311**	**1,216,805**	**+ 163,506**
V.—EASTERN STATES AGENCY—									
BHURTPUR—									
Bhurtpur City	67,553	66,163	+ 1,390	37,337	36,580	+ 757	30,216	29,583	+ 633
Bhurtpur Tehsil	40,431	41,340	— 909	21,929	22,276	— 347	18,502	19,064	— 562
Uchain	47,735	48,849	— 1,114	25,585	26,224	— 639	22,150	22,625	— 475
Akhaigarh	45,695	46,974	— 1,279	25,635	25,784	— 149	20,060	21,190	— 1,130
Bayana	75,126	76,559	— 1,433	40,646	41,326	— 680	34,480	35,233	— 753
Bhosawar	82,663	80,852	+ 1,811	44,134	43,086	+ 1,048	38,529	37,766	+ 763
Pahari	27,737	29,801	— 2,064	15,038	15,718	— 680	12,699	14,083	— 1,384
Deeg	62,725	63,928	— 1,203	34,315	34,707	— 392	28,410	29,221	— 811
Rupbas	30,186	34,134	— 3,948	16,351	18,765	— 2,414	13,835	15,369	— 1,534
Kama	44,058	40,375	+ 3,683	23,444	21,470	+ 1,974	20,614	18,905	+ 1,709
Kumbeir	51,180	45,382	+ 5,798	27,478	24,306	+ 3,172	23,702	21,076	+ 2,626
Gopalgarh	40,791	45,535	— 4,744	21,595	25,558	— 3,963	19,196	19,977	— 781
Nagur	23,943	25,266	— 1,323	13,986	14,381	— 395	9,957	10,885	— 928
TOTAL	639,323	645,158	— 5,335	347,473	350,181	+ 2,708	292,350	294,977	— 2,627
Bhurtpur Railway	478	...	+ 478	355	...	+ 355	123	...	+ 123
Europeans, etc., in Bhurtpur	2	...	+ 2	2	...	+ 2	...	...	...
Population of 1881 cannot be accounted for	...	382	— 382	...	294	— 294	...	88	— 88
GRAND TOTAL, BHURTPUR	**640,303**	**645,540**	**— 5,237**	**347,830**	**350,475**	**— 2,645**	**292,473**	**295,065**	**— 2,592**
KARAULI—									
Karauli City	23,110	25,607	— 2,497	11,761	12,995	— 1,234	11,349	12,612	— 1,263
Hazur Tehsil	37,821	35,864	+ 1,957	20,832	20,040	+ 792	16,989	15,824	+ 1,165
Jirota	31,611	29,039	+ 2,572	17,035	15,640	+ 1,395	14,576	13,399	+ 1,177
Machilpura	24,981	23,857	+ 1,124	13,670	13,079	+ 591	11,311	10,778	+ 533
Mandril	23,139	20,179	+ 2,960	12,404	10,988	+ 1,416	10,735	9,191	+ 1,544
Utgir	15,911	14,124	+ 1,787	8,845	7,903	+ 942	7,066	6,221	+ 845
TOTAL	156,573	148,670	+ 7,903	84,547	80,645	+ 3,902	72,026	68,025	+ 4,001
TOTAL EUROPEANS, ETC., IN KARAULI	14	...	+ 14	8	...	+ 8	6	...	+ 6
GRAND TOTAL, KARAULI	**156,587**	**148,670**	**+ 7,917**	**84,555**	**80,645**	**+ 3,910**	**72,032**	**68,025**	**+ 4,007**
DHOLPUR—									
Gird Tehsil	76,607	68,191	+ 8,416	45,512	37,714	+ 7,798	31,095	30,477	+ 618
Bari	54,564	48,847	+ 5,717	29,989	27,145	+ 2,844	24,575	21,702	+ 2,873
Basheri	48,732	47,202	+ 1,530	26,902	26,402	+ 500	21,830	20,800	+ 1,030
Kolari	46,831	39,392	+ 7,439	24,955	21,332	+ 3,623	21,876	18,060	+ 3,816
Rajakhera	34,532	28,997	+ 5,535	19,366	16,258	+ 3,108	15,166	12,739	+ 2,427
Sir-Muttra	18,458	17,028	+ 1,430	10,280	9,491	+ 789	8,178	7,537	+ 641
TOTAL	279,724	249,657	+ 30,067	157,004	138,342	+ 18,662	122,720	111,315	+ 11,405
Europeans, etc.	5	...	+ 5	4	...	+ 4	1	...	+ 1
INDIAN MIDLAND RAILWAY—									
Dholpur	115	...	+ 115	83	...	+ 83	32	...	+ 32
Mania Station	46	...	+ 46	32	...	+ 32	14	...	+ 14
GRAND TOTAL, DHOLPUR STATE	**279,890**	**249,657**	**+ 30,233**	**157,123**	**138,342**	**+ 18,781**	**122,767**	**111,315**	**+ 11,452**
GRAND TOTAL, EASTERN STATES AGENCY	**1,076,780**	**1,043,867**	**+ 32,913**	**589,508**	**569,462**	**+ 20,046**	**487,272**	**474,405**	**+128,675**

TABLE II.—Variation in the population since the Census of 1881—*contd.*

	Both Sexes.			Males.			Females.		
	1891.	1881.	Variation.	1891.	1881.	Variation.	1891.	1881.	Variation.
1	2	3	4	5	6	7	8	9	10
VI.—ALWAR AGENCY—									
Alwar—									
Alwar	141,157	121,074	+ 20,083	74,703	64,495	+ 10,208	66,454	56,579	+ 9,875
Bansur	65,203	64,055	+ 1,148	34,866	34,235	+ 631	30,337	29,820	+ 517
Bahror	69,419	60,678	+ 8,741	35,898	31,613	+ 4,285	33,521	29,065	+ 4,456
Govindgarh	21,694	19,615	+ 2,079	11,310	10,193	+ 1,117	10,384	9,422	+ 962
Kathumbar	38,964	34,349	+ 4,615	20,783	18,337	+ 2,446	18,181	16,012	+ 2,169
Kishengarh	61,671	52,448	+ 9,223	32,033	27,512	+ 4,521	29,638	24,936	+ 4,702
Luchmangarh	60,479	50,982	+ 9,497	31,516	26,847	+ 4,669	28,963	24,135	+ 4,828
Mundawar	56,886	54,272	+ 2,614	29,870	28,357	+ 1,513	27,016	25,915	+ 1,101
Rajgarh	88,901	76,207	+ 12,694	46,536	39,777	+ 6,759	42,365	36,430	+ 5,935
Ramgarh	47,912	42,470	+ 5,442	25,155	22,548	+ 2,607	22,757	19,922	+ 2,835
Thanaghazi	54,561	50,939	+ 3,622	28,674	26,966	+ 1,708	25,887	23,973	+ 1,914
Tijara	52,570	49,451	+ 3,119	27,930	26,143	+ 1,787	24,640	23,308	+ 1,332
Nimrana Estate	7,340	6,386	+ 954	3,894	3,361	+ 533	3,446	3,025	+ 421
Total	766,757	682,926	+ 83,831	403,168	360,384	+ 42,784	363,589	322,542	+ 41,047
Total Railway	971	...	+ 971	700	...	+ 700	271	...	+ 271
Total Europeans, etc.	58	...	+ 58	30	...	+ 30	28	...	+ 28
GRAND TOTAL, ALWAR AGENCY	**767,786**	**682,926**	**+ 84,860**	**403,898**	**360,384**	**+ 43,514**	**363,888**	**322,542**	**+ 41,346**
VII.—HARAOWTI AND TONK AGENCY—									
Tonk (Rajputana)—									
Tonk	114,298	94,672	+ 19,626	59,591	49,250	+ 10,341	54,707	45,422	+ 9,285
Aligarh	19,623	16,892	+ 2,731	10,466	8,386	+ 2,080	9,157	8,506	+ 651
Nimbahera	64,888	58,615	+ 6,273	33,609	30,620	+ 2,989	31,279	27,995	+ 3,284
Total	198,809	170,179	+ 28,630	103,666	88,256	+ 15410	95,143	81,923	+ 13,220
Total Railway	122	...	+ 122	84	...	+ 84	38	...	+ 38
Total Europeans, &c.	3	...	+ 3	2	...	+ 2	1	...	+ 1
GRAND TOTAL	**198,934**	**170,179**	**+ 28,755**	**103,752**	**88,256**	**+ 15,496**	**95,182**	**81,923**	**+ 13,259**
Detached Tracts of Tonk under Central India—									
Chabra	46,473	45,541	+ 932	24,290	23,973	+ 317	22,183	21,568	+ 615
Parawa	40,806	39,286	+ 1,520	21,567	20,926	+ 641	19,239	18,360	+ 879
Sironj	93,856	83,023	+ 10,833	50,488	43,714	+ 6,774	43,368	39,309	+ 4,459
Total	181,135	167,850	+ 13,285	96,345	88,613	+ 7,732	84,790	79,237	+ 5,553
GRAND TOTAL, TONK STATE	**380,069**	**338,029**	**42,040**	**200,097**	**176,869**	**+ 23,228**	**179,972**	**161,160**	**+ 18,812**
Bundi—									
Bundi	22,544	20,744	+ 1,800	11,980	9,977	+ 2,003	10,564	10,767	– 203
Taragarh	5,492	4,111	+ 1,381	2,882	2,397	+ 485	2,610	1,714	+ 896
Patan	28,252	24,602	+ 3,650	14,674	12,811	+ 1,863	13,578	11,791	+ 1,787
Kapran	9,235	8,543	+ 692	4,793	4,304	+ 489	4,442	4,239	+ 203
Gandowli	39,760	33,433	+ 6,327	20,821	17,424	+ 3,397	18,939	16,009	+ 2,930
Ajitgarh	4,634	3,667	+ 967	2,532	1,976	+ 556	2,102	1,691	+ 411
Deyi	42,940	38,098	+ 4,842	22,452	19,991	+ 2,461	20,488	18,107	+ 2,381
Nænwa	6,093	5,254	+ 839	3,148	2,749	+ 399	2,945	2,505	+ 440
Gotra	43,527	37,180	+ 6,347	23,051	19,254	+ 3,797	20,476	17,926	+ 2,550
Hindoli	41,857	34,758	+ 7,099	22,420	18,526	+ 3,894	19,437	16,232	+ 3,205
Selore	51,341	44,311	+ 7,030	27,280	23,694	+ 3,586	24,061	20,617	+ 3,444
Total	295,675	254,701	+ 40,974	156,033	133,103	+ 22,930	139,642	121,598	+ 18,044
Shahpura—									
Phooliya (Shahpura)	63,646	51,750	+ 11,896	33,243	27,217	+ 6,026	30,403	24,533	+ 5,870
Total	63,646	51,750	+ 11,896	33,243	27,217	+ 6,026	30,403	24,533	+ 5,870
GRAND TOTAL, HARAOWTI AND TONK AGENCY	**739,390**	**644,480**	**+ 94,910**	**389,373**	**337,189**	**+ 52,184**	**350,017**	**307,291**	**+ 42,726**

TABLE II.—Variation in the population since the Census of 1881—*concld.*

	Both Sexes.			Males.			Females.		
	1891.	1881.	Variation.	1891.	1881.	Variation.	1891.	1881.	Variation.
1	2	3	4	5	6	7	8	9	10
VIII.—JHALLAWAR AGENCY—									
JHALLAWAR—									
Jhalrapatan (Chaoni)	23,363	20,303	+ 3,060	12,126	10,866	+ 1,260	11,237	9,437	+ 1,800
Jhalrapatan (Town)	10,783	11,469	— 686	5,680	6,042	— 362	5,103	5,427	— 324
Patan (Pergana)	17,494	17,146	+ 348	9,219	9,236	— 17	8,275	7,910	+ 365
Chechat	25,066	25,110	— 44	13,184	13,314	— 130	11,882	11,796	+ 86
Suket	16,424	16,461	— 37	8,610	8,495	+ 115	7,814	7,966	— 152
Asnawar	9,600	10,236	— 636	5,170	5,522	— 352	4,430	4,714	— 284
Bakani	28,195	28,615	— 420	14,999	15,225	— 226	13,196	13,390	— 194
Iklera	16,673	15,827	+ 936	8,837	8,377	+ 460	7,926	7,450	+ 476
Ghatoli	16,007	14,645	+ 1,362	8,560	7,880	+ 680	7,447	6,765	+ 682
Chipa Barod	34,225	37,389	— 3,164	18,020	19,862	— 1,842	16,205	17,527	— 1,322
Manohar Thana	27,796	23,784	+ 4,012	14,563	12,650	+ 1,913	13,233	11,134	+ 2,099
TOTAL OF CENTRAL JHALLAWAR	225,716	220,985	+ 4,731	118,968	117,469	+ 1,459	106,748	103,516	+ 3,232
Pachpahar	18,173	20,665	— 2,492	9,631	11,182	— 1,551	8,542	9,483	— 941
Awar	15,575	16,441	— 686	8,475	9,019	— 544	7,280	7,422	— 142
Dag	26,205	26,558	— 352	14,345	14,906	— 561	11,861	11,652	+ 209
Gungdhar	30,821	28,549	+ 1,272	16,816	16,212	+ 604	14,005	13,337	+ 668
TOTAL OF CHOMAHLLA	90,955	93,213	— 2,258	49,267	51,319	— 2,052	41,688	41,894	— 206
Uprehti	13,361	15,054	— 1,693	6,993	8,063	— 1,070	6,368	6,991	— 623
Taleti	13,551	11,236	+ 2,315	7,244	6,188	+ 1,056	6,307	5,048	+ 1,259
TOTAL SHAHABAD	26,912	26,290	+ 622	14,237	14,251	— 14	12,675	12,039	+ 636
TOTAL JHALLAWAR	343,583	340,488	+ 3,095	182,472	183,039	— 567	161,111	157,449	+ 3,662
TOTAL EUROPEANS, ETC.	18	...	+ 18	6	...	+ 6	12	...	+ 12
GRAND TOTAL, JHALLAWAR AGENCY	**343,601**	**340,488**	**+ 3,113**	**182,478**	**183,039**	**— 561**	**161,123**	**157,449**	**+ 3,674**
IX.—KOTAH AGENCY—									
KOTAH—									
Kotah City and suburbs	38,620	40,309	— 1,689	2,003	2,907	— 904	18,617	19,402	— 785
Nizamats—									
Anta	32,810	31,081	+ 1,729	16,914	16,089	+ 825	15,896	14,992	+ 904
Baran	37,889	39,556	— 1,667	19,286	20,273	— 987	18,603	19,283	— 680
Barodh	23,358	22,630	+ 728	12,134	11,859	+ 275	11,224	10,771	+ 453
Digod	22,055	20,632	+ 1,423	11,624	10,770	+ 854	10,431	9,862	+ 569
Etwah	23,109	21,834	+ 1,275	11,949	11,435	+ 514	11,160	10,399	+ 761
Ghataoli	20,069	19,333	+ 736	10,562	10,246	+ 316	9,507	9,087	+ 420
Kanwas	27,599	26,753	+ 846	14,196	14,037	+ 159	13,403	12,716	+ 687
Khanpur	26,372	24,407	+ 1,965	13,798	12,617	+ 1,181	12,574	11,790	+ 784
Kishangunj	28,992	27,544	+ 1,448	15,392	14,446	+ 946	13,600	13,098	+ 502
Kunjer	21,583	23,691	— 2,108	11,146	12,429	— 1,283	10,437	11,262	— 825
Ladpura	42,290	43,972	— 1,682	21,814	23,032	— 1,218	20,476	20,940	— 464
Mangrol	31,984	33,307	— 1,323	16,451	17,413	— 962	15,533	15,894	— 361
Sangod	32,565	31,411	+ 1,154	16,921	16,395	+ 526	15,644	15,016	+ 628
Shergarh	28,313	28,485	— 172	14,699	14,965	— 266	13,614	13,520	+ 94
Taruj	32,928	30,038	+ 2,890	17,228	15,838	+ 1,319	15,700	14,200	+ 1,500
Kotries—									
Antarda	4,219	3,857	+ 362	2,203	2,003	+ 200	2,016	1,854	+ 162
Balwan	2,888	2,349	+ 539	1,562	1,288	+ 274	1,326	1,061	+ 265
Gainta	4,727	4,677	+ 50	2,425	2,371	+ 54	2,302	2,306	— 4
Indargarh	26,208	24,264	+ 1,944	13,681	12,740	+ 941	12,537	11,524	+ 1,003
Karwar	2,525	2,814	— 289	1,285	1,453	— 168	1,240	1,361	— 121
Khataoli with Farera	8,088	6,850	+ 1,238	4,198	3,517	+ 681	3,890	3,333	+ 557
Pipalda with Phusod	7,072	7,481	— 409	3,648	3,801	— 153	3,424	3,680	— 256
TOTAL KOTAH	526,263	517,275	+ 8,988	273,119	269,924	+ 3,195	253,144	247,351	+ 5,793
TOTAL EUROPEANS, ETC.	4	...	+ 4	2	...	+ 2	2	...	+ 2
GRAND TOTAL, KOTAH STATE	**526,267**	**517,275**	**+ 8,992**	**278,121**	**269,924**	**+ 3,197**	**253,146**	**247,851**	**+ 5,795**
GRAND TOTAL, (including attached tracts of Tonk in Central India, and those of Central India in Meywar, but excluding the unenumerated Bhils of Meywar and Dungarpur	**12,200,097**	**10,149,286**	**+ 2,050,811**	**6,451,263**	**5,485,161**	**+ 966,102**	**5,748,834**	**4,664,125**	**+ 1,084,709**

RAJPUTANA AGENCY.

CENSUS OF 1891.

PROVINCIAL TABLE III.

Statement showing the distribution of the Population according to Religion, by Parganas, Tehsils or other administrative divisions.

Table III.—Religious distribution of Population—Rajputana Agency.

Summary of

Names of Agencies, States, etc.	Total Population.			Hindus.			Aryas.			Mussalmans.		
	Total.	Males.	Females.	Total.	Males.	Females.	Total.	Males.	Females.	Total.	Males.	Females.
1	2	3	4	5	6	7	8	9	10	11	12	13
I.—MEYWAR RESIDENCY—												
Meywar	1,709,781	893,842	815,939	1,314,194	688,795	625,399	1	1	...	59,125	31,484	27,641
Banswara	186,043	95,460	90,583	63,6[illegible]4	32,204	31,480	...	...	...	4,795	2,491	2,304
Dungarpur	98,448	49,444	49,004	87,017	43,808	43,209	...	...	...	4,314	2,229	2,085
Partabgurh	87,975	45,842	42,133	50,209	26,137	24,072	...	...	...	4,937	2,815	2,122
Khaerwara Cantonment	648	588	60	599	549	50	...	...	...	33	30	3
Kotra Cantonment	150	147	3	21	21	...	...	...	...	10	10	...
Total Meywar Residency	2,083,045	1,085,323	997,722	1,515,724	791,514	724,210	1	1	...	73,214	39,059	34,155
II.—WESTERN RAJPUTANA STATES RESIDENCY—												
Marwar	2,519,868	1,324,934	1,194,934	2,173,567	1,149,506	1,024,061	155	115	40	178,611	95,376	83,235
½ Sambhar Joint Jurisdiction	8,310	4 543	3,767	6,201	3,392	2,809	1	1	...	2,001	1,087	914
Total Marwar	2,528,178	1,329,477	1,198,701	2,179,768	1,152,898	1,026,870	156	116	40	180,612	96,463	84,149
Sirohi	186,025	97,280	88,745	162,000	85,987	76,013	...	...	...	4,912	2,879	2,033
Jesalmir	115,701	68,699	53,002	84,740	45,265	39,475	...	...	...	29,443	16,761	12,682
Erinpura Cantonment	1,859	1,286	573	1,567	1,075	492	...	...	...	263	189	74
Abu Sanitarium	92	56	36	59	36	23	...	...	...	8	4	4
Total Western Rajputana States Residency	2,831,855	1,490,798	1,341,057	2,428,134	1,285,261	1,142,873	156	116	40	215,238	116,296	98,942
III.—JEYPORE RESIDENCY—												
Jeypore	2,815,655	1,501,222	1,314,433	2,570,984	1,372,302	1,198,682	146	100	46	196,740	103,576	93,164
½ Sambhar Joint Jurisdiction	8,311	4,544	3,767	6,201	3,393	2,808	2	2	...	2,001	1,088	913
Total Jeypore	2,823,966	1,505,766	1,318,200	2,577,185	1,375,695	1,201,490	148	102	46	198,741	104,664	94,077
Kishengurh	125,516	65,038	60,478	110,499	57,258	53,241	7	4	3	9,429	4,944	4,485
Lawa	3,360	1,728	1,632	2,972	1,517	1,455	...	...	...	160	91	69
Total Jeypore Residency	2,952,842	1,572,532	1,380,310	2,690,656	1,434,470	1,256,186	155	106	49	208,330	109,699	98,631
IV.—HARAOWTI AND TONK AGENCY—												
Tonk	198,934	103,752	95,182	162,795	85,182	77,613	...	...	...	29,504	14,988	14,516
Detached Tracts of Tonk in Central India	181,135	96,345	84,790	163,909	87,007	76,902	...	...	...	15,030	8,171	6,859
Total Tonk	380,069	200,097	179,972	326,704	172,189	154,514	...	...	...	44,534	23,159	21,375
Bundi	295,675	156,033	139,642	276,055	145,657	130,398	...	...	...	11,606	6,139	5,467
Shahpura	63,646	33,243	30,403	58,154	30,404	27,750	...	...	...	3,136	1,638	1,498
Total Haraowti and Tonk Agency	739,390	389,373	350,017	660,913	348,250	312,663	...	...	...	59,276	30,936	28,340
V.—EASTERN STATES AGENCY—												
Bharatpur	640,303	347,830	292,473	528,629	287 899	240,730	...	...	...	107,260	57,598	49,662
Karauli	156,587	84,555	72,032	147,282	79,749	67,533	...	...	...	8,933	4,598	4,335
Dholpur	279,890	157,123	122,767	259,787	146,556	113,231	..	...	...	17,423	9,082	8,341
Total Eastern States Agency	1,076,780	589,508	487,272	935,658	514,204	421,494	...	...	...	133,616	71,278	62,338
VI.—BIKANIR AGENCY	831,955	440,046	391,909	724,940	385,153	339,777	58	27	31	80,029	43,107	36,922
VII.—ALWAR „	767,786	403,898	363,888	582,690	307,063	275,627	...	...	...	180,426	94,411	86,015
VIII.—KOTAH „	526,267	273,121	253,146	486,944	252,833	234,111	...	...	...	33,921	17,450	16,471
IX.—JHALLAWAR „	343,601	182,478	161,123	317,674	168,779	148,895	1	1	...	21,707	11,438	10,269
Total Rajputana Agency	12,153,521	6,427,077	5,726,444	10,343,373	5,487,537	4,855,836	371	251	120	1,005,757	533,674	472,083
Detached Tracts of Gungapur and Nundwas of Central India in Meywar	18,118	9,711	8,407	12,994	6,996	5,998	...	...	...	624	336	288
Add unenumerated Bhils of—												
(i) Meywar	134,429	67,214	67,215	...	...	...	...	...	...	...	...	...
(ii) Kushalgurh	25,598	13,045	12,553	...	...	...	...	...	...	...	...	...
(iii) Dungarpur	66,952	33,476	33,476	...	...	...	...	...	...	...	...	...
(iv) Sirohi (Grassias)	2,860	1,430	1,430	...	...	...	...	...	...	...	...	...
Total unenumerated	229,839	115,165	114,674	...	...	...	...	...	...	...	...	...
GRAND TOTAL	2,401,478	6,551,953	5,849,525	10,356,367	5,494,533	4,861,834	371	251	120	1,006,381	534,010	472,371

Provincial Table III.

Jains.			Christians.			Animistic.			Jews.			Parsis.			Sikhs.			No Religion.		
Total.	Males.	Females.	Total.	Males.	Females.	Total.	Males.	Females.	Total.	Males.	Females.	Total.	Males.	Females.	Total.	Males.	Females.	Total.	Males.	Females.
14	15	16	17	18	19	20	21	22	23	24	25	26	27	28	29	30	31	32	33	34
92,902	48,508	44,394	115	70	45	243,428	124,973	118,455	...	...	...	16	11	5	...	...	...	...	...	...
5,998	2,908	3,090	...	...	...	111,566	57,857	53,709	...	...	...	...	...	...	...	...	...	...	...	...
7,117	3,407	3,710	...	...	...	...	...	...	...	...	...	...	...	...	...	...	...	...	...	...
6,119	3,188	2,931	1	1	...	26,705	13,699	13,006	...	...	...	4	2	2	...	...	...	...	...	...
...	...	...	16	9	7	...	...	...	...	...	...	...	...	...	...	...	...	...	...	...
...	...	...	6	3	3	113	113	...	...	...	...	...	...	...	...	...	...	...	...	...
112,136	58,011	54,125	138	83	55	381,812	196,642	185,170	...	...	...	20	13	7	...	...	...	...	...	...
167,270	79,786	87,484	186	105	81	...	...	...	2	1	1	44	24	20	33	21	12	...	...	...
83	50	33	24	13	11	...	...	...	...	...	...	...	...	...	...	...	...	...	...	...
167,353	79,836	87,517	210	118	92	...	...	...	2	1	1	44	24	20	33	21	12	...	...	...
18,513	8,059	10,454	459	271	188	...	...	...	12	7	5	129	77	52	...	...	...	...	...	...
1,518	673	845	...	...	...	...	...	...	...	...	...	...	...	...	...	...	...	...	...	...
...	...	...	20	13	7	...	...	...	...	...	...	...	...	...	...	...	...	...	...	...
...	...	...	25	16	9	...	...	...	...	...	...	...	...	...	9	9	...	...	...	...
187,384	88,568	98,816	714	418	296	...	...	...	14	8	6	173	101	72	42	30	12	...	...	...
47,024	24,840	22,184	658	350	308	...	...	...	1	1	...	25	14	11	75	37	38	2	2	...
83	49	34	24	12	12	...	...	...	...	...	...	...	...	...	...	...	...	...	...	...
47,107	24,889	22,218	682	362	320	...	...	...	1	1	...	25	14	11	75	37	38	2	2	...
5,550	2,815	2,735	21	11	10	...	...	...	...	...	...	5	3	2	5	3	2	...	...	...
228	120	108	...	...	...	...	...	...	...	...	...	...	...	...	...	...	...	...	...	...
52,885	27,824	25,061	703	373	330	...	...	...	1	1	...	30	17	13	80	40	40	2	2	...
6,622	3,574	3,048	13	8	5	...	...	...	...	...	...	...	...	...	...	...	...	...	...	...
2,189	1,162	1,027	7	5	2	...	...	...	...	...	...	...	...	...	...	...	...	...	...	...
8,811	4,736	4,075	20	13	7	...	...	...	...	...	...	...	...	...	...	...	...	...	...	...
8,011	4,235	3,776	...	...	...	...	...	...	...	...	...	3	2	1	...	...	...	...	...	...
2,353	1,198	1,155	2	2	...	...	...	...	...	...	...	1	1	...	...	...	...	...	...	...
19,175	10,169	9,006	22	15	7	...	...	...	...	...	...	4	3	1	...	...	...	...	...	...
4,408	2,329	2,079	6	4	2	...	...	...	...	...	...	...	...	...	...	...	...	...	...	...
359	201	158	13	7	6	...	...	...	...	...	...	...	...	...	...	...	...	...	...	...
2,649	1,465	1,184	6	5	1	...	...	...	...	...	...	...	...	...	25	15	10	...	...	...
7,416	3,995	3,421	25	16	9	...	...	...	...	...	...	...	...	...	25	15	10	...	...	...
26,268	11,278	14,990	21	13	8	...	...	...	...	...	...	9	3	6	630	455	175	...	...	...
4,495	2,326	2,169	166	93	73	...	...	...	...	...	...	2	1	1	7	4	3	...	...	...
5,169	2,724	2,445	55	26	29	...	...	...	...	...	...	...	...	...	178	88	90	...	...	...
4,047	2,169	1,878	18	6	12	...	...	...	...	...	...	...	...	...	154	85	69	...	...	...
418,975	207,064	211,911	1,862	1,043	819	381,812	196,642	185,170	15	9	6	238	138	100	1,116	717	399	2	2	...
832	459	373	...	...	...	3,668	1,920	1,748	...	...	...	...	...	...	...	...	...	...	...	...
...	...	...	...	...	...	134,429	67,214	67,215	...	...	...	...	...	...	...	...	...	...	...	...
...	...	...	...	...	...	25,598	13,045	12,553	...	...	...	...	...	...	...	...	...	...	...	...
...	...	...	...	...	...	66,952	33,476	33,476	...	...	...	...	...	...	...	...	...	...	...	...
...	...	...	...	...	...	2,860	1,430	1,430	...	...	...	...	...	...	...	...	...	...	...	...
...	...	...	...	...	...	220,839	115,165	114,674	...	...	...	...	...	...	...	...	...	...	...	...
419,807	207,523	212,284	1.862	1,043	819	615.319	313,727	301,592	15	9	6	238	138	100	1,116	717	399	2	2	...

PROVINCIAL

TABLE III.—Statement showing the Distribution of

Names of States and Agencies	Total Population.			Hindus.			Aryas.			Mussalmans.		
	Total.	Males.	Females.	Total.	Males.	Females.	Total.	Males.	Females.	Total.	Males.	Females.
1	2	3	4	5	6	7	8	9	10	11	12	13
I.—MEYWAR RESIDENCY—												
Meywar—												
Oodeypore	73,439	38,795	34,644	45,293	24,048	21,245	...	...	...	9,778	5,149	4,629
Meja	5,099	2,663	2,436	4,366	2,281	2,085	...	...	...	100	57	43
Parsoli	8,477	4,502	3,975	7,490	3,997	3,493	...	...	...	119	64	55
Sardargarh	6,583	3,433	3,150	5,140	2,694	2,446	...	...	...	122	65	57
Kankrowli	8,294	4,258	4,036	6,294	3,260	3,034	...	...	...	291	145	146
Kelwara	44,662	23,686	20,976	32,253	17,204	15,049	...	...	...	391	239	152
Bansi	4,617	2,378	2,239	3,552	1,819	1,733	...	...	...	103	54	49
Amet	16,506	8,623	7,883	12,867	6,777	6,090	...	...	...	348	173	175
Jharol	8,110	4,259	3,851	6,999	3,660	3,339	...	...	...	88	70	18
Kanor	15,786	8,173	7,613	12,889	6,696	6,193	...	...	...	493	268	225
Delwara	30,099	15,704	14,395	21,507	11,211	10,296	...	...	...	420	239	181
Shivrati	9,487	4,945	4,542	7,254	3,799	3,455	...	...	...	45	27	18
Bijeypur	10,030	5,234	4,796	6,569	3,433	3,136	...	...	...	91	60	31
Banera	36,804	19,136	17,668	30,839	16,057	14,782	...	...	...	2,077	1,084	993
Khamnor	34,249	17,994	16,255	25,210	13,307	11,903	...	...	...	217	123	94
Gogunda	13,972	7,275	6,697	8,175	4,276	3,899	...	...	...	116	67	49
Bidnor	27,519	14,713	12,806	23,147	12,398	10,749	...	...	...	636	347	289
Kurabar	25,452	13,260	12,192	16,922	8.858	8,064	...	...	...	246	150	96
Kotharia	15,364	7,994	7,370	12,139	6,352	5,787	...	...	...	183	101	82
Karjali	5,282	2,675	2,607	4,192	2,122	2,070	...	...	...	6	4	2
Nathdwara	21,661	11,301	10,360	16,660	8,729	7,931	...	...	...	822	434	388
Devasthan	41,696	21,628	20,068	30,966	16,114	14,852	...	...	...	383	248	135
Fatehgarh	1,303	695	608	1,063	571	492	...	...	...	17	9	8
Asinda	21,416	11,130	10,286	17,980	9,317	8,663	...	...	...	552	312	240
Hurra and Shimbhogarh	53,986	28,509	25,477	45,002	23,786	21,216	...	...	...	1,733	969	764
Kapasin	52,355	27,178	25,177	42,323	22,056	20,267	...	...	...	1,499	779	720
Bagor	12,568	6,556	6,012	10,761	5,641	5,120	...	...	...	255	122	133
Bijolia	14,949	7,719	7,230	10,784	5,613	5,171	...	...	...	174	105	69
Kanera	8,289	4,219	4,070	6,526	3,328	3,198	...	...	...	154	85	69
Deogarh	56,531	29,828	26,703	45,091	23,747	21,344	...	...	...	1,404	723	681
Bari Sadri	16,499	8,641	7.858	13,800	7,244	6,556	...	...	...	779	412	367
Begun	30,835	15,966	14,869	23,176	12,027	11,149	...	...	...	1,445	763	682
Magra Sarara	54,715	28,852	25,863	34,691	18 237	16,454	...	...	...	831	540	291
Dhariawad	6,162	3,090	3,072	4,845	2,388	2,457	...	...	...	121	77	44
Bedla	23,923	12,452	11,471	20,963	10,933	10,030	...	...	...	315	179	136
Sayra	23,543	12,326	11,217	14,433	7,652	6,781	...	...	...	67	44	23
Choti Sadri	48,060	24,788	23,272	34,086	17,539	16,547	...	...	...	1,397	799	598
Salumbar	55,009	28,022	26,987	36,276	18,461	17,815	...	...	...	1,246	611	635
Kotra Bhumat	7,648	4,189	3,459	6,574	3,561	3,013	...	...	...	421	274	147
Kherwara Bhumat	13,346	6,782	6,564	11,726	5,916	5,810	...	...	...	670	367	303
Rincher	7,103	3,761	3,342	5,379	2,839	2,540	...	...	...	46	25	21
Bhindar	24,899	12,774	12,125	17,368	8,957	8,411	...	...	...	1,336	711	625
Chitorgarh	116,348	60,534	55,814	96,463	50,215	46,248	...	...	...	3,744	1,987	1,757
Bhainsrorgarh	23,500	12,261	11,239	18,012	9,357	8,655	...	...	...	461	258	203
Bhilwara	96,443	50,313	46,130	82,500	43.228	39,672	...	...	...	4,743	2,550	2,193
Girva	93,316	48,142	45,174	46,298	23,999	22,299	...	...	...	8,384	4,242	4,142
Mandalgarh	84,472	44,651	39,821	72,656	38,596	34,060	...	...	...	2,941	1,518	1,423
Rasmi	46,757	24,363	22,389	39,233	20,536	18,697	...	...	...	1,418	734	684
Rajnagar	39,858	20,857	19,001	31,834	16,709	15,065	...	...	...	523	260	263
Sharan	99,929	52,228	47,701	82,108	43.027	39,081	...	...	...	2,305	1,178	1,127
Jahazpur	85,637	45,899	39,738	74,945	40,287	34,658	...	...	...	2,524	1,354	1,170
Kachola Shahpura	26,227	13,832	12,395	25,485	13,403	12,082	...	...	...	318	181	137
TOTAL MEYWAR DISTRICTS	**1,708,814**	**893,191**	**815,623**	**1,313,504**	**688,322**	**625,182**	...	...	...	**58,898**	**31,336**	**27,562**
MILITARY CANTONMENTS IN MEYWAR—												
Kherwara Cantonment	648	588	60	599	549	50	...	...	...	33	30	3
Kotra Cantonment	150	147	3	21	21	...	...	...	...	10	10	...
TOTAL CANTONMENTS	**798**	**735**	**63**	**620**	**570**	**50**	...	...	...	**43**	**40**	**3**
Railway Population in Meywar	932	633	299	650	473	217	1	1	...	227	148	79
European, etc., in Meywar	35	18	17	...	...	...	...	...	...	...	...	...
Detached tracts of Central India in Meywar *i.e.*, Nandwas Pargana of Indore State	5,840	3,122	2,718	3,249	1,758	1,491	...	...	...	74	43	31
Gungapur Pargana of Gwalior State	12,278	6,589	5,689	9,745	5,238	4,507	...	...	...	550	293	257
TOTAL ENUMERATED POPULATION	**1,728,697**	**904,288**	**824,409**	**1,327,808**	**696,361**	**631,447**	**1**	**1**	...	**59,792**	**31,860**	**27,932**
TOTAL UNENUMERATED BHILS IN MEYWAR	**134,429**	**67,214**	**67,215**	...	...	...	...	...	...	...	...	...
TOTAL RELIGIONS	**1,863,126**	**971,502**	**891,624**	**1,327,808**	**696 361**	**631,447**	**1**	**1**	...	**59,792**	**31,860**	**27,932**

TABLE.

the Population according to Religion.

Jains.			Christians.			Animistic.			Jews.			Parsis.			Sikhs.		
Total.	Males.	Females.	Total.	Males.	Females.	Total.	Males.	Females.	Total.	Males.	Females.	Total.	Males.	Females.	Total.	Males.	Females.
14	15	16	17	18	19	20	21	22	23	24	25	26	27	28	29	30	31
7,410	3,688	3,722	62	40	22	10,890	5,867	5,023	...	...	...	6	3	3	...	...	...
45	28	17	1	1	...	587	296	291	...	...	...	...	...	...	...	...	...
109	62	47	...	...	...	759	379	380	...	...	...	...	...	...	...	...	...
647	352	295	...	...	...	674	322	352	...	...	...	...	...	...	...	...	...
679	348	331	...	...	...	1,030	505	525	...	...	...	...	...	...	...	...	...
3,851	1,950	1,901	...	...	...	8,167	4,293	3,874	...	...	...	...	...	...	...	...	...
129	71	58	...	...	...	833	434	399	...	...	...	...	...	...	...	...	...
1,708	891	817	...	...	...	1,583	782	801	...	...	...	...	...	...	...	...	...
697	357	340	...	...	...	326	172	154	...	...	...	...	...	...	...	...	...
1,483	746	737	...	...	...	921	463	458	...	...	...	...	...	...	...	...	...
1,266	650	616	...	...	...	6,906	3,604	3,302	...	...	...	...	...	...	...	...	...
337	176	161	...	...	...	1,851	943	908	...	...	...	...	...	...	...	...	...
77	29	48	...	...	...	3,293	1,712	1,581	...	...	...	...	...	...	...	...	...
865	472	393	...	...	...	3,023	1,523	1,500	...	...	...	...	...	...	...	...	...
2,503	1,313	1,190	...	...	...	6,319	3,251	3,068	...	...	...	...	...	...	...	...	...
1,303	652	651	...	...	...	4,376	2,280	2,098	...	...	...	...	...	...	...	...	...
1,255	679	576	...	...	...	2,481	1,289	1,192	...	...	...	...	...	...	...	...	...
1,908	981	927	...	...	...	6,376	3,271	3,105	...	...	...	...	...	...	...	...	...
590	295	295	...	...	...	2,452	1,246	1,206	...	...	...	...	...	...	...	...	...
72	42	30	...	...	...	1,012	507	505	...	...	...	...	...	...	...	...	...
1,177	612	565	...	...	...	3,002	1,526	1,476	...	...	...	...	...	...	...	...	...
2,254	1,160	1,094	...	...	...	8,093	4,106	3,987	...	...	...	...	...	...	...	...	...
170	87	83	...	...	...	53	28	25	...	...	...	...	...	...	...	...	...
912	489	423	3	3	...	1,969	1,009	960	...	...	...	...	...	...	...	...	...
2,841	1,533	1,308	...	...	...	4,410	2,221	2,189	...	...	...	...	...	...	...	...	...
1,543	841	702	...	...	...	6,990	3,502	3,488	...	...	...	...	...	...	...	...	...
529	277	252	...	...	...	1,023	516	507	...	...	...	...	...	...	...	...	...
388	200	188	...	...	...	3,603	1,801	1,802	...	...	...	...	...	...	...	...	...
130	67	63	...	...	...	1,479	739	740	...	...	...	...	...	...	...	...	...
3,942	2,054	1,888	...	...	...	6,094	3,304	2,790	...	...	...	...	...	...	...	...	...
1,038	535	503	...	...	...	882	450	432	...	...	...	...	...	...	...	...	...
764	410	354	...	...	...	5,450	2,766	2,684	...	...	...	...	...	...	...	...	...
4,463	2,266	2,197	...	...	...	14,730	7,809	6,921	...	...	...	...	...	...	...	...	...
937	454	483	...	...	...	259	171	88	...	...	...	...	...	...	...	...	...
378	189	189	1	1	...	2,266	1,150	1,116	...	...	...	...	...	...	...	...	...
2,369	1,108	1,261	...	...	...	6,674	3,522	3,152	...	...	...	...	...	...	...	...	...
1,391	714	677	...	...	...	11,185	5,735	5,450	...	...	...	1	1	...	...	...	...
3,516	1,833	1,683	...	...	...	13,971	7,117	6,854	...	...	...	...	...	...	...	...	...
585	316	269	...	...	...	68	38	30	...	...	...	...	...	...	...	...	...
759	376	383	...	...	...	191	123	68	...	...	...	...	...	...	...	...	...
802	432	370	...	...	...	876	465	411	...	...	...	...	...	...	...	...	...
1,675	874	801	...	...	...	4,520	2,232	2.288	...	...	...	...	...	...	...	...	...
2,619	1,402	1,217	8	4	4	13,513	6,925	6,588	...	...	...	1	1	...	...	...	...
315	177	138	...	...	...	4,712	2,469	2,243	...	...	...	...	...	...	...	...	...
3,601	1,921	1,680	...	...	...	5,191	2,608	2,583	...	...	...	8	6	2	...	...	...
11,926	6,401	5,525	...	...	...	26,708	13,500	13,208	...	...	...	...	...	...	...	...	...
2,227	1,170	1,057	...	...	...	6,648	3,367	3,281	...	...	...	...	...	...	...	...	...
1,821	969	852	...	...	...	4,285	2,129	2,156	...	...	...	...	...	...	...	...	...
2,177	1,152	1,025	...	...	...	5,324	2,676	2,648	...	...	...	...	...	...	...	...	...
6,467	3,450	3,017	...	...	...	9,049	4,573	4,476	...	...	...	...	...	...	...	...	...
1,819	1,001	818	...	...	...	6,349	3,257	3,092	...	...	...	...	...	...	...	...	...
424	248	176	...	...	...	...	...	...	...	...	...	...	...	...	...	...	...
92,893	48,500	44,393	75	49	26	243,428	124,973	118,455	...	...	...	16	11	5	...	...	...
...	...	...	16	9	7	...	...	...	...	...	...	...	...	...	...	...	...
...	...	...	6	3	3	113	113	...	...	...	...	...	...	...	...	...	...
...	...	...	22	12	10	113	113	...	...	...	...	...	...	...	...	...	...
9	8	1	5	3	2	...	...	...	...	...	...	...	...	...	...	...	...
...	...	...	35	18	17	...	...	...	...	...	...	...	...	...	...	...	...
9	5	4	...	...	...	2,508	1,316	1,192	...	...	...	...	...	...	...	...	...
823	454	369	...	...	...	1,160	604	556	...	...	...	...	...	...	...	...	...
93,734	48,967	44,767	137	82	55	247,209	127,006	120,203	...	...	...	16	11	5	...	...	...
...	...	...	...	...	...	134,429	67,214	67,215	...	...	...	...	...	...	...	...	...
93,734	48,967	44,767	137	82	55	381,638	194,220	187,418	...	...	...	16	11	5	...	...	...

TABLE III.—Statement showing the Distribution of

Names of States and Agencies.	Total Population.			Hindus.			Aryas.			Mussalmans.		
	Total.	Males.	Females.	Total.	Males.	Females.	Total.	Males.	Females.	Total.	Males.	Females.
1	2	3	4	5	6	7	8	9	10	11	12	13
MEYWAR RESIDENCY— *contd.*												
Banswara—												
Banswara	180,268	92,540	87,728	59,440	30,087	29,353	...	...	...	4,283	2,189	2,094
Kushalgarh	5,775	2,920	2,855	4,244	2,117	2,127	...	...	...	512	302	210
Unenumerated Population	25,598	13,045	12,553	...	...	...	...	...	...	...	...	...
Total	31,373	15,965	15,408	4,244	2,117	2,127	...	...	...	512	302	210
GRAND TOTAL	211,641	108,505	103,136	63,684	32,204	31,480	...	...	...	4,795	2,491	2,304
Partabgarh—												
Partabgarh	87,975	45,842	42,133	50,209	26,137	24,072	...	...	...	4,937	2,815	2,122
Dungarpur—												
Dungarpur	11,401	5,496	5,905	8,785	4,302	4,483	...	...	...	1,668	772	896
Kanba	10,158	5,208	4,950	9,214	4,720	4,494	...	...	...	218	169	49
Ganeshpur	8,694	4,447	4,247	8,073	4,122	3,951	...	...	...	48	27	21
Ashpur	9,360	4,799	4,561	8,457	4,338	4,119	...	...	...	68	43	25
Pujpor	7,773	3,903	3,870	7,109	3,569	3,540	...	...	...	56	31	25
Nithava	10,790	5,440	5,350	9,922	5,012	4,910	...	...	...	39	26	13
Sagwara	10,663	5,293	5,370	8,208	4,059	4,149	...	...	...	1,269	656	613
Padwa	11,991	5,933	6,058	11,269	5,573	5,696	...	...	...	63	45	18
Galiakot	8,227	4,009	4,218	7,243	3,534	3,709	...	...	...	468	241	227
Dhambora	9,391	4,916	4,475	8,737	4,579	4,158	...	...	...	417	219	198
Total	98,448	49,444	49,004	87,017	43,808	43,209	...	...	..	4,314	2,229	2,085
Unenumerated Bhils of Dungarpur taken from Census, 1881	66,952	33,476	33,476	...	...	...	...	...	...	...	...	...
GRAND TOTAL	165,400	82,920	82,480	87,017	43,808	43,209	...	...	...	4,314	2,229	2,085
Total Meywar Residency	2,083,045	1,085,323	997,722	1,515,724	791,514	724,210	1	1	...	73,214	9,059	34,155
Detached Tracts of Central India in Meywar	18,118	9,711	8,407	12,994	6,996	5,998	...	...	...	624	336	288
GRAND TOTAL, MEYWAR RESIDENCY	2,101,163	1,095,034	1,006,129	1,528,718	798,510	730,208	1	1	...	73,838	39,395	34,443
II.—WESTERN RAJPUTANA STATES AGENCY—												
Marwar and Malani—												
Jodhpore City	61,759	31,663	30,096	42,990	21,987	21,003	18	8	10	13,676	7,051	6,625
" Kasba	18,646	11,664	16,982	15,385	9,513	5,872	66	64	2	2,549	1,726	823
" Pargana	246,962	131,134	115,828	226,997	120,938	106,059	1	1	...	10,879	5,816	5,063
Total	327,367	174,461	152,906	285,372	152,438	132,934	85	73	12	27,104	14,593	12,511
Nagore	252,257	130,640	121,617	223,179	116,966	106,213	15	7	8	19,505	9,470	10,035
Bali	212,479	109,179	193,300	179,969	94,540	85,429	1	1	...	3,695	2,105	1,590
Merta	205,704	107,089	98,615	186,826	97,545	89,281	...	...	...	11,291	5,754	5,537
Jalore	170,428	88,069	82,359	143,092	75,014	68,078	...	...	...	3,979	2,154	1,825
Sojat	141,782	73,597	68,185	122,192	63,800	58,392	1	1	...	5,734	3,017	2,717
Jaswantpura	111,550	58,517	53,033	98,468	51,954	46,514	...	...	...	3,228	1,822	1,406
Parbatsar	104,962	55,926	49,036	95,989	51,321	44,668	4	3	1	6,832	3,544	3,288
Sanchore	95,890	51,530	44,360	79,638	42,652	36,986	1	1	...	12,407	6,770	5,637
Jaitaran	87,635	45,720	41,915	75,303	39,482	35,821	...	...	...	5,797	3,088	2,709
Bilara	84,952	44,338	40,614	73,414	38,594	34,820	...	...	...	5,069	2,636	2,433
Phalodi	71,803	37,341	34,462	59,795	31,372	28,423	18	8	10	7,206	3,950	3,256
Shergarh	70,919	39,048	31,871	65,005	35,785	29,220	...	...	...	2,825	1,592	1,233
Siwana	64,747	33,425	31,322	55,286	28,716	26,570	...	...	...	1,175	670	505
Pali	58,463	29,949	28,514	46,372	23,990	22,382	...	...	...	5,776	2,974	2,802
Marote	56,806	30,710	26,096	53,015	28,665	24,350	1	1	...	1,325	731	594
Didwana	54,272	28,435	25,837	45,350	23,988	21,362	...	...	...	8,575	4,279	4,296
Pachbhadra	52,904	27,944	24,960	43,289	23,040	20,249	2	2	...	4,434	2,330	2,104
Nawa	31,538	16,721	14,817	25,760	13,606	12,154	...	...	...	3,968	2,174	1,794
Sheo	30,291	16,426	13,865	21,607	11,572	10,035	...	...	...	7,862	4,444	3,418
Sankra	10,074	5,675	4,399	7,280	4,105	3,175	...	...	...	2,794	1,570	1,224
Total Marwar	2,296,823	1,204,740	1,092,083	1,986,201	1,049,145	937,056	128	97	31	150,581	79,667	70,914
Malani	221,184	119,036	102,148	186,199	99,608	86,591	7	4	3	27,572	15,439	12,133
Total Marwar and Malani	2,518,007	1,323,776	1,194,231	2,172,400	1,148,753	1,023,647	135	101	34	178,153	95,106	83,047

the Population according to Religion —*contd.*

Jains.			Christians.			Animistic.			Jews.			Parsis.			Sikhs.		
Total.	Males.	Females.	Total.	Males.	Females.	Total.	Males.	Females.	Total.	Males.	Females.	Total.	Males.	Females.	Total.	Males.	Females.
14	15	16	17	18	19	20	21	22	23	24	25	26	27	28	29	30	31
5,406	2,627	2,779	...	...	...	111,139	57,637	53,502	...	...	...	...	...	...	...	...	...
592	281	311	...	...	...	427	220	207	...	...	...	...	...	...	...	...	...
...	...	...	...	...	...	25,598	13,045	12,553	...	...	...	...	...	...	...	...	...
592	281	311	...	...	...	26,025	13,265	12,760	...	...	...	...	...	...	...	...	...
5,998	2,908	3,090	...	...	...	137,164	70,902	66,262	...	...	...	...	...	...	...	...	...
6,119	3,188	2,931	1	1	...	26,705	13,699	13,006	...	...	...	4	2	2	...	...	...
948	422	526	...	...	...	...	...	...	...	...	...	...	...	...	...	...	...
726	319	407	...	...	...	...	...	...	...	...	...	...	...	...	...	...	...
573	298	275	...	...	...	...	...	...	...	...	...	...	...	...	...	...	...
835	418	417	...	...	...	...	...	...	...	...	...	...	...	...	...	...	...
608	303	305	...	...	...	...	...	...	...	...	...	...	...	...	...	...	...
829	402	427	...	...	...	...	...	...	...	...	...	...	...	...	...	...	...
1,186	578	608	...	...	...	...	...	...	...	...	...	...	...	...	...	...	...
659	315	344	...	...	...	...	...	...	...	...	...	...	...	...	...	...	...
516	234	282	...	...	...	...	...	...	...	...	...	...	...	...	...	...	...
237	118	119	...	...	...	...	...	...	...	...	...	...	...	...	...	...	...
7,117	3,407	3,710	...	...	...	...	...	...	...	...	...	...	...	...	...	...	...
...	...	...	...	...	...	66,952	33,476	33,476	...	...	...	...	...	...	...	...	...
7,117	3,407	3,710	...	...	...	66,952	33,476	33,476	...	...	...	...	...	...	...	...	...
112,136	58,011	54,125	138	83	55	381,812	196,642	185,170	...	...	...	20	13	7	...	...	...
832	459	373	...	...	...	3,668	1,920	1,748	...	...	...	...	...	...	...	...	...
112,968	58,470	54,498	138	83	55	385,480	198,562	186,912	...	...	...	20	13	7	...	...	...
5,040	2,594	2,446	23	18	5	...	...	...	...	...	...	9	4	5	3	1	2
604	337	267	14	8	6	...	...	...	...	...	...	25	13	12	3	3	...
9,085	4,379	4,706	...	...	...	...	...	...	...	...	...	...	...	...	...	...	...
14,729	7,310	7,419	37	26	11	...	...	...	...	...	...	34	17	17	6	4	2
9,558	4,197	5,361	...	...	...	...	...	...	...	...	...	...	...	...	...	...	...
28,792	12,511	16,281	9	9	...	...	...	...	...	...	...	3	3	...	10	10	...
7,587	3,790	3,797	...	...	...	...	...	...	...	...	...	...	...	...	...	...	...
23,357	10,901	12,456	...	...	...	...	...	...	...	...	...	...	...	...	...	...	...
13,847	6,772	7,075	8	7	1	...	...	...	...	...	...	...	...	...	...	...	...
9,854	4,741	5,113	...	...	...	...	...	...	...	...	...	...	...	...	...	...	...
2,137	1,058	1,079	...	...	...	...	...	...	...	...	...	...	...	...	...	...	...
3,844	2,107	1,737	...	...	...	...	...	...	...	...	...	...	...	...	...	...	...
6,535	3,150	3,385	...	...	...	...	...	...	...	...	...	...	...	...	...	...	...
6,469	3,108	3,361	...	...	...	...	...	...	...	...	...	...	...	...	...	...	...
4,784	2,011	2,773	...	...	...	...	...	...	...	...	...	...	...	...	...	...	...
3,089	1,671	1,418	...	...	...	...	...	...	...	...	...	...	...	...	...	...	...
8,273	4,033	4,240	...	...	...	...	...	...	...	...	...	...	...	...	13	6	7
6,315	2,985	3,330	...	...	...	...	...	...	...	...	...	...	...	...	...	...	...
2,463	1,312	1,151	1	1	...	...	...	...	...	...	...	...	...	...	1	...	1
347	168	179	...	...	...	...	...	...	...	...	...	...	...	...	...	...	...
5,179	2,572	2,607	...	...	...	...	...	...	...	...	...	...	...	...	...	...	...
1,809	940	869	...	...	...	...	...	...	...	...	...	1	1	...	...	...	...
822	410	412	...	...	...	...	...	...	...	...	...	...	...	...	...	...	...
...	...	...	...	...	...	...	...	...	...	...	...	...	...	...	...	...	...
159,790	75,747	84,043	55	43	12	...	...	...	...	...	...	38	21	17	30	20	10
7,406	3,985	3,421	...	...	...	...	...	...	...	...	...	...	...	...	...	...	...
167,196	79,732	87,464	55	43	12	...	...	...	...	...	...	38	21	17	30	20	10

TABLE III.—Statement showing the Distribution of

Names of States and Agencies.	Total Population.			Hindus.			Aryas.			Mussalmans.		
	Total.	Males.	Females.	Total.	Males.	Females.	Total.	Males.	Females.	Total.	Males.	Females.
1	2	3	4	5	6	7	8	9	10	11	12	13
WESTERN RAJPUTANA STATES AGENCY—*contd.*												
† Sambhar, Jeypore and Jodhpur Joint Jurisdiction	8,286	4,530	3,756	6,195	3,388	2,807	1	1	...	2,001	1,087	914
† Sambhar Railway	24	13	11	6	4	2	...	...	...	...	...	...
Total	8,310	4,543	3,767	6,201	3,392	2,809	1	1	...	2,001	1,087	914
Total R. M. Railway in Marwar	1,771	1,115	656	1,167	753	414	20	14	6	458	270	188
Europeans, etc., Jodhpur	32	16	16	...	...	...	...	...	...	...	...	...
Do. Nawa	23	11	12	...	...	...	...	...	...	...	...	...
Do. Didwana	12	6	6	...	...	...	...	...	...	...	...	...
Do. Pachbhadra	15	7	8	...	...	...	...	...	...	...	...	...
Do. Phalodi	8	3	5	...	...	...	...	...	...	...	...	...
Total Europeans, etc.	90	43	47	...	...	...	...	...	...	...	...	...
GRAND TOTAL, MARWAR STATE	2,528,178	1,329,477	1,198,701	2,179,768	1,152,898	1,026,870	156	116	40	180,612	96,463	84,149
Sirohi—												
Sirohi	7,136	3,525	3,611	5,501	2,754	2,747	...	...	...	390	236	154
Khooni	25,456	13,181	12,275	20,694	11,036	9,658	...	...	...	529	285	244
Magra	23,610	12,187	11,423	19,933	10,622	9,311	...	...	...	159	90	69
Jara Kharel	20,304	10,428	9,876	17,800	9,381	8,419	...	...	...	146	86	60
Pamera	19,235	9,893	9,342	17,655	9,218	8,437	...	...	...	115	72	43
Madar	18,777	9,853	8,924	16,411	8,640	7,771	...	...	...	568	342	226
Anadra	7,874	4,150	3,724	7,066	3,759	3,307	...	...	...	197	116	81
Abu*	3,612	2,044	1,568	3,089	1,755	1,334	...		...	342	195	147
Abu Road	4,438	2,465	1,973	3,166	1,748	1,418	...	...	...	1,003	554	449
Santpore	11,424	6,173	5,251	11,048	5,968	5,080	...	...	...	236	137	99
Rohera	18,259	9,290	8,969	16,627	8,554	8,073	...	...	...	221	143	78
Pindwara	20,670	10,964	9,706	19,129	10,262	8,867	...	...	...	155	89	66
Abu Civil Station	1,048	723	325	785	520	265	...	...	...	207	159	48
Total	1,81,843	94,876	86,967	1,58,904	84,217	74,687	...	...	...	4,268	2,504	1,764
Abu Sanitarium Population†	92	50	36	59	36	23	...	...	...	8	4	4
Europeans, etc., on Abu	165	98	67	...	...	...	...	...	...	...	...	...
Sirohi Railway	2,410	1,494	916	1,670	1,051	619	...	...	...	485	294	191
Erinpura Bazar	1,607	812	795	1,426	719	707	...	...	...	159	81	78
Erinpura Cantonment	1,859	1,286	573	1,567	1,075	492	...	...	...	263	189	74
Total Unenumerated Population of Bhakher (Grassia)	2,860	1,430	1,430	2,860	1,430	1,430	...	..	...	...	...	...
GRAND TOTAL, SIROHI STATE	190,836	100,052	90,784	166,486	88,528	77,958	...	...	...	5,183	3,072	2,111
Jesalmir—												
Total Jesalmir, State	115,701	62,699	53,002	84,740	45,265	39,475	...	...	...	29,443	16,761	12,682
TOTAL WESTERN RAJPUTANA STATES RESIDENCY	2,831,855	1,490,798	1,341,057	2,428,134	1,285,261	1,142,873	156	116	40	215,238	116,296	98,942
III.—BIKANIR—												
Anupgarh	8,507	4,631	3,876	3,782	2,071	1,711	...	...	...	4,718	2,553	2,165
Bahaderan	38,026	20,612	17,414	35,149	19,080	16,069	...	...	...	2,565	1,384	1,181
Bikanir City	50,037	24,705	25,332	36,290	17,849	18,441	...	...	...	9,273	4,898	4,375
Bikanir Suburbs	6,203	3,184	3,019	4,718	2,493	2,225	...	...	...	1,217	600	617
Bikanir Tahsil	149,053	78,638	70,415	132,632	70,187	62,445	1	1	...	9,305	5,120	4,185
Total	205,293	106,527	98,766	173,640	90,529	83,111	1	1	...	19,795	10,618	9,177
Churu	82,899	44,032	38,867	71,578	38,291	33,287	57	26	31	9,692	5,050	4,642
Dungargarh	44,007	22,603	21,404	41,053	21,158	19,895	...	...	...	1,121	633	488
Hanumangarh	37,459	20,405	17,054	29,010	15,728	13,282	...	...	...	7,828	4,282	3,546
Lun Karansar	65,224	35,010	30,214	56,354	30,224	26,130	...	...	...	7,581	4,206	3,375
Mirzawala	10,375	5,711	4,664	6,246	3,442	2,804	...	...	...	3,950	2,134	1,816
Nohar	80,311	43,002	37,309	74,457	39,830	34,627	...	...	...	5,405	2,945	2,460
Rajgarh	61,277	33,249	28,028	55,967	30,491	25,476	...	...	...	4,461	2,384	2,077
Ratangarh	60,267	31,666	28,601	54,619	28,983	25,636	...	...	...	3,694	1,957	1,737
Sardarshehr	44,911	23,313	21,598	39,656	20,909	18,747	...	...	...	2,814	1,499	1,315
Sujangarh	77,031	40,490	36,541	69,568	37,013	32,555	...	...	...	4,129	2,199	1,930
Suraatgarh	16,356	8,788	7,568	13,861	7,414	6,447	...	...	...	2,276	1,263	1,013
Total Europeans, etc., in Bikanir	12	7	5	...	...	...	...	...	...	...	...	...
GRAND TOTAL, BIKANIR AGENCY	831,955	440,046	391,909	724,940	385,163	339,777	58	27	31	80,029	43,107	36,922

* Villages and bazar on Abu included.

† Abu Military Population only.

the Population according to Religion —*contd.*

Jains.			Christians.			Animistic.			Jews.			Parsis.			Sikhs.		
Total.	Males.	Females.	Total.	Males.	Females.	Total.	Males.	Females	Total.	Males.	Females.	Total.	Males.	Females.	Total.	Males.	Females.
14	15	16	17	18	19	20	21	22	23	24	25	26	27	28	29	30	31
83	50	33	6	4	2	...	...	...	...	...	...	...	...	...	...	...	...
...	...	...	18	9	9	...	...	...	...	...	...	...	...	...	...	...	...
83	50	33	24	13	11	...	...	...	...	...	...	...	...	...	...	...	...
74	54	20	41	19	22	...	...	...	2	1	1	6	3	3	3	1	2
...	...	...	32	16	16	...	...	...	...	...	...	...	...	...	...	...	...
...	...	...	23	11	12	...	...	...	...	...	...	...	...	...	...	...	...
...	...	...	12	6	6	...	...	...	...	...	...	...	...	...	...	...	...
...	...	...	15	7	8	...	...	...	...	...	...	...	...	...	...	...	...
...	...	...	8	3	5	...	...	...	...	...	...	...	...	...	...	...	...
...	...	...	90	43	47	...	...	...	...	...	...	...	...	...	...	...	...
167,353	79,836	87,517	210	118	92	...	...	...	2	1	1	44	24	20	33	21	12
1,242	535	707	3	...	3	...	...	...	...	...	...	...	...	...	...	...	...
4,233	1,860	2,373	...	...	...	...	...	...	...	...	...	...	...	...	...	...	...
3,518	1,475	2,043	...	...	...	...	...	...	...	...	...	...	...	...	...	...	...
2,358	961	1,397	...	...	...	...	...	...	...	...	...	...	...	...	...	...	...
1,464	602	862	...	...	...	...	...	...	...	...	...	1	1	...	...	...	...
1,798	871	927	...	...	...	...	...	...	...	...	...	...	...	...	...	...	...
611	275	336	...	...	...	...	...	...	...	...	...	...	...	...	...	...	...
155	84	71	...	...	...	...	...	...	...	...	...	26	10	16	...	...	...
144	91	53	38	16	22	...	...	...	3	2	1	84	54	30	...	...	...
140	68	72	...	...	...	...	...	...	...	...	...	...	...	...	...	...	...
1,411	503	818	...	...	...	...	...	...	...	...	...	...	...	...	...	...	...
1,386	613	773	...	...	...	...	...	...	...	...	...	...	...	...	...	...	...
...	...	...	39	33	6	...	...	...	...	...	...	17	11	6	...	...	...
18,460	8,028	10,432	80	49	31	...	...	...	3	2	1	128	76	52	...	...	...
...	...	...	25	16	9	...	...	...	...	...	...	...	...	...	...	...	...
...	...	...	165	98	67	...	...	...	...	...	...	...	...	...	...	...	...
31	19	12	214	124	90	...	...	...	9	5	4	1	1	...	...	...	...
22	12	10	...	...	...	...	...	...	...	...	...	...	...	...	...	...	...
...	...	...	20	13	7	...	...	...	...	...	...	...	...	...	9	9	...
...	...	...	...	...	...	...	...	...	...	...	...	...	...	...	...	...	...
18,513	8,059	10,454	504	300	204	...	...	...	12	7	5	129	77	52	9	9	...
1,518	673	845	...	...	...	...	...	...	...	...	...	...	...	...	...	...	...
187,384	88,568	98,816	714	418	296	...	...	...	14	8	6	173	101	72	42	30	12
1	1	...	...	...	...	...	...	...	...	...	...	...	...	...	6	6	...
311	147	164	...	...	...	...	...	...	...	...	...	...	...	...	1	1	...
4,429	1,021	2,508	5	4	1	...	...	...	...	...	...	...	...	...	40	33	7
257	88	169	...	...	...	...	...	...	...	...	...	9	3	6	2	...	2
7,104	3,319	3,785	...	...	...	...	...	...	...	...	...	...	...	...	11	11	...
11,790	5,328	6,462	5	4	1	...	...	...	...	...	...	9	3	6	53	44	9
1,571	664	997	...	...	...	...	...	...	...	...	...	...	...	...	1	1	...
1,833	812	1,0[illegible]1	...	...	...	...	...	...	...	...	...	...	...	...	...	...	...
244	130	105	...	...	...	...	...	...	...	...	...	...	...	...	377	256	121
1,289	580	709	...	...	...	...	...	...	...	...	...	...	...	...	...	...	...
3	3	...	...	...	...	...	...	...	...	...	...	...	...	...	176	132	44
445	225	220	4	2	2	...	...	...	...	...	...	...	...	...	...	...	...
849	374	475	...	...	...	...	...	...	...	...	...	...	...	...	...	...	...
1,954	726	1,228	...	...	...	...	...	...	...	...	...	...	...	...	...	...	...
2,441	905	1,536	...	...	...	...	...	...	...	...	...	...	...	...	...	...	...
3,334	1,278	2,056	...	...	...	...	...	...	...	...	...	...	...	...	...	...	...
203	96	107	...	...	...	...	...	...	...	...	...	...	...	...	16	15	1
...	...	...	12	7	5	...	...	...	...	...	...	...	...	...	...	...	...
26,268	11,278	14,990	21	13	8	...	...	...	...	...	...	9	3	6	630	455	175

TABLE III.—Statement showing the Distribution of

Names of States and Agencies.	Total Population.			Hindus.			Aryas.			Mussalmans.		
	Total.	Males.	Females.	Total.	Males.	Females.	Total.	Males.	Females.	Total.	Males.	Females.
1	2	3	4	5	6	7	8	9	10	11	12	13
V.—JEYPORE RESIDENCY—												
Jeypore—												
Jeypore City	158,787	84,024	74,763	109,818	58,033	51,785	43	43	...	38,953	20,825	18,128
Total	158,787	84,024	74,763	109,818	58,033	51,785	43	43	...	38,953	20,825	18,128
Jeypore Tehsil	195,101	103,838	91,263	186,289	99,074	87,215	...	...	...	6,416	3,470	2,946
Jamua Ramgarh	153,055	80,786	72,269	146,455	77,345	69,110	...	...	...	5,977	3,098	2,879
Chaksu Tehsil	112,488	59,783	52,705	105,840	56,088	49,752	...	...	...	3,560	2,000	1,560
Kalegh	106,822	56,749	50,073	98,341	52,339	46,002	...	...	...	4,827	2,446	2,381
Total	567,466	301,156	266,310	536,925	284,846	252,079	...	...	...	20,780	11,014	9,766
Dausa Tehsil	124,203	65,776	58,427	120,588	63,798	56,790	...	...	...	3,156	1,723	1,433
Lalsote	102,360	54,050	48,310	99,613	52,554	47,059	...	...	...	2,281	1,235	1,046
Sikrai	26,103	13,905	12,198	25,468	13,556	11,912	...	...	...	598	330	268
Baswa	69,334	36,453	32,881	67,155	35,247	31,908	...	...	...	1,665	931	734
Total	322,000	170,184	151,816	312,824	165,155	147,669	...	...	...	7,700	4,219	3,481
Jhoonjhanu	207,538	111,718	95,820	181,202	98,293	82,909	...	...	...	25,789	13,136	12,653
Udeypore	62,768	35,385	27,383	60,019	34,030	25,989	...	...	...	2,745	1,351	1,394
Total	270,306	147,103	123,203	241,221	132,323	108,898	...	...	...	28,534	14,487	14,047
Sawai Ramgarh	127,269	70,001	57,268	122,218	67,158	55,060	...	...	...	4,957	2,785	2,172
Khandela	68,832	36,586	32,246	63,669	34,067	29,602	...	...	...	4,392	2,119	2,273
Baraith Tehsil	53,450	28,456	24,994	50,618	27,001	23,617	...	...	...	2,449	1,238	1,211
Total	249,551	135,043	114,508	236,505	128,226	108,279	...	...	...	11,798	6,142	5,656
Madhopur Tehsil	60,631	31,659	28,972	52,523	27,469	25,954	...	...	...	7,064	3,677	3,387
Barli "	69,463	36,762	32,701	64,967	34,370	30,597	...	...	...	2,981	1,564	1,417
Malarna	53,497	28,105	25,392	47,848	25,137	22,711	...	...	...	5,165	2,701	2,464
Khandar	33,499	17,790	15,709	32,656	17,359	15,297	...	...	...	641	341	300
Isarda	13,481	7,090	6,391	12,457	6,506	5,951	...	...	...	542	321	221
Barwara	12,264	6,448	5,816	11,117	5,818	5,299	...	...	...	705	396	309
Total	242,835	127,854	114,981	221,568	116,659	104,909	...	...	...	17,098	9,000	8,098
Hindown Tehsil	50,737	27,212	23,525	46,090	24,834	21,256	...	...	...	4,127	2,098	2,029
Toda Bhim "	43,991	23,225	20,766	41,122	21,800	19,322	...	...	...	2,649	1,304	1,345
Mahwa "	37,188	19,668	17,520	34,568	18,210	16,358	...	...	...	2,024	1,145	879
Walghat "	25,269	13,951	11,318	23,684	13,127	10,557	...	...	...	1,426	737	689
Ghonsla "	14,862	8,208	6,654	14,041	7,751	6,290	...	...	...	639	362	277
Ratanzillah "	14,858	8,095	6,763	13,968	7,611	6,357	...	...	...	763	424	339
Total	186,905	100,359	86,546	173,473	93,333	80,140	...	...	...	11,628	6,070	5,558
‡ Sambhar Joint Jurisdiction (Jeypore and Jodhpur)	8,287	4,532	3,755	6,195	3,389	2,806	2	2	...	2,001	1,088	913
‡ Sambhar 1 Railway	24	12	12	6	4	2	...	...	...	...	...	...
Total	8,311	4,544	3,767	6,201	3,393	2,808	2	2	...	2,001	1,088	913
Naraina Tehsil	33,147	17,565	15,582	28,841	15,265	13,576	...	...	...	2,772	1,481	1,291
Danta Ramgarh	82,522	44,719	37,803	77,158	41,827	35,331	...	...	...	3,447	1,907	1,540
Muazamabad	59,693	31,481	28,212	53,415	28,086	25,329	...	...	...	3,117	1,692	1,425
Total	175,362	93,765	81,597	159,414	85,178	74,236	...	...	...	9,336	5,080	4,256
Malpura Tehsil	76,643	40,180	36,463	70,039	36,631	33,408	...	...	...	3,733	1,984	1,749
Toda Rai Singh	62,904	33,145	29,759	58,465	30,796	27,669	...	...	...	2,060	1,127	933
Newai	39,660	21,171	18,489	37,086	19,780	17,306	...	...	...	1,174	646	528
Total	179,207	94,496	84,711	165,590	87,207	78,383	...	...	...	6,967	3,757	3,210
Gungapore Tehsil	44,687	23,558	21,129	42,181	22,213	19,968	...	...	...	2,380	1,268	1,112
Wazirpura	22,718	11,844	10,874	20,861	10,886	9,975	...	...	...	1,637	831	806
Bamaniawas Tehsil	13,811	7,200	6,611	13,243	6,905	6,338	...	...	...	467	243	224
Total	81,216	42,602	38,614	76,285	40,004	36,281		...	...	4,484	2,342	2,142
Kote Kasim	17,054	8,939	8,115	15,096	8,022	7,074	...	...	...	1,921	902	1,019
Total	17,054	8,939	8,115	15,096	8,022	7,074	...	...	...	1,921	902	1,019
Bandikui	4,297	2,303	1,994	3,757	2,021	1,736	...	...	...	473	245	228
Total	4,297	2,303	1,994	3,757	2,021	1,736	...	...	...	473	245	228

the Population according to Religion—*contd.*

Jains.			Christians.			Animistic.			Jews.			Parsis.			Sikhs.		
Total.	Males.	Females.	Total.	Males.	Females.	Total.	Males.	Females.	Total.	Males.	Females.	Total.	Males.	Females.	Total.	Males.	Females.
14	15	16	17	18	19	20	21	22	23	24	25	26	27	28	29	30	31
9,780	5,021	4,759	127	73	54	...	...	...	...	...	...	2	1	1	64	30	34
9,780	**5,021**	**4,759**	**127**	**73**	**54**	...	...	...	...	...	...	**2**	**1**	**1**	**64**	**30**	**34**
2,392	1,292	1,100	4	2	2	...	...	...	...	...	...	...	...	...	...	...	...
623	343	280	...	...	...	...	...	...	...	...	...	...	...	...	...	...	...
3,088	1,605	1,393	...	...	...	...	...	...	...	...	...	...	...	...	...	...	...
3,654	1,964	1,690	...	...	...	...	...	...	...	...	...	...	...	...	...	...	...
9,757	**5,294**	**4,463**	**4**	**2**	**2**	...	...	...	...	...	...	...	...	...	...	...	...
459	255	204	...	...	...	...	...	...	...	...	...	...	...	...	...	...	...
466	261	205	...	...	...	...	...	...	...	...	...	...	...	...	...	...	...
37	19	18	...	...	...	...	...	...	...	...	...	...	...	...	...	...	...
514	275	239	...	...	...	...	...	...	...	...	...	...	...	...	...	...	...
1,476	**810**	**666**	...	...	...	...	...	...	...	...	...	...	...	...	...	...	...
547	289	258	...	...	...	...	...	...	...	...	...	...	...	...	...	...	...
4	4	...	...	...	...	...	...	...	...	...	...	...	...	...	...	...	...
551	**293**	**258**	...	...	...	...	...	...	...	...	...	...	...	...	...	...	...
94	58	36	...	...	...	...	...	...	...	...	...	...	...	...	...	...	...
771	400	371	...	...	...	...	...	...	...	...	...	...	...	...	...	...	...
383	217	166	...	...	...	...	...	...	...	...	...	...	...	...	...	...	...
1,248	**675**	**573**	...	...	...	...	...	...	...	...	...	...	...	...	...	...	...
1,044	513	531	...	...	...	...	...	...	...	...	...	...	...	...	...	...	...
1,515	828	687	...	...	...	...	...	...	...	...	...	...	...	...	...	...	...
484	267	217	...	...	...	...	...	...	...	...	...	...	...	...	...	...	...
202	90	112	...	...	...	...	...	...	...	...	...	...	...	...	...	...	...
482	263	219	...	...	...	...	...	...	...	...	...	...	...	...	...	...	...
442	234	208	...	...	...	...	...	...	...	...	...	...	...	...	...	...	...
4,169	**2,195**	**1,974**	...	...	...	...	...	...	...	...	...	...	...	...	...	...	...
520	280	240	...	...	...	...	...	...	...	...	...	...	...	...	...	...	...
220	121	99	...	...	...	...	...	...	...	...	...	...	...	...	...	...	...
596	313	283	...	...	...	...	...	...	...	...	...	...	...	...	...	...	...
159	87	72	...	...	...	...	...	...	...	...	...	...	...	...	...	...	...
182	95	87	...	...	...	...	...	...	...	...	...	...	...	...	...	...	...
127	60	67	...	...	...	...	...	...	...	...	...	...	...	...	...	...	...
1,804	**956**	**848**	...	...	...	...	...	...	...	...	...	...	...	...	...	...	...
83	49	34	6	4	2	...	...	...	...	...	...	...	...	...	...	...	...
...	...	...	18	8	10	...	...	...	...	...	...	...	...	...	...	...	...
83	**49**	**34**	**24**	**12**	**12**	...	...	...	...	...	...	...	...	...	...	...	...
1,534	810	715	...	...	...	...	...	...	...	...	...	...	...	...	...	...	...
1,917	985	932	...	...	...	...	...	...	...	...	...	...	...	...	...	...	...
3,161	1,703	1,458	...	...	...	...	...	...	...	...	...	...	...	...	...	...	...
6,612	**3,507**	**3,105**	...	...	...	...	...	...	...	...	...	...	...	...	...	...	...
2,871	1,565	1,306	...	...	...	...	...	...	...	...	...	...	...	...	...	...	...
2,379	1,222	1,157	...	...	...	...	...	...	...	...	...	...	...	...	...	...	...
1 400	745	655	...	...	...	...	...	...	...	...	...	...	...	...	...	...	...
6,650	**3,532**	**3,118**	...	...	...	...	...	...	...	...	...	...	...	...	...	...	...
126	77	49	...	...	...	...	...	...	...	...	...	...	...	...	...	...	...
220	127	93	...	...	...	...	...	...	...	...	...	...	...	...	...	...	...
101	52	49	...	...	...	...	...	...	...	...	...	...	...	...	...	...	...
447	**256**	**191**	...	...	...	...	...	...	...	...	...	...	...	...	...	...	...
36	14	22	1	1	...	...	...	...	...	...	...	...	...	...	...	...	...
36	**14**	**22**	**1**	**1**	...	...	...	...	...	...	...	...	...	...	...	...	...
66	36	30	1	1	...	...	...	...	...	...	...	...	...	...	...	...	...
66	**36**	**30**	**1**	**1**	...	...	...	...	...	...	...	...	...	...	...	...	...

TABLE III.—Statement showing the Distribution of

Names of States and Agencies.	Total Population.			Hindus.			Aryas.			Mussalmans.		
	Total.	Males.	Females.	Total.	Males.	Females.	Total.	Males.	Females.	Total.	Males.	Females.
1	2	3	4	5	6	7	8	9	10	11	12	13
IV.—JEYPORE RESIDENCY—*contd.*												
Sikar	179,337	95,431	83,906	153,494	81,900	71,594	...	...	...	23,520	12,381	11,139
Khetri	131,377	70,578	60,799	121,139	65,341	55,798	...	...	...	10 197	5,216	4,981
Uniára	43,382	23,191	20,191	39,735	21,300	18,435	...	...	...	1,650	855	795
Total	354,096	189,200	164,856	314,368	168,541	145,827	...	...	...	35,367	18,452	16,515
Total	2,817,392½	1,501,571½	1,315,821	2,573,045	1,372,940½	1,200,104½	44½	44½	...	197,040	103,622½	93,417½
Total Jeypore Railway	6,455	4,123	2,332	4,140	2,754	1,386	103	57	46	1,701	1,041	660
Total Europeans, Etc.	118	71	47	...	...	...	...	...	...	...	...	...
GRAND TOTAL, JEYPORE STATE	2,823,966	1,505,766	1,318,200	2,577,185	1,375,695	1,201,490	148	102	46	198,741	104,664	94,077
Kishengarh—												
Kishengarh City	15,363	7,954	7 409	10,421	5,399	5,022	7	4	3	3,350	1,807	1,543
District Kishengarh	32,266	16,861	15,405	28,770	15,000	13,770	...	...	...	2,515	1,208	1,217
„ Rupnagar	24,656	12,724	11,932	-2,305	11,582	10,723	...	...	...	1,382	680	693
„ Araeen	24,277	12 589	11,688	22,850	11,835	11,015	...	...	...	539	290	249
„ Sarwar	28,860	14,842	14,018	26,077	13,389	12,688	...	...	...	1,625	845	780
Total	125,422	64,970	60,452	110,423	57,205	53,218	7	4	3	9,411	4,929	4,482
Total Kishengarh Railway	94	68	26	76	53	23	...	...	...	18	15	3
GRAND TOTAL, KISHENGARH STATE	125,516	65,038	60,478	110,499	57,258	53,241	7	4	3	9,429	4,944	4,485
Lawa—												
Lawa	3,360	1,728	1,632	2,972	1,517	1,455	...	...	...	160	91	69
GRAND TOTAL, JEYPORE RESIDENCY	2,952,842	1,572,532	1,380,310	2,690,656	1,434,470	1,256,186	155	106	49	208,330	109,699	98,631
V.—EASTERN STATES AGENCY—												
Bhartpur—												
Bhartpur City	67,553	37,337	30,216	49,860	27,710	22,150	...	...	...	16,540	9,038	7,502
Bhartpur Tehsil	40,431	21,929	18,502	38,415	20,795	17,620	...	...	...	1,932	1,089	843
Uchain	47,735	25,585	22,150	43,047	23,124	19,923	...	...	...	4,239	2,214	2,025
Akhaïgarh	45,695	25,635	20,060	42,957	24,214	18,743	...	...	...	2,461	1,269	1,192
Bayana	75,126	40,646	34,480	70,605	38,262	32,343	...	...	...	4,194	2,208	1,986
Bhusawar	82,663	44,134	38,529	77,135	41,290	35,845	...	...	...	4,969	2,559	2,410
Pahari	27,737	15,038	12,699	9,566	5,224	4,342	...	...	...	18,072	9,761	8,311
Deeg	62,725	34,315	28,410	55,283	30,332	24,951	...	...	...	7,011	3,746	3,265
Rupbas	30,186	16,351	13,835	27,656	14,984	12,672	...	..	...	2,512	1,357	1,155
Kama	44,058	23,444	20,614	28,606	15,193	13 413	...	...	...	14,888	7,956	6,932
Kumheir	51,180	27,478	23,702	48,056	25,878	22,178	....	...	...	2,790	1,427	1,363
Gopalgarh	40,791	21,595	19,196	19,109	10,138	8,971	...	...	...	21,587	11,402	10,185
Nagur	23,943	13,986	9,957	17,986	10,482	7,504	...	...	...	5,940	3,493	2,447
Total	639,823	347,473	292,350	528,281	287,626	240,655	...	...	...	107,135	57,519	49,616
Bhartpur Railway	478	355	123	348	273	75	...	...	...	125	79	46
Europeans, etc., in Bhartpur	2	2	..	...	...	...	...	...	...	...	...	...
GRAND TOTAL, BHARTPUR STATE	640,303	347,830	292,473	528 629	287,899	240,730	...	...	...	107,260	57,598	49,662
Karauli—												
Karauli City	23,111	11,762	11,349	17,423	9,004	8,419	...	...	...	5,352	2,579	2,773
Hazur Tehsil	37,821	20,832	16,989	36,808	20,239	16,569	...	...	...	1,006	586	420
Jirota „	31,611	17,035	14,576	30,574	16,451	14,123	...	...	...	1,030	577	453
Machilpur „	24,981	13,670	11,311	24,274	13,287	10,987	...	...	...	707	383	324
Mandrail „	23,139	12,404	10,735	22,509	12,066	10,443	...	...	...	626	335	291
Utgir „	15,911	8,845	7,066	15,694	8,702	6,992	...	...	...	212	138	74
Total	156,574	84,548	72,026	147,282	79,749	67,533	...	...	...	8,933	4,598	4,335
Europeans, etc., in Karauli	13	7	6	...	...	...	...	...	...	...	...	...
GRAND TOTAL, KARAULI STATE	156,587	84,555	72,032	147,282	79,749	67,533	...	...	...	8,933	4,598	4,335

of the Population according to Religion—*contd.*

Jains.			Christians.			Animistic.			Jews.			Parsis.			Sikhs.			No Religion.		
Total.	Males.	Females.	Total.	Males.	Females.	Total.	Males.	Females.	Total.	Males.	Females.	Total.	Males.	Females.	Total.	Males.	Females.	Total.	Males.	Females.
14	15	16.	17	18	19	20	21	22	23	24	25	26	27	28	29	30	31	32	33	34
2,323	1,150	1,173	...	...	...	...	...	...	...	...	...	...	...	...	...	...	...	...	...	...
29	17	12	8	1	7	...	...	...	...	...	...	4	3	1	...	...	...	...	...	...
1,997	1,036	961	...	...	...	...	...	...	...	...	...	...	...	...	...	...	...	...	...	...
4,349	2,203	2,146	8	1	7	...	...	...	...	...	...	4	3	1	...	...	...	...	...	...
47,028	24,841	22,187	165	88	77	...	...	...	...	...	...	6	4	2	64	30	34	...	...	...
79	48	31	400	204	196	...	...	...	1	1	...	19	10	9	11	7	4	1	1	...
...	...	...	117	70	47	...	...	...	...	...	...	...	...	...	...	...	...	1	1	...
47,107	24,889	22,218	682	362	320	...	...	...	1	1	...	25	14	11	75	37	38	2	2	...
1,562	732	830	18	9	9	...	...	...	...	...	...	5	3	2	...	...	...	...	...	...
976	560	416	...	...	...	...	...	...	...	...	...	...	...	...	5	3	2	...	...	...
966	451	515	3	2	1	...	...	...	...	...	...	...	...	...	...	...	...	...	...	...
888	464	424	...	...	...	...	...	...	...	...	...	...	...	...	...	...	...	...	...	...
1,158	608	550	...	...	...	...	...	...	...	...	...	...	...	...	...	...	...	...	...	...
5,550	2,815	2,735	21	11	10	...	...	...	...	...	...	5	3	2	5	3	2	...	...	...
...	...	...	...	...	...	...	...	...	...	...	...	...	...	...	...	...	...	...	...	...
5,550	2,815	2,735	21	11	10	...	...	...	...	...	...	5	3	2	5	3	2	...	...	...
228	120	108	...	...	...	...	...	...	...	...	...	...	...	...	...	...	...	...	...	...
52,885	27,824	25,061	703	373	330	...	...	...	1	1	...	30	17	13	80	40	40	2	2	...
1,151	587	564	2	2	...	...	...	...	...	...	...	...	...	...	...	...	...	...	...	...
84	45	39	...	...	...	...	...	...	...	...	...	...	...	...	...	...	...	...	...	...
449	247	202	...	...	...	...	...	...	...	...	...	...	...	...	...	...	...	...	...	...
277	152	125	...	...	...	...	...	...	...	...	...	...	...	...	...	...	...	...	...	...
327	176	151	...	...	...	...	...	...	...	...	...	...	...	...	...	...	...	...	...	...
559	285	274	...	...	...	...	...	...	...	...	...	...	...	...	...	...	...	...	...	...
99	53	46	...	...	...	...	...	...	...	...	...	...	...	...	...	...	...	...	...	...
431	237	194	...	...	...	...	...	...	...	...	...	...	...	...	...	...	...	...	...	...
18	10	8	...	...	...	...	...	...	...	...	...	...	...	...	...	...	...	...	...	...
564	295	269	...	...	...	...	...	...	...	...	...	...	...	...	...	...	...	...	...	...
334	173	161	...	...	...	...	...	...	...	...	...	...	...	...	...	...	...	...	...	...
95	55	40	...	...	...	...	...	...	...	...	...	...	...	...	...	...	...	...	...	...
17	11	6	...	...	...	...	...	...	...	...	...	...	...	...	...	...	...	...	...	...
4,405	2,326	2,079	2	2	...	...	...	...	...	...	...	...	...	...	...	...	...	...	...	...
3	3	...	2	...	2	...	...	...	...	...	...	...	...	...	...	...	...	...	...	...
...	...	...	2	2	...	...	...	...	...	...	...	...	...	...	...	...	...	...	...	...
4,408	2,329	2,079	6	4	2	...	...	...	...	...	...	...	...	...	...	...	...	...	...	...
336	179	157	...	...	...	...	...	...	...	...	...	...	...	...	...	...	...	...	...	...
7	7	...	...	...	...	...	...	...	...	...	...	...	...	...	...	...	...	...	...	...
7	7	...	...	...	...	...	...	...	...	...	...	...	...	...	...	...	...	...	...	...
...	...	...	...	...	...	...	...	...	...	...	...	...	...	...	...	...	...	...	...	...
4	3	1	...	...	...	...	...	...	...	...	...	...	...	...	...	...	...	...	...	...
5	5	...	...	...	...	...	...	...	...	...	...	...	...	...	...	...	...	...	...	...
359	201	158	...	...	...	...	...	...	...	...	...	...	...	...	...	...	...	...	...	...
...	...	...	13	7	6	...	...	...	...	...	...	...	...	...	...	...	...	...	...	...
359	201	158	13	7	6	...	...	...	...	...	...	...	...	...	...	...	...	...	...	...

TABLE III.—Statement showing the Distribution

Names of States and Agencies.	Total Population.			Hindus.			Aryas.			Mussalmans.		
	Total.	Males.	Females.	Total.	Males.	Females.	Total.	Males.	Females.	Total.	Males.	Females.
1	2	3	4	5	6	7	8	9	10	11	12	13
EASTERN STATES AGENCY—												
Dholpur—												
Gird Tehsil	76,607	45,512	31,095	68,937	41,442	27,495	...	...	...	6,780	3,602	3,178
Bari "	54,564	29,989	24,575	49,705	27,658	22,047	...	...	...	4,837	2,321	2,516
Basheri "	48,732	26,902	21,830	47,130	25,993	21,137	...	...	...	1,600	907	693
Kolari "	46,831	24,955	21,876	44,808	23,859	20,949	...	...	...	2,019	1,092	927
Raja Khera	34,532	19,366	15,166	31,639	17,764	13,875	...	...	...	1,137	606	531
Sir Muthra	18,458	10,280	8,178	17,442	9,750	7,692	...	...	...	1,016	530	486
Total	279,724	157,004	122,720	259,661	146,466	113,195	...	...	...	17,389	9,058	8,331
Europeans, etc., in Dholpur	5	4	1	...	...	...	...	...	...	...	...	...
Indian Midland Railway—												
Dholpur	115	83	32	85	61	24	...	...	...	29	21	8
Mania Station	46	32	14	41	29	12	...	...	...	5	3	2
GRAND TOTAL, DHOLPUR STATE	279,890	157,123	122,767	259,787	146,556	113,231	...	...	...	17,423	9,082	8,341
GRAND TOTAL, EASTERN STATES AGENCY	1,076,780	589,508	487,272	935,698	514,204	421,494	...	...	...	133,616	71,278	62,338
VI.—ALWAR AGENCY—												
Alwar	141,157	74,703	66,454	93,562	49,479	44,083	...	...	...	46,222	24,516	21,706
Bansar	65,203	34,866	30,337	62,332	33,393	28,939	...	...	...	2,828	1,447	1,381
Bahror	69,419	35,898	33,521	65,308	33,917	31,391	...	...	...	4,056	1,955	2,101
Govindgarh	21,694	11,310	10,384	11,060	5,744	5,316	...	...	...	10,549	5,523	5,026
Kathumbar	38,964	20,783	18,181	35,498	18,852	16,646	...	...	...	3,034	1,709	1,325
Kishengarh	61,671	32,033	29,638	31,283	16,342	14,941	...	...	...	30,388	15,691	14,697
Luchmangarh	60,479	31,516	28,963	48,882	25,506	23,376	...	...	...	10,847	5,611	5,236
Mandawar	56,886	29,870	27,016	47,112	24,861	22,251	...	...	...	9,774	5,009	4,765
Rajgarh	88,901	46,536	42,365	83,258	43,647	39,611	...	...	...	5,259	2,677	2,582
Ramgarh	47,912	25,155	22,757	19,110	9,933	9,177	...	...	...	27,979	14,807	13,172
Thanaghazi	54,561	28,674	25,887	52,640	27,693	24,947	...	...	...	1,573	796	777
Tijara	52,570	27,930	24,640	24,802	13,387	11,415	...	...	...	27,468	14,397	13,071
Nimrana	7,340	3,894	3,446	7,128	3,789	3,339	...	...	...	212	105	107
Total	766,757	403,168	363,589	581,975	306,543	275,432	...	...	...	180,189	94,243	85,946
Total Railway	971	700	271	715	520	195	...	...	...	237	168	69
Total Europeans, etc.	58	30	28	...	...	...	...	...	...	...	...	...
GRAND TOTAL, ALWAR AGENCY	767,786	403,898	363,888	582,690	307,063	275,627	...	...	...	180,426	94,411	86,015
VII.—HARAOWTI AND TONK AGENCY—												
Tonk (Rajputana)—												
Tonk	114,298	59,591	54,707	85,774	45,140	40,634	...	...	...	25,104	12,618	12,491
Aligarh	19,623	10,466	9,157	17,164	9,118	8,046	...	...	...	1,621	876	745
Nimbahera	64,888	33,609	31,279	59,774	30,862	28,912	...	...	...	2,741	1,478	1,263
Total Tonk	158,809	103,666	95,143	162,712	85,120	77,592	...	...	...	29,466	14,967	14,499
Total Railway	122	84	38	83	62	21	...	...	...	38	21	17
Total Europeans, etc.	3	2	1	...	...	...	...	...	...	...	...	...
Total Rajputana (Tonk)	198,934	103,752	95,182	162,795	85,182	77,613	...	...	...	29,504	14,988	14,516
Detached Tracts of Rajputana under Central India—												
Chabra	46,473	24,290	22,183	43,556	22,835	20,721	...	...	...	2,670	1,313	1,357
Parwa	40,866	21,567	19,299	36,935	19,593	17,342	...	...	...	2,538	1,283	1,255
Sironj	93,856	50,488	43,368	83,418	44,579	38,839	...	...	...	9,822	5,575	4,247
Total	181,135	96,345	84,790	163,909	87,007	76,902	...	...	...	15,030	8,171	6,859
GRAND TOTAL, TONK STATE	380,069	200,097	179,972	326,704	172,189	154,515	...	...	...	44,534	23,159	21,375
Bundi—												
Bundi	22,544	11,980	10,564	17,009	9,085	7,924	...	...	...	4,575	2,413	2,162
Taragarh	5,492	2,882	2,610	5,253	2,749	2,504	...	...	...	89	53	36
Patan	28,252	14,674	13,578	27,233	14,114	13,119	...	...	...	666	362	304
Kapran	9,235	4,793	4,442	8,514	4,406	4,108	...	...	...	450	231	219
Gundowli	39,760	20,821	18,939	38,550	20,163	18,387	...	...	...	504	276	228
Ajitgarh	4,634	2,532	2,102	4,528	2,472	2,056	...	...	...	20	14	6
Deyi	42,940	22,452	20,488	39,849	20,874	18,975	...	...	...	1,093	534	559
Naenwa	6,093	3,148	2,945	4,316	2,232	2,084	...	...	...	923	472	451
Gotra	43,527	23,057	20,476	41,351	21,877	19,474	...	...	...	946	515	431
Hindoli	41,857	22,420	19,437	39,645	21,267	18,378	...	...	...	1,451	755	696
Selore	51,341	27,280	24,061	49,807	26,418	23,389	...	...	...	889	514	375
Total	295,675	156,033	139,642	276,055	145,657	130,398	...	...	...	11,606	6,139	5,467

of the Population according to Religion—*contd.*

Jains.			Christians.			Animistic.			Jews.			Parsis.			Sikhs.		
Total.	Males.	Females.	Total.	Males.	Females.	Total.	Males.	Females.	Total.	Males.	Females.	Total.	Males.	Females.	Total.	Males.	Females.
14	15	16	17	18	19	20	21	22	23	24	25	26	27	28	29	30	31
865	453	412	...	...	...	...	...	...	...	...	...	...	...	...	25	15	10
22	10	12	...	...	...	...	...	...	...	...	...	...	...	...	...	...	...
2	2	...	...	...	...	...	...	...	...	...	...	...	...	...	...	...	...
4	4	...	...	...	...	...	...	...	...	...	...	...	...	...	...	...	...
1,756	996	760	...	...	...	...	...	...	...	...	...	...	...	...	...	...	...
...	...	...	...	...	...	...	...	...	...	...	...	...	...	...	...	...	...
2,649	1,465	1,184	...	...	...	...	...	...	...	...	...	...	...	...	25	15	10
...	...	...	5	4	1	...	...	...	...	...	...	...	...	...	...	...	...
...	...	...	1	1	...	...	...	...	...	...	...	...	...	...	...	...	...
...	...	...	...	...	...	...	...	...	...	...	...	...	...	...	...	...	...
2,649	1,465	1,184	6	5	1	...	...	...	...	...	...	...	...	...	25	15	10
7,416	3,995	3,421	25	16	9	...	...	...	...	...	...	...	...	...	25	15	10
1,268	647	621	103	60	43	...	...	...	...	...	...	2	1	1	...	...	...
43	26	17	...	...	...	...	...	...	...	...	...	...	...	...	...	...	...
55	26	29	...	...	...	...	...	...	...	...	...	...	...	...	...	...	...
85	43	42	...	...	...	...	...	...	...	...	...	...	...	...	...	...	...
432	222	210	...	...	...	...	...	...	...	...	...	...	...	...	...	...	...
...	...	...	...	...	...	...	...	...	...	...	...	...	...	...	...	...	...
750	399	351	...	...	...	...	...	...	...	...	...	...	...	...	...	...	...
...	...	...	...	...	...	...	...	...	...	...	...	...	...	...	...	...	...
384	212	172	...	...	...	...	...	...	...	...	...	...	...	...	...	...	...
823	415	408	...	...	...	...	...	...	...	...	...	...	...	...	...	...	...
348	185	163	...	...	...	...	...	...	...	...	...	...	...	...	...	...	...
300	146	154	...	...	...	...	...	...	...	...	...	...	...	...	...	...	...
...	...	...	...	...	...	...	...	...	...	...	...	...	...	...	...	...	...
4,488	2,321	2,167	103	60	43	...	...	...	...	...	...	2	1	1	...	...	...
7	5	2	5	3	2	...	...	...	...	...	...	...	...	...	7	4	3
...	...	...	58	30	28	...	...	...	...	...	...	...	...	...	...	...	...
4,495	2,326	2,169	166	93	73	...	...	...	...	...	...	2	1	1	7	4	3
3,410	1,832	1,578	10	6	4	...	...	...	...	...	...	...	...	...	...	...	...
338	472	366	...	...	...	...	...	...	...	...	...	...	...	...	...	...	...
2,373	1,269	1,104	...	...	...	...	...	...	...	...	...	...	...	...	...	...	...
6,621	3,573	3,048	10	6	4	...	...	...	...	...	...	...	...	...	...	...	...
1	1	...	...	...	...	...	...	...	...	...	...	...	...	...	...	...	...
...	...	...	3	2	1	...	...	...	...	...	...	...	...	...	...	...	...
6,622	3,574	3,048	13	8	5	...	...	...	...	...	...	...	...	...	...	...	...
247	142	105	...	...	...	...	...	...	...	...	...	...	...	...	...	...	...
1,333	691	642	...	...	...	...	...	...	...	...	...	...	...	...	...	...	...
609	329	280	7	5	2	...	...	...	...	...	...	...	...	...	...	...	...
2,189	1,162	1,027	7	5	2	...	...	...	...	...	...	...	...	...	...	...	...
8,811	4,736	4,075	20	13	7	...	...	...	...	...	...	...	...	...	...	...	...
957	480	477	...	...	...	...	...	...	...	...	...	3	2	1	...	...	...
150	80	70	...	...	...	...	...	...	...	...	...	...	...	...	...	...	...
353	198	155	...	...	...	...	...	...	...	...	...	...	...	...	...	...	...
271	156	115	...	...	...	...	...	...	...	...	...	...	...	...	...	...	...
706	382	324	...	...	...	...	...	...	...	...	...	...	...	...	...	...	...
86	46	40	...	...	...	...	...	...	...	...	...	...	...	...	...	...	...
1,998	1,044	954	...	...	...	...	...	...	...	...	...	...	...	...	...	...	...
854	444	410	...	...	...	...	...	...	...	...	...	...	...	...	...	...	...
1,230	659	571	...	...	...	...	...	...	...	...	...	...	...	...	...	...	...
761	398	363	...	...	...	...	...	...	...	...	...	...	...	...	...	...	...
645	348	297	...	...	...	...	...	...	...	...	...	...	...	...	...	...	...
8,011	4,235	3,776	...	...	...	...	...	...	...	...	...	3	2	1	...	...	...

TABLE III.—Statement showing the Distribution

Names of States and Agencies.	Total Population.			Hindus.			Aryas.			Mussalmans.		
	Total.	Males.	Females.	Total.	Males.	Females.	Total.	Males.	Females.	Total.	Males.	Females.
1	2	3	4	5	6	7	8	9	10	11	12	13
HARAOWTI AND TONK AGENCY—*contd.*												
Shahpura—												
Kachola Pargana of Shahpura included under Meywar	26,227	*13,832*	12,395	25,485	*13,403*	12,082	...	...	...	318	*181*	137
Phoolya Pargana (Shahpura)	63,646	*33,243*	30,403	58,154	*30,404*	27,750	...	...	...	3,136	*1,638*	1,498
Total Shahpura State	...	...	...	...	...	...	...	...	...	...	...	...
GRAND TOTAL, HARAOWTI AND TONK AGENCY	739,390	389,373	350,017	660,913	348,250	312,663	...	...	...	59,276	30,936	28,340
VIII.—JHALLAWAR AGENCY—												
Jhalrapatan (Chaoni)	23,363	*12,126*	11,237	15,459	*8,167*	7,292	..	...	...	7,375	*3,690*	3,685
Jhalrapatan (Town)	10,783	*5,680*	5,103	7,820	*4,140*	3,680	...	...	...	2,185	*1,133*	1,052
Pargana Patan	17,494	*9,219*	8,275	17,266	*9,055*	8,211	...	...	...	220	*158*	62
Chechat	25,066	*13,184*	11,882	23,961	*12,584*	11,377	1	*1*	...	1,058	*573*	485
Suket	16,424	*8,610*	7,814	15,831	*8,273*	7,558	...	...	...	530	*303*	227
Asnawar	9,600	*5,170*	4,430	9,329	*4,992*	4,337	...	...	..	257	*173*	84
Bakani	28,195	*14,999*	13,196	26,847	*14,244*	12,603	...	...	...	1,127	*624*	503
Iklera	16,763	*8,837*	7,926	15,862	*8,313*	7,549	...	...	...	741	*428*	313
Ghatoli	16,007	*8 560*	7,447	15,507	*8,295*	7,212	..	...	...	491	*261*	230
Chipa Barod	34,225	*18,020*	16,205	32,576	*17,168*	15,408	...	...	...	1,487	*771*	716
Manohar Thana	27,796	*14,563*	13,233	25,814	*13,509*	12,305	...	...	...	1,901	*1,015*	886
Total Central Jhallawar	225,716	118,968	106,748	206,272	108,740	97,532	1	1	...	17,372	9,129	8,243
Pachpahar	18,173	*9,631*	8,542	17,026	*9,009*	8,017	...	...	...	787	*427*	360
Awar	15,755	*8,475*	7,280	14,743	*7,913*	6,830	...	...	...	510	*282*	228
Dag	26,206	*14,345*	11,861	24,631	*13,503*	11,128	...	...	...	864	*460*	404
Gangdhar	30,821	*16,816*	14,005	29,175	*15,963*	13,212	...	...	...	1,095	*559*	536
Total of Chomahla	50,955	*49,267*	41,688	85,575	*46,388*	39,187	...	...	...	3,256	*1,728*	1,528
Uprehti	13,361	*6,093*	6,368	12,915	*6,721*	6,194	...	...	...	442	*269*	173
Taleti	13,551	*7,244*	6,307	12,912	*6,930*	5,982	...	...	...	637	*312*	325
Total of Shahabad	26,912	*14,237*	12,675	25,827	*13,651*	12,176	...	...	...	1,079	*581*	498
Total	343,583	182,472	161,111	317,674	163,779	148,895	1	1	...	21,707	11,438	10,269
Total Europeans, etc.	18	*6*	12	...	...	...	...	...	...	...	...	...
GRAND TOTAL, JHALLAWAR AGENCY	343,601	182,478	161,123	317,674	168,779	148,895	1	1	...	21,707	11,438	10,269
IX.—KOTAH—												
Kotah City and Suburbs	38,620	*20,003*	18,617	28,123	*14,673*	13,450	...	...	...	9,806	*4,950*	4,856
Nizamats—												
Anta	32,810	*16,914*	15,896	31,141	*16,107*	15,034	...	..	...	1,611	*771*	840
Baran	37,889	*19,286*	18,603	35,364	*18,029*	17,335	...	...	...	2,358	*1,178*	1,180
Barodh	23,358	*12,134*	11,224	22,105	*11,500*	10,605	...	...	...	1,086	*546*	540
Digod	22,055	*11,624*	10,431	20,904	*11,004*	9,900	...	...	...	934	*504*	430
Etawah	23,109	*11,949*	11,160	22,014	*11,364*	10,650		...	...	731	*388*	343
Ghatoli	20,069	*10,562*	9,507	19,085	*10,007*	9,078	...	...	...	645	*375*	270
Kanwas	27,599	*14,196*	13,403	26,224	*13,459*	12,765	...	...	...	1,233	*657*	576
Khanpur	26,372	*13,798*	12,574	25,154	*13,121*	12,033	...	...	...	1,023	*588*	435
Kishenganj	28,992	*15,392*	13,600	28,000	*14,847*	13,153	...	...	...	900	*501*	399
Kunjer	21,583	*11,146*	10,437	20,813	*10,744*	10,069	...	...	...	598	*306*	292
Ladpura	42,290	*21,814*	20,476	38,154	*19,780*	18,374	...	...	...	3,405	*1,668*	1,737
Mangrol	31,984	*16,451*	15,533	29,362	*15,091*	14,271	...	...	...	2,384	*1,232*	1,152
Sangod	32,565	*16,921*	15,644	30,757	*15,977*	14,780	...	...	...	1,636	*849*	787
Shergarh	28,313	*14,699*	13,614	26,435	*13,736*	12,699	...	...	...	1,695	*872*	823
Taraj	32,928	*17,228*	15,700	31,788	*16,617*	15,171	...	...	...	733	*397*	336

of the Population according to Religion —*contd.*

Jains.			Christians.			Animistic.			Jews.			Parsis.			Sikhs.		
Total.	Males.	Females.	Total.	Males.	Females.	Total.	Males.	Females.	Total.	Males.	Females.	Total.	Males.	Females.	Total.	Males.	Females.
14	15	16	17	18	19	20	21	22	23	24	25	26	27	28	29	30	31
424	248	176	...	...	...	...	...	...	...	...	...	...	...	...	...	...	...
2,353	1,198	1,155	2	2	...	...	...	...	...	...	...	1	1	...	...	...	...
...	...	...	...	...	...	...	...	...	...	...	...	...	...	...	...	...	...
19,175	10,169	9.006	22	15	7	...	...	...	...	...	...	4	3	1	...	...	...
412	204	208	...	...	...	...	...	...	...	...	...	...	...	...	117	65	52
777	406	371	...	...	...	...	...	...	...	...	...	...	...	...	1	1	...
8	6	2	...	...	...	...	...	...	...	...	...	...	...	...	...	...	...
46	26	20	...	...	...	...	...	...	...	...	...	...	...	...	...	...	...
61	32	29	...	...	...	...	...	...	...	...	...	...	...	...	2	2	...
14	5	9	...	...	...	...	...	...	...	...	...	...	...	...	...	...	...
221	131	90	...	...	...	...	...	...	...	...	...	...	...	...	...	...	...
160	96	64	...	...	...	...	...	...	...	...	...	...	...	...	...	...	...
9	4	5	...	...	...	...	...	...	...	...	...	...	...	...	...	...	...
162	81	81	...	...	...	...	...	...	...	...	...	...	...	...	...	...	...
81	39	42	...	...	...	...	...	...	...	...	...	...	...	...	...	...	...
1,951	1,030	921	...	...	...	...	...	...	...	...	...	...	...	...	120	68	52
35	191	161	...	...	...	...	...	...	...	...	...	...	...	...	8	4	4
48	272	216	...	...	...	...	...	...	...	...	...	...	...	...	14	8	6
701	378	323	...	...	...	...	...	...	...	...	...	...	...	...	10	4	6
549	293	256	...	...	...	...	...	...	...	...	...	...	...	...	2	1	1
2,090	1,134	956	...	...	...	...	...	...	...	...	...	...	...	...	34	17	17
4	3	1	...	...	...	...	...	...	...	...	...	...	...	...	...	...	...
2	2	...	...	...	...	...	...	...	...	...	...	...	...	...	...	...	...
6	5	1	...	...	...	...	...	...	...	...	...	...	...	...	...	...	...
4,047	2,169	1,878	...	...	...	...	...	...	...	...	...	...	...	...	154	85	69
...	...	...	18	6	12	...	...	...	...	...	...	...	...	...	...	...	...
4,047	2,169	1,878	18	6	12	...	...	...	...	...	...	...	...	...	154	35	69
464	270	194	49	22	27	...	...	...	...	...	...	...	...	...	178	88	90
58	36	22	...	...	...	...	...	...	...	...	...	...	...	...	...	...	...
167	79	88	...	...	...	...	...	...	...	...	...	...	...	...	...	...	...
167	88	79	...	...	...	...	...	...	...	...	...	...	...	...	...	...	...
217	116	101	...	...	...	...	...	...	...	...	...	...	...	...	...	...	...
364	197	167	...	...	...	...	...	...	...	...	...	...	...	...	...	...	...
339	180	159	...	...	...	...	...	...	...	...	...	...	...	...	...	...	...
142	80	62	...	...	...	...	...	...	...	...	...	...	...	...	...	...	...
195	89	106	...	...	...	...	...	...	...	...	...	...	...	...	...	...	...
92	44	48	...	...	...	...	...	...	...	...	...	...	...	...	...	...	...
172	96	76	...	...	...	...	...	...	...	...	...	...	...	...	...	...	...
731	366	365	...	...	...	...	...	...	...	...	...	...	...	...	...	...	...
238	128	110	...	...	...	...	...	...	...	...	...	...	...	...	...	...	...
172	95	77	...	...	...	...	...	...	...	...	...	...	...	...	...	...	...
183	91	92	...	...	...	...	...	...	...	...	...	...	...	...	...	...	...
407	214	193	...	...	...	...	...	...	...	...	...	...	...	...	...	...	...

TABLE III.—Statement showing the Distribution

Names of States and Agencies.	Total Population.			Hindus.			Aryas.			Mussalmans.		
	Total.	Males.	Females.	Total.	Males.	Females.	Total.	Males.	Females.	Total.	Males.	Females.
1	2	3	4	5	6	7	8	9	10	11	12	13
Kotries—												
Antarda	4,219	2,203	2,016	3,952	2,071	1,881	...	...	...	127	63	64
Balwan	2,888	1,562	1,326	2,724	1,466	1,258	...	...	...	134	78	56
Gainta	4,727	2,425	2,302	4,456	2,298	2,158	...	...	...	267	124	143
Indargarh	26,208	13,681	12,527	23,834	12,409	11,425	...	...	...	1,613	865	748
Karwar	2,525	1,285	1,240	2.320	1,177	1,143	...	...	...	178	94	84
Khatoli with Farara	8,088	4,198	3,890	7,544	3,910	3,634	...	...	...	485	260	225
Pipalda with Phusod	7,072	3,648	3,424	6,691	3,446	3,245	...	...	...	339	184	155
Total Kotah	526,263	273,119	253,144	486,944	252,833	234,111	...	...	...	33,921	17,450	16,471
Europeans, etc., in Kotah	4	2	2	...	...	...	...	...	...	...	...	...
GRAND TOTAL, KOTAH AGENCY	526,267	273,121	253,146	486,944	252,833	234,111	...	...	...	33,921	17,450	16,471
GRAND TOTAL, RAJPUTANA (including the Central India, portion of Tonk, the detached areas of Central India, and the unenumerated population)	12,401,478	6,551,953	5,849,525	10,356,367	5,494,533	4,861,834	371	251	120	1,006,381	534,010	472,371

of the Population according to Religion —*concld.*

Jains.			Christians.			Animistic.			Jews.			Parsis.			Sikhs.			No Religion.		
Total.	Males.	Females.	Total.	Males.	Females.	Total.	Males.	Females.	Total.	Males.	Females.	Total.	Males.	Females.	Total.	Males.	Females.	Total.	Males.	Females.
14	15	16	17	18	19	20	21	22	23	24	25	26	27	28	29	30	31	32	33	34
140	69	71	...	...	...	...	...	...	...	...	...	...	...	...	...	...	...	...	...	...
30	18	12	...	...	...	...	...	...	...	...	...	...	...	...	...	...	...	...	...	...
4	3	1	...	...	...	...	...	...	...	...	...	...	...	...	...	...	...	...	...	...
759	405	354	2	2	...	...	...	...	...	...	...	...	...	...	...	...	...	...	...	...
27	14	13	...	...	...	...	...	...	...	...	...	...	...	...	...	...	...	...	...	...
59	28	31	...	...	...	...	...	...	...	...	...	...	...	...	...	...	...	...	...	...
42	18	24	...	...	...	...	...	...	...	...	...	...	...	...	...	...	...	...	...	...
5,169	2,724	2,445	51	24	27	...	...	...	...	...	...	...	...	...	178	88	90	...	...	...
...	...	...	4	2	2	...	...	...	...	...	...	...	...	...	...	...	...	...	...	...
5,169	2,724	2,445	55	26	29	...	...	...	...	...	...	...	...	...	178	88	90	...	...	...
419,807	207,523	212,284	1,862	1,043	819	615,319	313,727	301,592	15	9	6	238	138	100	1,116	717	399	2	2	...

RAJPUTANA AGENCY.

CENSUS OF 1891.

PROVINCIAL TABLE IV.

Statement of Population for Towns with more than 5,000 inhabitants, arranged territorially, *by Political Charges.*

Table IV.—Population for Towns—Rajputana Agency.

Summary of Provincial Table IV.

Names of Agency, States, etc.	Total Population.			Males.			Females.		
	1891.	1881.	Variation.	1891.	1881.	Variation.	1891.	1881.	Variation.
1	2	3	4	5	6	7	8	9	10
I.—MEYWAR RESIDENCY—									
Meywar	131,302	111,008	+ 20,294	68,451	57,460	+ 10,991	62,851	53,548	+ 9,303
Banswara	8,234	7,908	+ 326	3,998	4,055	— 57	4,236	3,853	+ 383
Dungarpur	6,431	6,449	— 18	3,003	3,213	— 210	3,428	3,236	+ 192
Partabgarh	14,819	12,430	+ 2,389	7,906	6,314	+ 1,592	6,913	6,116	+ 797
Total Meywar Residency	160,786	137,795	+ 22,991	83,358	71,042	+ 12,316	77,428	66,753	+ 10,675
II.—WESTERN RAJPUTANA STATES RESIDENCY—									
Marwar	268,927	207,306	+ 61,621	134,940	108,480	+ 26,460	133,987	98,826	+ 35,161
Sirohi	8,782	5,699	+ 3,083	4,667	3,015	+ 1,652	4,115	2,684	+ 1,431
Jesalmir	10,509	10,965	— 456	5,015	5,241	— 226	5,494	5,724	— 230
Total Western Rajputana States Residency	288,218	223,970	+ 64,248	144,622	116,736	+ 27,886	143,596	107,234	+ 36,362
III.—JEYPORE RESIDENCY—									
Jeypore	473,866	411,876	+ 61,990	248,619	214,310	+ 34,309	225,247	197,566	+ 27,681
Kishengarh	26,372	25,850	+ 522	13,537	13,041	+ 496	12,835	12,809	+ 26
Lawa	...	...	...	...	...	...	...	...	...
Total Jeypore Residency	500,238	437,726	+ 62,512	262,156	227,351	+ 34,805	238,082	210,375	+ 27,707
IV.—HARAOWTI AND TONK AGENCY (RAJPUTANA)—									
Tonk	51,426	47,015	+ 4,411	26,021	23,903	+ 2,118	25,405	23,112	+ 2,293
Detached tracts of Tonk in Central India	24,790	25,077	— 287	13,225	12,915	— 310	11,565	12,162	— 597
Total Tonk State	76,216	72,092	+ 4,124	39,246	36,818	+ 2,428	36,970	35,274	+ 1,696
Bundi	28,637	25,998	+ 2,639	15,128	12,726	+ 2,402	13,509	13,272	+ 237
Shahpura	11,718	10,647	+ 1,071	5,930	5,381	+ 549	5,788	5,266	+ 522
Total Haraowti and Tonk Agency	116,571	108,737	+ 7,834	60,304	54,925	+ 5,379	56,267	53,812	+ 2,455
V.—EASTERN STATES AGENCY—									
Bharatpur	123,605	124,944	— 1,339	66,752	66,824	— 72	56,853	58,120	— 1,267
Karauli	23,124	25,607	— 2,483	11,769	12,995	— 1,226	11,355	12,612	— 1,257
Dholpur	34,821	33,654	+ 1,167	18,259	17,556	+ 703	16,562	16,098	+ 464
Total Eastern States Agency	181,550	184,205	— 2,655	96,780	97,375	— 595	84,770	86,830	— 2,060
VI.—BIKANIR AGENCY	119,323	87,130	+ 32,193	59,158	44,943	+ 14,215	60,165	42,187	+ 17,978
VII.—ALWAR "	90,815	88,032	+ 2,783	47,836	46,155	+ 1,681	42,979	41,877	+ 1,102
VIII.—KOTAH "	56,451	58,896	— 2,445	28,992	30,450	— 1,458	27,459	28,446	— 987
IX.—JHALLAWAR "	34,164	31,772	+ 2,392	17,812	16,908	+ 904	16,352	14,864	+ 1,488
Total Rajputana Agency	1,548,116	1,358,263	+ 189,853	801,018	705,885	+ 95,133	747,098	652,378	+ 94,720
Detached tract of Gungapur of Gwalior in Meywar	6,761	5,590	+ 1,171	3,721	2,974	+ 747	3,040	2,616	+ 424
GRAND TOTAL	1,554,877	1,363,853	+ 191,024	804,739	708,859	+ 95,880	750,138	654,994	+ 95,144

PROVINCIAL TABLE.

TABLE IV.—Statement of Population for Towns with more than 5,000 inhabitants arranged territorially.

Town.	State.		Total Population.			Males.			Females.		
			1891.	1881.	Variation.	1891.	1881.	Variation.	1891.	1881.	Variation.
1	2	3	4	5	6	7	8	9	10	11	12
I.—MEYWAR RESIDENCY—											
Oodeypore	MEYWAR.		46,693	38,214	+ 8,479	24,873	20,168	+ 4,705	21,820	+ 18,046	+ 3,774
Kapasin			5,514	4,975	+ 539	2,909	2,630	+ 279	2,605	+ 2,345	+ 260
Nathdwara			9,331	8,458	+ 873	4,877	4,388	+ 489	4,454	+ 4,070	+ 384
Banera			5,760	4,718	+ 1,042	2,886	2,383	+ 503	2,874	+ 2,335	+ 539
Deogarh			7,400	6,846	+ 554	3,635	3,607	+ 28	3,765	+ 3,239	+ 526
Salumbar			6,029	5,574	+ 455	2,952	2,788	+ 164	3,077	+ 2,786	+ 291
Choti Sadri			5,368	4,521	+ 847	2,709	2,347	+ 362	2,659	+ 2,174	+ 485
Begun			5,882	5,641	+ 241	2,988	2,910	+ 78	2,894	+ 2,731	+ 163
Bhindar			6,750	6,522	+ 268	3,434	3,368	+ 66	3,356	+ 3,154	+ 202
Bhilwara			10,343	8,175	+ 2,168	5,485	4,034	+ 1,451	4,858	+ 4,141	+ 717
Pur			6,800	5,757	+ 1,043	3,450	2,799	+ 651	3,350	+ 2,958	+ 392
Chitore			9,354	6,931	+ 2,423	4,955	3,586	+ 1,369	4,399	+ 3,345	+ 1,054
Railway Population			932	...	+ 932	633	...	+ 633	299	+ ...	+ 299
Jehazpur			5,106	4,676	+ 430	2,665	2,452	+ 213	2,441	+ 2,224	+ 217
Total Meywar			131,302	111,008	+ 20,294	68,451	57,460	+ 10,991	62,851	+ 53,548	+ 9,303
Gungapur of Gwalior (in Central India)			6,761	5,590	+ 1,171	3,721	2,974	+ 747	3,040	2,616	+ 424
Total			138,063	116,598	+ 21,465	72,172	60,434	+ 11,738	65,891	56,164	+ 9,727
Banswara	BANSWARA.		8,234	7,908	+ 326	3,998	4,055	— 57	4,236	3,853	+ 383
Dungarpur	DUNGARPUR.		6,431	6,449	— 18	3,003	3,213	— 210	3,428	3,236	+ 192
Partabgarh	PARTABGARH.		14,819	12,430	+ 2,389	7,906	6,314	+ 1,592	6,913	6,116	+ 797
Total Meywar Residency			160,786	137,795	+ 22,991	83,358	71,042	+ 12,316	77,428	66,752	+ 10,675
Detached tract of Gungapur of Central India in Meywar			6,761	5,590	+ 1,171	3,721	2,974	+ 747	3,040	2,616	+ 424
Grand Total, Meywar Residency			167,547	143,385	+ 241,622	87,079	74,016	+ 13,063	80,468	69,369	+ 11,099
II.—WESTERN RAJPUTANA STATES RESIDENCY—											
Jodhpore	MARWAR.		61,849	57,211	+ 4,638	31,706	30,205	+ 1,501	30,143	27,006	+ 3,137
Railway Population (R.M.)			1,771	...	+ 1,771	1,115	...	+ 1,115	656	...	+ 656
Pokaran			7,895	6,467	+ 1,428	3,893	3,266	+ 627	4,002	3,201	+ 801
Bali (Godwar)			5,354	4,438	+ 916	2,617	2,358	+ 259	2,737	2,080	+ 657
Sadri			7,596	3,640	+ 3,956	3,656	2,012	+ 1,644	3,940	1,628	+ 2,312
Nimaj			5,744	4,371	+ 1,373	2,928	2,164	+ 764	2,816	2,207	+ 609
Sojat			12,624	10,394	+ 2,230	6,060	5,121	+ 939	6,564	5,273	+ 1,291
Pali			17,150	13,345	+ 3,805	8,535	6,880	+ 1,655	8,615	6,465	+ 2,150
Nawa			5,126	4,142	+ 984	2,742	2,205	+ 537	2,384	1,937	+ 447
Kuchawan			12,816	13,052	— 236	6,527	6,931	— 404	6,289	6,121	+ 168
Pachbhadra			5,125	4,271	+ 854	2,656	2,239	+ 417	2,469	2,032	+ 437
Balotra			5,435	...	+ 5,435	2,762	...	+ 2,762	2,673	...	+ 2,673
Nagore			17,191	14,067	+ 3,124	8,418	7,121	+ 1,297	8,773	6,946	+ 1,827
Mundwa			5,213	4,265	+ 948	2,602	2,167	+ 435	2,611	2,098	+ 513
Ladnu			7,404	5,183	+ 2,221	3,482	2,598	+ 884	3,922	2,585	+ 1,337
Kuchera			5,022	3,237	+ 1,785	2,310	1,796	+ 514	2,712	1,441	+ 1,271
Merta			7,135	6,682	+ 453	3,654	3,397	+ 257	3,481	3,285	+ 196
Kalu			5,182	4,439	+ 743	2,651	2,340	+ 311	2,531	2,099	+ 432
Rian			5,517	3,633	+ 1,884	2,850	2,076	+ 774	2,667	1,557	+ 1,110
Didwana			11,376	6,617	+ 4,759	5,768	3,423	+ 2,345	5,608	3,194	+ 2,414
Bhinmal			5,736	5,224	+ 512	2,906	2,715	+ 191	2,830	2,509	+ 321
Bilara			11,384	7,699	+ 3,685	5,996	3,923	+ 2,073	5,388	3,776	+ 1,612
Pipar			8,153	6,608	+ 1,545	3,924	3,466	+ 458	4,229	3,142	+ 1,087
Jalore			9,656	6,394	+ 3,262	4,768	3,287	+ 1,481	4,888	3,107	+ 1,781
Phalodi			10,497	9448	+ 1,049	4,811	5,126	— 315	5,686	4,322	+ 1,364
Lohawat			5,366	2,479	+ 2,887	2,802	1,664	+ 1,138	2,564	815	+ 1,749
Badmere			5,610	...	+ 5,610	2,801	...	+ 2,801	2,809	...	+ 2,809
Total Marwar			268,927	207,306	+ 61,621	134,940	108,480	+ 26,460	133,987	98,826	+ 35,161

TABLE IV.—Statement of Population for Towns with more than 5,000 inhabitants arranged territorially—*contd.*

Town.	State.		Total Population. 1891.	Total Population. 1881.	Total Population. Variation.	Males. 1891.	Males. 1881.	Males. Variation.	Females. 1891.	Females. 1881.	Females. Variation.
1	2	3	4	5	6	7	8	9	10	11	12
WESTERN RAJPUTANA STATES RESIDENCY—*contd.*											
Sirohi	SIROHI.		6,207	5,699	+ 508	3,075	3,015	+ 60	3,132	2,684	+ 448
European and Eurasian population			165	...	+ 165	98	...	+ 98	67	...	+ 67
Railway Population			2,410	...	+ 2,410	1,494	...	+ 1,494	916	...	+ 916
Total Sirohi			8,782	5,699	+ 3,083	4,667	3,015	+ 1,652	4,115	2,684	+ 1,431
Jesalmir	JESALMIR.		10,509	10,695	— 456	5,015	5,241	— 226	5,494	5,724	— 230
Total Western Rajputana States Residency			**288,218**	**223,970**	**+ 64,248**	**144,622**	**116,736**	**+ 27,886**	**143,596**	**107,234**	**+ 36,362**
III.—BIKANIR AGENCY—											
Bikanir	BIKANIR.		56,252	43,283	+ 12,969	27,896	21,409	+ 6,487	28,356	21,874	+ 6,482
Churu			14,014	10,666	+ 3,348	6,910	5,403	+ 1,507	7,104	5,263	+ 1,841
Nuhar			5,655	3,784	+ 1,871	2,894	2,080	+ 814	2,761	1,704	+ 1,057
Rajgarh			4,677	3,726	+ 951	2,346	2,131	+ 215	2,331	1,595	+ 736
Ratangarh			10,536	7,580	+ 2,956	5,123	3,871	+ 1,252	5,413	3,709	+ 1,704
Reni			6,553	5,198	+ 1,355	3,249	2,878	+ 371	3,304	2,320	+ 984
Sardarshahr			9,196	5,824	+ 3,372	4,463	2,919	+ 1,544	4,733	2,905	+ 1,828
Sujangarh			9,781	5,238	+ 4,543	4,824	3,169	+ 1,655	4,957	2,069	2,888
Suratgarh			2,659	1,831	+ 828	1,453	1,083	+ 370	1,206	748	+ 458
Total			119,323	87,130	+ 32,193	59,158	44,943	+ 14,215	60,165	42,187	+ 17,978
IV.—JEYPORE RESIDENCY—											
Jeypore City	JEYPORE.		158,905	142,578	+ 16,327	84,095	75,332	+ 8,763	74,810	67,246	+ 7,564
Railway population			6,455	...	+ 6,455	4,123	...	+ 4,123	2,332	...	+ 2,332
Sambhar Joint Jurisdiction (Railway) population			48	...	+ 48	25	...	+ 25	23	...	+ 23
Chomu			8,570	3,928	+ 4,642	4,351	2,075	+ 2,276	4,219	1,853	+ 2,366
Samod			6,582	3,676	+ 2,906	3,386	1,862	+ 1,524	3,196	1,814	+ 1,382
Lawan			5,326	3,744	+ 1,582	2,686	1,922	+ 764	2,640	1,822	+ 818
Chaksu			7,870	6,219	+ 1,651	4,589	3,436	+ 1,153	3,281	2,783	+ 498
Dausa			8,416	7,384	+ 1,032	4,518	3,760	+ 758	3,898	3,624	+ 274
Lalsote			8,163	8,743	— 580	4,021	4,366	— 345	4,142	4,377	— 235
Baswa			6,117	5,791	+ 326	3,230	2,980	+ 250	2,887	2,811	+ 76
Bhandarez			5,473	4,829	+ 644	2,753	2,358	+ 395	2,720	2,471	+ 249
Bisau			8,041	6,546	+ 1,495	4,047	3,257	+ 790	3,094	3,289	+ 705
Surajgarh			5,561	5,250	+ 311	2,761	2,597	+ 164	2,800	2,653	+ 147
Nawalgarh			12,567	10,032	+ 2,535	6,267	5,166	+ 1,101	6,300	4,866	+ 1,434
Jhoon Jhunu			12,267	9,538	+ 2,729	6,387	5,064	+ 1,323	5,880	4,474	+ 1,406
Singhana			5,901	5,559	+ 642	2,770	2,447	+ 323	3,131	2,812	+ 319
Udeypore			10,343	9,161	+ 1,182	6,562	5,618	+ 944	3,781	3,543	+ 238
Nimka Thana			5,733	2,711	+ 3,022	3,323	1,379	+ 1,944	2,410	1,332	+ 1,078
Khandela			10,067	7,949	+ 2,118	4,980	4,138	+ 842	5,087	3,811	+ 1,276
Bairath			5,748	5,649	+ 99	2,912	2,825	+ 87	2,836	2,824	+ 12
Sawai Madhopore			13,972	14,075	— 103	7,143	6,980	+ 162	6,829	7,095	— 266
Hindown			12,996	12,761	+ 235	6,780	6,786	— 6	6,216	5,975	+ 241
Toda Bhim			7,053	7,142	— 89	3,682	3,684	— 2	3,371	3,458	— 87
Sambhar			12,362	10,794	+ 1,568	6,802	5,824	+ 978	5,560	4,970	+ 590
Naraina			5,071	4,974	+ 97	2,668	2,688	— 20	2,403	2,286	+ 117
Sri Madhopore			6,130	6,847	— 717	3,094	3,804	— 710	3,036	3,043	— 7
Malpura			8,345	8,212	+ 133	4,336	4,469	— 133	4,009	3,743	+ 266
Toda Rai Singh			5,649	5,546	+ 103	2,927	3,189	— 262	2,722	2,357	+ 365
Newai			5,832	4,501	+ 1,331	3,569	2,279	+ 1,290	2,263	2,222	+ 41
Gungapore			5,880	5,880	...	3,108	2,989	+ 119	2,772	2,891	— 119
Bamaniawas			5,806	6,125	— 319	3,014	3,123	— 109	2,792	3,002	— 210
Sikar			19,897	17,739	+ 2,158	10,624	9,418	+ 1,206	9,273	8,321	+ 952
Fatehpore			16,560	14,731	+ 1,849	7,932	7,183	+ 749	8,648	7,548	+ 1,100
Ramgarh			12,197	11,313	+ 884	5,980	5,488	+ 492	6,217	5,825	+ 392
Lachmangarh			9,507	8,713	+ 794	4,656	4,209	+ 447	4,851	4,504	+ 347
Khetri			8,418	5,283	+ 3,135	4,420	2,592	+ 1,828	3,998	2,691	+ 1,307
Cherawa			6,701	5,489	+ 1,212	3,382	2,629	+ 753	3,319	2,860	+ 459
Kote			7,589	8,084	— 495	3,796	3,973	— 177	3,793	4,111	— 318
Uniara			5,728	4,680	+ 1,048	2,920	2,421	+ 499	2,808	2,259	+ 549
Total			473,866	411,876	+ 61,990	248,619	214,310	+ 34,309	225,247	197,566	+ 27,681
Kishengarh	KISHENGARH.		15,363	14,824	+ 539	7,954	7,513	+ 441	7,409	7,311	+ 98
Railway population			94	...	+ 94	68	...	+ 68	26	...	+ 26
Roopnagar			5,011	5,665	— 654	2,486	2,782	— 296	2,525	2,883	— 358
Sarwar			5,904	5,361	+ 543	3,029	2,746	+ 283	2,875	2,615	+ 260
Total			26,372	25,850	+ 522	13,537	13,041	+ 496	12,835	12,809	+ 26
GRAND TOTAL, JEYPORE RESIDENCY			**500,238**	**437,726**	**+ 62,512**	**262,156**	**227,351**	**+ 34,805**	**238,082**	**210,375**	**+ 27,707**

TABLE IV.—Statement of Population for Towns with more than 5,000 inhabitants arranged territorially—*contd.*

Town.	State.		Total Population. 1891.	1881.	Variation.	Males. 1891.	1881.	Variation.	Females. 1891.	1881.	Variation.
1	2	3	4	5	6	7	8	9	10	11	12
V.—EASTERN STATES AGENCY—											
BHARATPUR	BHARATPUR.		67,555	66,163	+ 1,392	37,339	36,580	+ 759	30,216	29,583	+ 633
Do. Railway	BHARATPUR.		478	...	+ 478	355	...	+ 355	123	...	+ 123
Bayana	BHARATPUR.		8,085	8,758	— 673	4,154	4,388	— 234	3,931	4,370	— 439
Bhosawar	BHARATPUR.		7,419	6,480	+ 939	3,778	3,326	+ 452	3,641	3,154	+ 487
Weir	BHARATPUR.		6,824	7,210	— 386	3,509	3,629	— 120	3,315	3,581	— 266
Deeg	BHARATPUR.		15,166	15,828	— 662	8,223	8,105	+ 118	6,943	7,723	— 780
Kama	BHARATPUR.		11,417	13,199	— 1,782	5,951	6,999	— 1,048	5,466	6,200	— 734
Kumheir	BHARATPUR.		6,661	7,306	— 645	3,443	3,797	— 354	3,218	3,509	— 291
TOTAL			123,605	124,944	— 1,339	66,752	66,824	— 72	56,853	58,120	— 1,267
KARAULI	KARAULI.		23,124	25,607	— 2,483	11,769	12,995	— 1,226	11,355	12,612	— 1,257
DHOLPUR	DHOLPUR.		9,624	15,833	— 6,209	4,791	8,537	— 3,746	4,833	7,296	— 2,463
Indian Midland Railway	DHOLPUR.		115	...	+ 115	83	...	+ 83	32	...	+ 32
Damanpur	DHOLPUR.		6,204	...	+ 6,204	3,381	..	+ 3,381	2,823	...	+ 2,823
Bari	DHOLPUR.		12,002	11,547	+ 545	6,273	5,669	+ 604	5,819	5,878	— 59
Raja Khera	DHOLPUR.		6,786	6,274	+ 512	3,731	3,350	+ 381	3,055	2,924	+ 131
TOTAL			34,821	33,654	+ 1,167	18,259	17,556	+ 703	16,562	16,058	+ 464
GRAND TOTAL, EASTERN STATES AGENCY			181,550	184,205	— 2,655	96,780	97,375	— 595	84,770	86,830	— 2,06
VI.—ALWAR AGENCY—											
Alwar	ALWAR		51,427	49,867	+ 1,560	27,764	26,544	+ 1,220	23,663	23,323	+ 340
Railway	ALWAR		971	...	+ 971	700	...	+ 700	271	...	+ 271
Rajgarh	ALWAR		10,302	9,749	+ 553	5,084	4,957	+ 127	5,218	4,792	+ 426
Tijara	ALWAR		7,049	7,723	— 674	3,543	3,001	— 358	3,506	3,822	— 316
Behror	ALWAR		5,719	5,533	+ 186	2,810	2,818	— 8	2,909	2,715	+ 194
Govindgarh	ALWAR		5,243	4,989	+ 254	2,688	2,529	+ 159	2,555	2,460	+ 95
Ramgarh	ALWAR		5,099	5,101	— 2	2,649	2,695	— 36	2,450	2,416	+ 34
Rampur	ALWAR		5,005	5,070	— 65	2,558	2,721	— 123	2,407	2,349	+ 58
TOTAL			90,815	88,032	+ 2,783	47,836	46,155	+ 1,681	42,979	41,877	+ 1,102
VII.—JHALRAPATAN—											
Jhalrapatan (Chaoni)	JHALLAWAR		23,381	20,303	+ 3,078	12,132	10,866	+ 1,266	11,249	9,437	+ 1,812
„ (Town)	JHALLAWAR		10,783	11,469	— 686	5,680	6,042	— 362	5,103	5,427	— 324
TOTAL			34,164	31,772	+ 2,392	17,812	16,908	+ 904	16,352	14,864	+ 1,488
VIII.—HARAOWTI AND TONK AGENCY—											
TONK	TONK IN RAJPUTANA.		45,947	40,726	+ 5,221	23,205	20,447	+ 2,758	22,742	20,279	+ 2,463
Railway population	TONK IN RAJPUTANA.		122	...	+ 122	84	...	+ 84	38	...	+ 38
Nimbahera	TONK IN RAJPUTANA.		5,357	6,289	— 932	2,732	3,456	— 724	2,625	2,833	— 208
Chabra	TONK IN CENTRAL INDIA.		7,426	8,040	— 614	3,730	4,314	— 584	3,696	3,726	— 3
Parawa	TONK IN CENTRAL INDIA.		5,627	5,681	— 54	2,819	2,976	— 157	2,808	2,705	+ 10
Seronj	TONK IN CENTRAL INDIA.		11,737	11,356	+ 381	6,676	5,625	+ 1,051	5,061	5,731	— 67
TOTAL			76,216	72,052	+ 4,124	39,246	36,818	+ 2,428	36,970	35,274	+ 169
BUNDI	BUNDI.		22,544	20,744	+ 1,800	11,980	9,977	+ 2,003	10,564	10,767	— 203
Naenwa	BUNDI.		6,093	5,254	+ 839	3,148	2,749	+ 399	2,945	2,505	+ 440
TOTAL			28,637	25,998	+ 2,639	15,128	12,726	+ 2,402	13,509	13,272	+ 237
SHAHPURA—*Phooliya*—(Shahpura)	SHAHPURA.		11,718	10,647	+ 1,071	5,930	5,381	+ 549	5,788	5,266	+ 522
GRAND TOTAL, HARAOWTI AND TONK AGENCY			116,571	108,737	+ 7,834	60,304	54,925	+ 5,379	56,267	53,812	+ 2,455

TABLE IV.—Statement of Population for Towns with more than 5,000 inhabitants arranged territorially—*concld.*

Town.	State.		Total Population.			Males.			Females.		
			1891.	1881.	Variation.	1891.	1881.	Variation.	1891.	1881.	Variation.
1	2	3	4	5	6	7	8	9	10	11	12
IX.—KOTAH—											
Kotah	Kotah.		38,624	40,270	− 1,646	20,005	20,868	− 863	18,619	19,402	− 783
Baran	Kotah.		7,067	7,714	− 647	3,503	3,900	− 397	3,564	3,814	− 250
Mangrol	Kotah.		5,714	5,906	− 192	2,937	3,104	− 167	2,777	2,802	− 25
Sangod	Kotah.		5,046	5,006	+ 40	2,547	2,578	− 31	2,499	2,428	+ 71
Total			56,451	58,896	− 2,445	28,992	30,450	− 1,458	27,459	28,446	− 987
GRAND TOTAL (including detached Towns of Tonk in Central India, and Gungapur of Gwalior in Meywar).	Rajputana.		1,554,877	1,363,853	+191,024	804,739	708,859	+ 95,880	750,138	654,994	+ 95,14

RAJPUTANA AGENCY.

CENSUS OF 1891.

PROVINCIAL TABLE V.

Statement showing Musalmans by Sects and by Parganas, Tehsils or other administrative divisions.

Summary of Provincial Table V.

Name of Agency.	Total Musalmans.			Sunnies.			Sihahs.			Others and Unspecified.		
	Total.	Males.	Females.	Total.	Males.	Females.	Total.	Males.	Females.	Total	Males.	Females.
1	2	3	4	5	6	7	8	9	10	11	12	13
I.—MEYWAR RESIDENCY—												
Meywar	59,125	31,484	27,641	51,598	27,549	24,049	7,300	3,787	3,513	227	148	79
Banswara	4,795	2,491	2,304	4,021	2,047	1,974	774	444	330	...	...	...
Dingarpur	4,314	2,229	2,085	2,808	1,496	1,312	1,506	733	773	...	...	...
Partabgarh	4,937	2,815	2,122	4,250	2,443	1,807	687	372	315	...	...	...
Kherwara Cantonment	33	30	3	...	...	...	...	...	...	33	30	3
Kotra Cantonment	10	10	...	...	...	...	...	...	...	10	10	...
Total Meywar Residency	73,214	39,059	34,155	62,677	33,535	29,142	10,267	5,336	4,931	270	188	82
II.—WESTERN RAJPUTANA STATES RESIDENCY.												
Marwar	178,611	95,376	83,235	177,097	94,531	82,566	1,056	575	481	458	270	188
½ Sambhar Joint Jurisdiction	2,001	1,087	914	2,000	1,086	914	1	1	...	...	...	...
Total Marwar	180,612	96,463	84,149	179,097	95,617	83,480	1,057	576	481	458	270	188
Sirohi	4,912	2,879	2,033	2,743	1,690	1,053	106	49	57	2,063	1,140	923
Jesalmir	29,443	16,761	12,682	29,313	16,677	12,636	130	84	46	...	...	...
Erinpura Cantonment	263	189	74	...	...	...	...	...	...	263	189	74
Abu Sanitarium	8	4	4	...	...	...	...	...	...	8	4	4
Total Western Rajputana States Residency	215,238	116,296	98,942	211,153	113,984	97,169	1,293	709	584	2,792	1,603	1,189
III.—JEYPORE RESIDENCY—												
Jeypore	196,741	103,577	93,164	193,495	101,737	91,758	1,544	798	746	1,702	1,042	660
½ Sambhar Joint Jurisdiction	2,000	1,087	913	2,000	1,087	913	...	...	...	...	...	...
Total Jeypore	198,741	104,664	94,077	195,495	102,824	92,671	1,544	798	746	1,702	1,042	660
Kishengarh	9,429	4,944	4,485	9,411	4,929	4,482	...	...	...	18	15	3
Lawa Thakurate	160	91	69	160	91	69	...	...	...	...	...	...
Total Jeypore Residency	208,330	109,699	98,631	205,066	107,844	97,222	1,544	798	746	1,720	1,057	663
IV.—HARAOWTI AND TONK AGENCY—												
Tonk (Rajputana)	29,504	14,988	14,516	29,410	14,929	14,481	56	38	18	38	21	17
Detached tracts of Tonk in Central India	15,030	8,171	6,859	14,668	7,977	6,691	362	194	168	...	...	...
Total Tonk State	44,534	23,159	21,375	44,078	22,906	21,172	418	232	186	38	21	17
Bundi	11,606	6,139	5,467	11,488	6,076	5,412	118	63	55	...	...	...
Shahpura Estate	3,136	1,638	1,498	3,136	1,638	1,498	...	...	...	...	...	...
Total Haraowti and Tonk Agency	59,276	30,936	28,340	58,702	30,620	28,082	536	295	241	38	21	17
V.—EASTERN STATES AGENCY—												
Bharatpur	107,260	57,598	49,662	104,057	56,150	47,907	3,078	1,369	1,709	125	79	46
Karauli	8,933	4,598	4,335	8,905	4,584	4,321	28	14	14	...	...	...
Dholpur	17,423	9,082	8,341	16,725	8,704	8,021	664	354	310	34	24	10
Total Eastern States Agency	133,616	71,278	62,338	129,687	69,438	60,249	3,770	1,737	2,033	159	103	56
VI.—BIKANIR AGENCY	80,029	43,107	36,922	79,959	43,090	36,909	30	17	13	...	...	...
VII.—ALWAR "	180,426	94,411	86,015	178,982	93,733	85,249	1,207	510	697	237	168	69
VIII.—JHALLAWAR AGENCY	21,707	11,438	10,269	20,603	10,832	9,771	1,104	606	498	...	...	...
IX.—KOTAH "	33,921	17,450	16,471	33,529	17,248	16,281	392	202	190	...	...	...
Total Rajputana Agency	1,005,757	533,674	472,083	980,398	520,324	460,074	20,143	10,210	9,933	5,216	3,140	2,076
Detached tracts of Gungapur and Nundwas of Central India in Meywar	624	336	288	...	...	...	...	...	...	624	336	288
GRAND TOTAL	1,006,381	534,010	472,371	980,398	520,324	460,074	20,143	10,210	9,933	5,840	3,476	2,364

TABLE V.—Statement showing Musalmans by Sects.

States.	Total Musalmans.			Sunnis.			Siahs.			Others and Unspecified.		
	Total.	Males.	Females.	Total.	Males.	Females.	Total.	Males.	Females.	Total.	Males.	Females.
1	2	3	4	5	6	7	8	9	10	11	12	13
MEYWAR RESIDENCY—												
Meywar—												
Oodeypore	9,778	5,149	4,629	7,738	4,240	3,498	2,040	909	1,131	...	...	...
Meja	100	57	43	100	57	43	...	...	...	...	...	...
Parsoli	119	64	55	119	64	55	...	...	...	...	...	...
Sirdargarh	122	65	57	121	64	57	1	1	...	...	...	...
Kankrowli	291	145	146	263	133	130	28	12	16	...	...	...
Kelwara	391	239	152	389	237	152	2	2	...	...	...	...
Bansi	103	54	49	102	53	49	1	1	...	...	...	...
Amet	348	173	175	288	131	157	60	42	18	...	...	...
Jharol	88	70	18	59	43	16	29	27	2	...	...	...
Kanor	493	268	225	377	208	169	116	60	56	...	...	...
Delwara	420	239	181	410	229	181	10	10	...	...	...	...
Shiwrati	45	27	18	44	26	18	1	1	...	...	...	...
Bijeypore	91	60	31	91	60	31	...	...	...	...	...	...
Banera	2,077	1,084	993	2,034	1,084	950	43	...	43	...	...	...
Khamnor	217	123	94	204	111	93	13	12	1	...	...	...
Gogunda	116	67	49	98	49	49	18	18	...	...	...	...
Bidnor	636	347	289	636	347	289	...	...	...	...	...	...
Kurabar	246	150	96	238	144	94	8	6	2	...	...	...
Kotharia	183	101	82	183	101	82	...	...	...	...	...	...
Karjali	6	4	2	6	4	2	...	...	...	...	...	...
Nathdwara	822	434	388	739	378	361	83	56	27	...	...	...
Devasthan	383	248	135	356	229	127	27	19	8	...	...	...
Fatehgarh	17	9	8	17	9	8	...	...	...	...	...	...
Asind	552	312	240	552	312	240	...	...	...	...	...	...
Hurra and Shimbhugarh	1,733	969	764	1,733	969	764	...	...	...	...	...	...
Kapasin	1,499	779	720	1,499	779	720	...	...	...	...	...	...
Bagor	255	122	133	255	122	133	...	...	...	...	...	...
Bijolia	174	105	69	122	103	69	2	2	...	...	...	...
Kanera	154	85	69	153	84	69	1	1	...	...	...	...
Deogarh	1,404	723	681	1,373	703	670	31	20	11	...	...	...
Bari Sadri	779	412	367	597	230	367	182	182	...	...	...	...
Begun	1,445	763	682	1,441	761	680	4	2	2	...	...	...
Magra Sarara	831	540	291	787	497	290	44	43	1	...	...	...
Dhariavad	121	77	44	118	75	43	3	2	1	...	...	...
Bedla	315	179	136	315	179	136	...	...	...	...	...	...
Sayra	67	44	23	64	41	23	3	3	...	...	...	...
Choti Sadri	1,397	799	598	1,371	782	589	26	17	9	...	...	...
Salumbar	1,246	611	635	1,028	500	528	218	111	107	...	...	...
Kotra Bhumat	421	274	147	346	206	140	75	68	7	...	...	...
Kherwara Bhumat	670	367	303	614	311	303	56	56	...	...	...	...
Rincher	46	25	21	46	25	21	...	...	...	...	...	...
Bhindar	1,336	711	625	930	518	412	406	193	213	...	...	...
Chitorgarh	3,744	1,987	1,757	3,644	1,962	1,682	100	25	75	...	...	...
Bhainsorgarh	461	258	203	461	258	203	...	...	...	...	...	...
Bhilwara	4,743	2,550	2,193	4,681	2,513	2,168	62	37	25	...	...	...
Girva	8,384	4,242	4,142	4,818	2,419	2,399	3,566	1,823	1,743	...	...	...
Mandalgarh	2,941	1,518	1,423	2,941	1,518	1,423	...	...	...	...	...	...
Rasmi	1,418	734	684	1,418	734	684	...	...	...	...	...	...
Rajnagar	523	260	263	504	250	254	19	10	9	...	...	...
Sahran	2,305	1,178	1,127	2,305	1,178	1,127	...	...	...	...	...	...
Jahazpur	2,524	1,354	1,170	2,514	1,345	1,169	10	9	1	...	...	...
Kachola Shahpura	318	181	137	306	174	132	12	7	5	...	...	...
Total	58,898	31,336	27,562	51,598	27,549	24,049	7,300	3,787	3,513	...	...	...
Kherwara Cantonment	33	30	3	...	...	...	...	...	...	33	30	3
Kotra Cantonment	10	10	...	...	...	...	...	...	...	10	10	...
Railway in Meywar	227	148	79	...	...	...	...	...	...	227	148	79
Total Meywar Districts	59,168	31,524	27,644	51,598	27,549	24,049	7,300	3,787	3,513	270	188	82
Detached tracts of Central India in Meywar— Nudwas Pargana, Indore State	74	43	31	...	...	...	...	...	...	74	43	31
Gungapur Pargana of Gwalior State	550	293	257	...	...	...	...	...	...	550	293	257
Detached tracts of Gungapur and Nundwas under Meywar	624	336	288	...	...	...	...	...	...	624	336	288
GRAND TOTAL OF MEYWAR STATE	59,792	31,860	27,932	51,598	27,549	24,049	7,300	3,787	3,513	894	524	370
Banswara—												
Banswara	4,283	2,189	2,094	3,709	1,868	1,841	574	321	253	...	...	...
Kushalgarh	512	302	210	312	179	133	200	123	77	...	...	...
Partabgarh—												
Partabgarh	4,937	2,815	2,122	4,250	2,443	1,807	687	372	315	...	...	...

TABLE V.—Statement showing Musalmans by Sects —*contd.*

STATES.	TOTAL MUSALMANS.			SUNNIS.			SIAHS.			OTHERS AND UNSPECIFIED.		
	Total.	Males.	Females.	Total.	Males.	Females.	Total.	Males.	Females.	Total.	Males.	Females.
1	2	3	4	5	6	7	8	9	10	11	12	13
MEYWAR RESIDENCY—												
DUNGARPUR—												
Dungarpur	1,668	772	896	1,353	628	725	315	144	171	...	...	...
Kanaba	218	169	49	193	144	49	25	25	...	...	...	...
Ganeshpura	48	27	21	48	27	21	...	...	...	...	...	...
Ashpur	68	43	25	68	43	25	...	...	...	...	...	...
Pujpur	56	31	25	52	27	25	4	4	...	...	...	...
Nethava	39	26	13	39	26	13	...	...	...	...	...	...
Sagwada	1,269	656	613	415	264	151	854	392	462	...	...	...
Padwa	63	45	18	50	35	15	13	10	3	...	...	...
Galiakot	468	241	227	212	120	92	256	121	135	...	...	...
Dhambora	417	219	198	378	182	196	39	37	2	...	...	...
GRAND TOTAL	4,314	2.229	2,085	2,808	1,496	1,312	1,506	733	773	...	...	...
Total Meywar Residency	73,214	39,059	34,155	62,677	33,535	29 142	10,267	5.336	4,931	270	188	82
DETACHED TRACTS OF CENTRAL INDIA UNDER MEYWAR	624	336	288	...	...	...	...	...	...	624	336	288
GRAND TOTAL, MEYWAR RESIDENCY	73,838	39,395	34,443	62,677	33,535	29,142	10,267	5,336	4,931	894	524	370
WESTERN RAJPUTANA STATES RESIDENCY—												
MARWAR AND MALANI—												
Jodhpore City	13,676	7,051	6,625	13,674	7,049	6,625	2	2	...	...	...	...
Do. Kasba	2,549	1,726	823	2,549	1,726	823	...	...	...	...	...	...
Do. Pargana	10,879	5,816	5,063	10,879	5,816	5,063	...	...	...	...	...	...
TOTAL	27,104	14,593	12,511	27,102	14,591	12,511	2	2	...	...	...	...
Nagore	19,505	9,470	10,035	19,493	9,465	10,028	12	5	7	...	...	...
Bali	3,695	2,105	1,590	3,685	2,095	1,590	10	10	...	...	...	...
Merta	11,291	5,754	5,537	11,124	5,679	5.445	167	75	92	...	...	...
Jalore	3,979	2,154	1,825	3,979	2,154	1,825	...	...	...	...	...	...
Sojat	5,734	3,017	2.717	5,686	2,984	2,702	48	33	15	...	...	...
Jaswantpura	3,228	1,822	1,406	3,068	1,736	1,332	160	86	74	...	...	...
Parbatsar	6,834	3,544	3,288	6,805	3.530	3,275	27	14	13	...	...	...
Sanchore	12,407	6,770	5,637	12,094	6,596	5,498	133	174	139	...	...	...
Jaltaran	5,797	3,088	2,709	5,764	3,066	2,698	33	22	11	...	...	...
Bilara	5,069	2,636	2,433	5,069	2,636	2,433	...	...	...	...	...	...
Phalodi	7,206	3,950	3,256	7,206	3.950	3,256	...	...	...	...	...	...
Shergarh	2,825	1,592	1,233	2,814	1,585	1,229	11	7	4	...	...	...
Siwana	1,175	670	505	1,166	661	505	9	9	...	...	...	...
Pali	5,776	2,974	2,802	5,765	2,970	2,795	11	4	7	...	...	...
Marote	1,325	731	594	1,325	731	594	...	...	...	...	...	...
Didwana	8,575	4,279	4,296	8,565	4,274	4,291	10	5	5	...	...	...
Pachbhadra	4,434	2,330	2,104	4,434	2,330	2,104	...	...	...	...	...	...
Nawa	3,968	2,174	1.794	3,968	2,174	1,794	...	...	...	...	...	...
Sheo	7,862	4.444	3,418	7,684	4,322	3,362	178	122	56	...	...	...
Sankra	2,794	1,570	1,224	2,794	1,570	1,224	...	...	...	...	...	...
TOTAL	150,581	79,667	70,914	149,590	79,099	70,491	991	568	423	...	...	...
Malani	27,572	15,439	12,133	27,507	15,432	12,075	65	7	58	...	...	...
TOTAL MARWAR, MALANI	178,153	95,106	83,047	177,097	94,531	82,566	1,056	575	481	...	...	...
½ Sambhar, Jeypore and Jodhpur Joint Jurisdiction	2,001	1,087	914	2,000	1,086	914	1	1	...	...	...	...
½ Sambhar Railway	...	...	...	...	...	...	...	...	...	...	...	...
R. M. Railway in Marwar	458	270	188	...	...	...	...	...	...	458	270	188
GRAND TOTAL	180,612	96,463	84.149	179,097	95,617	83,480	1.057	576	481	458	270	
SIROHI—												
Sirohi	390	236	154	249	151	98	...	...	...	141	85	56
Khooni	529	285	244	297	136	161	...	...	...	232	149	83
Magra	159	90	69	66	43	23	...	...	...	93	47	46
Jaro Kharel	146	86	60	74	57	17	...	...	...	72	29	43
Pamera	115	72	43	44	31	13	7	2	5	64	39	25
Madar	568	342	226	385	264	121	19	11	8	164	67	97
Anadra	197	116	81	100	66	34	26	9	17	71	41	30
Abu	342	195	147	245	128	117	27	13	14	70	54	16
Abu Road	1,003	554	449	733	457	276	27	14	13	243	83	160
Santpur	236	137	99	117	81	36	...	...	...	119	56	63
Rohera	221	143	78	135	91	44	...	...	...	86	52	34

TABLE V.—Statement showing Musalmans by Sects—*contd.*

States.	Total Musalmans.			Sunnis.			Siahs.			Others and Unspecified.		
	Total.	Males.	Females.	Total.	Males.	Females.	Total.	Males.	Females.	Total.	Males.	Females.
1	2	3	4	5	6	7	8	9	10	11	12	13
WESTERN RAJPUTANA STATES RESIDENCY—*continued.*												
Sirohi—*contd.*												
Pindwara	155	89	66	87	62	25	...	...	...	68	27	41
Abu Civil Station	207	159	48	109	78	31	...	...	...	98	81	17
Erinpura Bazar	159	81	78	102	45	57	...	...	...	57	36	21
Total	4,427	2,585	1,842	2,743	1,690	1,053	106	49	57	1,578	846	732
Abu Sanitiarium P.	8	4	4	...	...	...	...	...	...	8	4	4
Sirohi Railway	485	294	191	...	...	...	...	...	...	485	294	191
Erinpura Cantonment	263	189	74	...	...	...	...	...	...	263	189	74
GRAND TOTAL, SIROHI STATE	5,183	3,072	2,111	2,743	1,690	1,053	106	49	57	2,334	1,333	1,001
Jesalmir	29,443	16,761	12,682	29,313	16,677	12,636	130	84	46	...	...	...
GRAND TOTAL, WESTERN RAJPUTANA STATES RESIDENCY	215,238	116,296	98,942	21,153	113,984	97,169	1,293	709	584	2,792	1,603	1,189
Bikanir—												
Anupgarh	4,718	2,553	2,165	4,718	2,553	2,165	...	...	...	...	...	...
Bahaderan	2,565	1,384	1,181	2,565	1,384	1,181	...	...	...	...	...	...
Bikanir City	9,273	4,898	4,375	9,252	4,886	4,366	21	12	9	...	...	...
Bikanir Suburbs	1,217	600	617	1,217	600	617	...	...	...	...	...	...
Bikanir Tehsil	9,305	5,120	4,185	9,305	5,120	4,185	...	...	...	...	...	...
Total	19,795	10,618	9,177	19,774	10,606	9,168	21	12	9	...	...	...
Churu	9,692	5,050	4,642	9,692	5,050	4,642	...	...	...	...	...	...
Dungargarh	1,121	633	488	1,121	633	488	...	...	...	...	...	...
Hanumangarh	7,828	4,282	3,546	7,821	4,279	3,542	7	3	4	...	...	...
Lunkaransar	7,581	4,206	3,375	7,581	4,206	3,375	...	...	...	...	...	...
Mirzawala	3,950	2,134	1,816	3,948	2,132	1,816	2	2	...	...	...	...
Nohar	5,405	2,945	2,460	5,405	2,945	2,460	...	...	...	...	...	...
Rajgarh	4,461	2,384	2,077	4,461	2,384	2,077	...	...	...	...	...	...
Ratangarh	3,694	1,957	1,737	3,694	1,957	1,737	...	...	...	...	...	...
Sardarshahr	2,814	1,499	1,315	2,814	1,499	1,315	...	...	...	...	...	...
Sujangarh	4,129	2,199	1,939	4,129	2,199	1,930	...	...	...	...	...	...
Suratgarh	2,276	1,263	1,013	2,276	1,263	1,013	...	...	...	...	...	...
GRAND TOTAL, BIKANIR STATE	80,029	43,107	36,922	79,999	43,090	36,909	30	17	13	...	...	...
JEYPORE RESIDENCY—												
Jeypore—												
Jeypore City	38,953	20,825	18,128	38,252	20,453	17,799	701	372	329	...	...	...
Total	38,953	20,825	18,128	38,252	20,453	17,799	701	372	329	...	...	...
Jeypore Tehsil	6,416	3,470	2,946	6,398	3,458	2,940	18	12	6	...	...	...
Jamua Ramgarh	5,977	3,098	2,879	5,977	3,098	2,879	...	...	...	...	...	...
Chaksu Tehsil	3,560	2,000	1,560	3,560	2,000	1,560	...	...	...	...	...	...
Kalegh	4,827	2,446	2,381	4,827	2,446	2,381	...	...	...	...	...	...
Total	20,780	11,014	9,766	20,762	11,002	9,760	18	12	6	...	...	...
Dausa Tehsil	3,156	1,723	1,433	3,133	1,709	1,424	23	14	9	...	...	...
Lalsote	2,281	1,235	1,046	2,278	1,233	1,045	3	2	1	...	...	...
Sikrai	598	330	268	595	327	268	3	3	...	...	...	...
Baswa	1,665	931	734	1,660	930	730	5	1	4	...	...	...
Total	7,700	4,219	3,481	7,666	4,199	3,467	34	20	14	...	...	...
Jhoonjhnu	25,789	13,136	12,653	25,778	13,130	12,648	11	6	5	...	...	...
Udeypore	2,745	1,351	1,394	2,708	1,334	1,374	37	17	20	...	...	...
Total	28,534	14,487	14,047	28,486	14,464	14,022	48	23	25	...	...	...
Sawai Ramgarh	4,957	2,785	2,172	4,946	2,776	2,170	11	9	2	...	...	...
Khandela	4,392	2,119	2,273	4,392	2,119	2,273	...	...	...	...	...	...
Bairath Tehsil	2,449	1,238	1,211	2,449	1,238	1,211	...	...	...	...	...	...
Total	11,798	6,142	5,656	11,787	6,133	5,654	11	9	2	...	...	...

TABLE V.—Statement showing Musalmans by Sects —*contd.*

States.	Total Musalmans.			Sunnis.			Siahs.			Others and Unspecified.		
	Total.	Males.	Females.	Total.	Males.	Females.	Total.	Males.	Females.	Total.	Males.	Females.
1	2	3	4	5	6	7	8	9	10	11	12	13
JEYPORE RESIDENCY—*contd.*												
Madhopur Tehsil	7,064	3,677	3,387	7,053	3,672	3,381	11	5	6	...	...	...
Barli	2,981	1,564	1,417	2,981	1,564	1,417	...	...	...	...	...	...
Malarna	5,165	2,701	2,464	5,155	2,696	2,459	10	5	5	...	...	...
Khandar	641	341	300	641	341	300	...	...	...	...	...	...
Isarda Thikana	542	321	221	542	321	221	...	...	...	...	...	...
Barwara	705	396	309	705	396	309	...	...	...	...	...	...
Total	17,098	9,000	8,098	17,077	8,990	8,087	21	10	11	...	...	...
Hindone Tehsil	4,127	2,098	2,029	4,058	2,064	1,994	69	34	35	...	...	...
Toda Bhim	2,649	1,304	1,345	2,632	1,294	1,338	17	10	7	...	...	...
Malwa Tehsil	2,024	1,145	879	1,982	1,120	862	42	25	17	...	...	...
Walghat	1,426	737	689	1,426	737	689	...	...	...	...	...	...
Ghonsla	639	362	277	635	361	274	4	1	3	...	...	...
Ratanzilla	763	424	339	756	419	337	7	5	2	...	...	...
Total	11,628	6,070	5,558	11,489	5,995	5,494	139	75	64	...	...	...
½ Sambhar Railway	1	1	...	...	...	...	...	...	...	1	1	...
½ Sambhar Joint Jurisdiction	2,000	1,087	913	2,000	1,087	913	...	...	...	...	...	...
Nairana Tehsil	2,772	1,481	1,291	2,772	1,481	1,291	...	...	...	...	...	...
Danta Ramgarh	3,447	1,907	1,540	3,309	1,820	1,489	138	87	51	...	...	...
Muazamabad	3,117	1,692	1,425	3,110	1,689	1,421	7	3	4	...	...	...
Total	11,337	6,168	5,169	11,191	6,077	5,114	145	50	55	1	1	...
Malpura Tehsil	3,733	1,984	1,749	3,733	1,984	1,749	...	...	...	...	...	...
Toda Rai Singh	2,060	1,127	933	2,060	1,127	933	...	...	...	...	...	...
Newai	1,174	646	528	1,174	646	528	...	...	...	...	...	...
Total	6,967	3,757	3,210	6,967	3,757	3,210	...	...	...	...	...	...
Gungapur Tehsil	2,380	1,268	1,112	2,360	1,257	1,103	20	11	9	...	...	...
Vazirpur	1,637	831	806	1,602	814	788	35	17	18	...	...	...
Bamaniawas	467	243	224	467	243	224	...	...	...	...	...	...
Total	4,484	2,342	2,142	4,429	2,314	2,115	55	28	27	...	...	...
Kote Kasim	1,921	902	1,019	1,702	822	880	219	80	139	...	...	...
Total	1,921	902	1,019	1,702	822	880	219	80	139	...	...	...
Bandikui	473	245	228	473	245	228	...	...	...	...	...	...
Total	473	245	228	473	245	228	...	...	...	...	...	...
Sikar	23,520	12,381	11,139	23,378	12,306	11,072	142	75	67	...	...	...
Khetri	10,197	5,216	4,981	10,197	5,216	4,981	...	...	...	...	...	...
Uniara	1,650	855	795	1,639	851	788	11	4	7	...	...	...
Total	35,367	18,452	16,915	35,214	18,373	16,841	153	.79	74	..	...	...
Total	197,040	103,623	93.417	195,495	102,824	92,671	1,544	798	746	1	1	...
Total Jeypore Residency	1,701	1,041	660	...	...	...	...	...	...	1,701	1,041	660
GRAND TOTAL	198,741	104,664	94,077	195,495	102,824	92,671	1,544	798	746	1,702	1,042	660
Kishengarh—												
Kishengarh City	3,350	1,807	1,543	3,350	1,807	1,543	...	...	...	...	...	...
District Kishengarh	2,515	1,298	1,217	2,515	1,298	1,217	...	...	...	...	...	...
" Rupnagar	1,382	689	693	1,382	689	693	...	...	...	...	...	...
" Araeen	539	290	249	539	290	249	...	...	...	...	...	...
" Sarwar	1,625	845	780	1,625	845	780	...	...	...	...	...	...
Total	9,411	4,929	4,482	9,411	4,929	4,482	...	...	...	...	...	...
Total Kishengarh Railway	18	15	3	...	...	...	...	...	...	18	15	3
GRAND TOTAL, KISHENGARH	9,429	4,944	4,485	9,411	4,929	4,482	...	...	...	18	15	3
Lawa—												
Lawa	160	91	69	160	91	69	...	..	...	...	...	...
GRAND TOTAL, JEYPORE RESIDENCY	208,330	109,699	98,631	205,066	107,844	97,222	1,544	798	746	1,720	1,057	663

TABLE V.—Statement showing Musalmans by Sects —*contd.*

States.	Total Musalmans.			Sunnis.			Siahs.			Others and Unspecified.		
	Total.	Males.	Females.	Total.	Males.	Females.	Total.	Males.	Females.	Total.	Males.	Females.
1	2	3	4	5	6	7	8	9	10	11	12	13
EASTERN STATES AGENCY—												
Bharatpur—												
Bharatpur City	16,540	9,038	7,502	15,610	8,725	6,885	930	313	617	...	...	...
Bharatpur Tehsil	1,932	1,089	843	1,880	1,062	818	52	27	25	...	...	...
Uchain "	4,239	2,214	2,025	3,111	1,694	1,417	1,128	520	608	...	...	...
Akhaygarh "	2,461	1,269	1,192	2,456	1,265	1,191	5	4	1	...	...	...
Bayana "	4,194	2,208	1,986	4,028	2,121	1,907	166	87	79	...	...	...
Bhusawar "	4,969	2,559	2,410	4,968	2,558	2,410	1	1	...	...	...	...
Pahari	18,072	9,761	8,311	18,044	9,742	8,302	28	19	9	...	...	...
Deeg	7,011	3,746	3,265	6,902	3,686	3,216	109	60	49	...	...	...
Rupbas	2,512	1,357	1,155	2,441	1,330	1,111	71	27	44	...	...	...
Kama	14,888	7,956	6,932	14,510	7,761	6,749	378	195	183	...	...	...
Kumhair	2,790	1,427	1,363	2,615	1,334	1,281	175	93	82	...	...	...
Gopalgarh	21,587	11,402	10,185	21,559	11,383	10,176	28	19	9	...	...	...
Nagur	5,940	3,493	2,447	5,933	3,489	2,444	7	4	3	...	...	...
Total	107,135	57,519	49,616	104,057	56,150	47,907	3,078	1,369	1,709	...	...	...
Bhartpur Railway	125	79	46	...	...	..	...	...	...	125	79	46
GRAND TOTAL	107,260	57,598	49,662	104,057	56,150	47,907	3,078	1,369	1,709	125	79	46
Karauli—												
Karauli City	5,352	2,579	2,773	5,332	2,570	2,762	20	9	11	...	...	...
Hazur Tehsil	1,006	586	420	998	581	417	8	5	3	...	...	...
Jirota "	1,030	577	453	1,030	577	453	...	...	...	...	...	...
Machilpura "	707	383	324	707	383	324	...	...	...	...	...	...
Mandrail "	626	335	291	626	335	291	...	...	...	...	...	...
Utgir "	212	138	74	212	138	74	...	...	...	...	...	...
GRAND TOTAL	8,933	4,598	4,335	8,905	4,584	4,321	28	14	14	...	...	...
Dholpur—												
Gird Tehsil	6,780	3,602	3,178	6,386	3,383	3,003	394	219	175	...	...	...
Bari "	4,837	2,321	2,516	4,641	2,228	2,413	196	93	103	...	...	...
Basheri "	1,600	907	693	1,552	882	670	48	25	23	...	...	...
Kolari "	2,019	1,092	927	2,002	1,083	919	17	9	8	...	...	...
Rjakhera "	1,137	606	531	1,128	598	530	9	8	1	...	...	...
Sir Muthra Tehsil	1,016	530	486	1,016	530	468	...	...	...	...	...	...
Total	17,389	9,058	8,331	16,725	8,704	8,021	664	354	310	...	...	...
Indian Midland Railway—												
Dholpur	29	21	8	...	...	...	...	...	...	29	21	8
Mania Station	5	3	2	...	...	...	...	...	...	5	3	2
GRAND TOTAL	17,423	9,082	8,341	16,725	8,704	8,021	664	354	310	34	24	10
GRAND TOTAL, EASTERN STATES AGENCY	133,616	71,278	62,338	129,687	69,438	60,249	3,770	1.737	2.033	159	103	56
Alwar—												
Alwar	46,222	24,516	21,706	45,308	24,123	21,185	914	393	521	...	...	...
Baosur	2,828	1,447	1,381	2,822	1,446	1,376	6	1	5	...	...	...
Bahror	4,056	1,955	2,101	4,054	1,953	2,101	2	2	...	...	...	...
Govindgarh	10,549	5,523	5,026	10,539	5,518	5,021	10	5	5	...	...	...
Kathumbar	3,034	1,709	1,325	3,034	1,709	1,325	...	...	...	...	...	...
Kishengarh	30,388	15,691	14,697	30,168	15,611	14,557	220	80	140	...	...	...
Luchmangarh	10,847	5,611	5,236	10,845	5,610	5,235	2	1	1	...	...	...
Mandawar	9,774	5,009	4,765	9,774	5,009	4,765	...	...	...	...	...	...
Rajgarh	5,259	2,677	2,582	5,249	2,672	2,577	10	5	5	...	...	...
Ramgarh	27,979	14,807	13,172	27,979	14,807	13,172	...	...	...	...	...	...
Thanaghazi	1,573	796	777	1,573	796	777	...	...	...	...	...	...
Tijara	27,468	14,397	13,071	27,425	14,374	13,051	43	23	20	...	...	...
Nimrana	212	105	107	212	105	107	...	..	...	...	...	...
Total	180,189	94,243	85,946	178,982	93,733	85,249	1,207	510	697	...	...	...
Alwar Ra'lway	237	168	69	...	...	...	...	...	...	237	168	69
GRAND TOTAL, ALWAR AGENCY	180,426	94,411	86,015	178,982	93,733	85,249	1,207	510	697	237	168	69

TABLE V.—Statement showing Musalmans by Sects—*contd.*

States.	Total Musalmans.			Sunnis.			Siahs.			Others and Unspecified.		
	Total.	Males.	Females.	Total.	Males.	Females.	Total.	Males.	Females.	Total.	Males.	Females.
1	2	3	4	5	6	7	8	9	10	11	12	13
HARAOWTI AND TONK AGENCY—												
Tonk—												
Tonk (Rajputana)	25,104	12,613	12,491	25,092	12,605	12,487	12	8	4	...	...	...
Aligarh	1,621	876	745	1,621	876	745	...	...	...	...	...	...
Nimbahera	2,741	1,478	1,263	2,697	1,448	1,249	44	30	14	...	...	...
Total Railway	38	21	17	...	...	...	...	...	...	38	21	17
Total Rajputana, Tonk	29,504	14,988	14,516	29,410	14,929	14,481	56	38	18	38	21	17
Chabra	2,670	1,313	1,357	2,658	1,307	1,351	12	6	6	...	...	...
Parawa	2,538	1,283	1,255	2,517	1,269	1,248	21	14	7	...	...	...
Sironj	9,822	5,575	4,247	9,493	5,401	4,092	329	174	155	...	...	...
Total Central India, Tonk	15,030	8,171	6,859	14,668	7,977	6,691	362	194	168	...	...	...
GRAND TOTAL	44,534	23,159	21,375	44,078	22,906	21,172	418	232	186	38	21	17
Bundi—												
Bundi	4,575	2,413	2,162	4,460	2,353	2,107	115	60	55	...	...	...
Taragarh	89	53	36	89	53	36	...	...	...	...	...	...
Patan	666	362	304	666	362	304	...	...	...	...	...	...
Kapran	450	231	219	448	229	219	2	2	...	...	...	...
Gandowli	504	276	228	504	276	228	...	...	...	...	...	...
Ajitgarh	20	14	6	20	14	6	...	...	...	...	...	...
Deyi	1,093	534	559	1,093	534	559	...	...	...	...	...	...
Nænwa	923	472	451	923	472	451	...	...	...	...	...	...
Gotra	946	515	431	946	515	431	...	...	...	...	...	...
Hindoli	1,451	755	696	1,450	754	696	1	1	...	...	...	...
Selore	889	514	375	889	514	375	...	...	...	...	...	...
Total Bundi	11,606	6,139	5,467	11,488	6,076	5,412	118	63	55	...	...	...
Shahpura Estate—												
Kachola Pargana of Shahpura, included under Meywar	318	181	13	306	174	132	12	7	5	...	...	...
Phooliya Pargana of Shahpura	3,136	1,638	1,498	3,136	1,638	1,498	...	...	...	...	...	...
GRAND TOTAL	3,454	1,819	1,635	3,442	1,812	1,630	12	7	5	...	...	...
GRAND TOTAL, HARAOWTI AND TONK AGENCY, EXCLUDING KACHOLA	59,276	30,936	28,340	58,702	30,620	28,082	536	295	241	38	21	17
Jhallawar—												
Jhalrapatan (Chaoni)	7,375	3,690	3,685	7,282	3,631	3,651	93	59	34	...	...	...
Jhalrapatan (Town)	2,185	1,133	1,052	1,539	788	751	646	345	301	...	...	...
Pargana Patan	220	158	62	194	142	52	26	16	10	...	...	...
Chechat	1,058	573	485	992	532	460	66	41	25	...	...	...
Suket	530	303	227	501	284	217	29	19	10	...	...	...
Asnawar	257	173	84	248	169	79	9	4	5	...	...	...
Bakanir	1,127	624	503	1,103	609	494	24	15	9	...	...	...
Iklera	741	428	313	731	425	306	10	3	7	...	...	...
Ghatoli	491	261	230	491	261	230	...	...	...	...	...	...
Chipa Barod	1,487	771	716	1,423	748	675	64	23	41	...	...	...
Manohar Thana	1,901	1,015	886	1,893	1,010	883	8	5	3	...	...	...
Total Central Jhallawar	17,372	9,129	8,243	16,397	8,599	7,798	975	530	445	...	...	...
Pachpahar	787	427	360	749	405	344	38	22	16	...	...	...
Awar	510	282	228	501	277	224	9	5	4	...	...	...
Dag	864	460	404	855	452	403	9	8	1	...	...	...
Gangdhar	1,095	559	536	1,024	519	505	71	40	31	...	...	...
Total Chomahla	3,256	1,728	1,528	3,129	1,653	1,476	127	75	52	...	...	...
Uprethi	442	260	173	440	268	172	2	1	1	...	...	...
Taleti	637	312	325	637	312	325	...	...	...	...	...	...
Total Shahabad	1,079	581	498	1,077	580	497	2	1	1	...	...	...
GRAND TOTAL	21,707	11,438	10,269	20,603	10,832	9,771	1,104	606	498	...	...	...

TABLE V.—Statement showing Musalmans by Sects—*contd.*

States.	Total Musalmans.			Sunnis.			Siahs.			Others and Unspecified.		
	Total.	Males.	Females.	Total.	Males.	Females.	Total.	Males.	Females.	Total.	Males.	Females.
1	2	3	4	5	6	7	8	9	10	11	12	13
Kotah—												
Kotah	9,806	*4,950*	4,856	9,586	*4,838*	4,748	220	*112*	108	...	...	...
Nizamats—												
Anta	1,611	*771*	840	1,611	*771*	840	...	...	...	...	...	...
Baran	2,358	*1,178*	1,180	2,247	*1,123*	1,124	111	*55*	56	...	...	...
Barod	1,086	*546*	540	1,086	*546*	540	...	...	...	...	...	...
Digod	934	*504*	430	934	*504*	430	...	...	...	...	...	...
Etawah	731	*588*	343	731	*388*	343	...	...	...	...	...	...
Ghatoli	645	*375*	270	645	*375*	270	...	...	...	...	...	...
Kanwas	1,233	*657*	576	1,233	*657*	576	...	...	...	...	...	...
Khanpur	1,023	*588*	435	1 023	*588*	435	...	...	...	...	...	...
Kishanganj	900	*501*	399	899	*500*	399	1	*1*	...	...	...	...
Kunjer	598	*306*	292	598	*306*	292	...	...	...	...	...	...
Ladpura	3,405	*1,668*	1,737	3,381	*1,656*	1,725	24	*12*	12	...	...	...
Mangrol	2,384	*1,232*	1,152	2,376	*1,226*	1,150	8	*6*	2	...	...	...
Sangod	1,636	*849*	787	1,609	*833*	776	27	*16*	11	...	...	...
Shergarh	1,695	*872*	823	1,694	*872*	822	1	...	1	...	...	...
Taraj	733	*397*	336	733	*397*	336	...	...	...	...	...	...
Total Nizamats	20,972	10,832	10,140	20,800	10,742	10,058	172	50	82	...	...	...
Kotries—												
Antarda	127	*63*	64	127	*63*	64	...	...	...	...	...	...
Balwan	134	*78*	56	134	*78*	56	...	...	...	...	...	...
Gainta	267	*124*	143	267	*124*	143	...	...	...	...	...	...
Indargarh	1,613	*865*	748	1,613	*865*	748	...	...	...	...	...	...
Karwar	178	*04*	84	178	*94*	84	...	...	...	...	...	...
Khatoh with Farara	485	*260*	225	485	*260*	225	...	...	...	...	...	...
Pipalda with Phusod	339	*184*	155	339	*184*	155	...	...	...	...	...	...
GRAND TOTAL, KOTAH STATE	33,921	17,450	16,471	33,529	17,248	16,281	392	202	190	...	...	...
GRAND TOTAL	1,006,381	534,010	472,371	980,398	520,324	460,074	20,143	10,210	9,933	5,840	3,476	2,364

RAJPUTANA AGENCY.

CENSUS OF 1891.

PROVINCIAL TABLE VI.

Statement showing the Sub-divisions of Rajputs, by territorial units.

ABSTRACT.

	Sub-divisions of Rajputs.	Total Strength.		
		Total.	Males.	Females.
I	Gehlote or Sesodia	76,853	41,494	35,359
II	Yadu or Jadun	94,445	53,987	40,458
III	Rahtore	173,909	102,534	71,375
IV	Kachhawaha or Cushawah	106,705	68,677	38,028
V	Parwar or Panwar	42,553	24,021	18,532
VI	Chohan or Hara	101,820	54,817	47,003
VII	Chalook or Solanki	13,555	7,348	6,207
VIII	Prithihara or Parihara	11,694	5,926	5,768
IX	Châorā	74	39	35
X	Takshac or Tâk	101	31	70
XI	Katti	94	63	31
XII	Jhalla Macwahana	4,800	2,915	1,885
XIII	Gohell	150	77	73
XIV	Dabi	226	122	104
XV	Gor	6,259	3,511	2,748
XVI	Dor or Doda	730	308	422
XVII	Gherwal or Bundella	236	135	101
XVIII	Bir-goojar	4,267	2,214	2,053
XIX	Sengar	768	373	395
XX	Sikarwal	4,045	1,930	2,115
XXI	Beis, Byce or Bans	805	474	331
XXII	Dahia	183	69	114
XXIII	Dahima	30	19	11
XXIV	Miscellaneous	25,355	13,541	11,814
XXV	Others and unspecified	79,211	43,126	36,085
	Total	(a) 748,868	427,751	321,117

Note.—The clan of a married Rajput woman was entered in the Enumeration Schedules after that of her father and not her husband.

(a) Excluding the figures for the States of Banswara and Partabgarh which States have not furnished the caste details.

In addition to the Rajput population entered in this table, there are 6,375 males and 5,561 females subject to the Tonk Durbar residing in detached tracts of Chabra, Parawa, and Sironj, under Central India Agency.

The total number of Rajputs in the whole of Tonk State is 16,440, sub-divided into the following clans:—

	Sub-division or Sept.		Strength.		
			Total.	Males.	Females.
1	Gehlote or Sesodia		2,132	1,148	984
2	Yadun		458	273	185
3	Rathore		2,031	1,128	903
4	Kachhawaha		3,327	1,603	1,724
5	Panwar (Parwar)		1,319	822	497
6	Chohan		2,484	1,296	1,188
7	Solanki		1,313	681	632
8	Prithihara (Parihara)		803	674	129
9	Bundella		307	144	163
10	Sengar		1,145	487	658
11	Sikarwal		110	46	64
12	Beis		96	68	28
13	Pachoria	Miscellaneous septs.	361	257	104
14	Tarwaria		110	77	33
15	Raizada		124	20	104
16	Bharwas		320	219	101
	Total		16,440	8,943	7,497

The 136,949 Rajputs returned in Meywar are inclusive of 396 males and 322 females of detached tracts of Nandwas of Indore and Gungapur of Gwalior under Central India Agency.

* Excluding the figures for the detached tracts of Central India in Meywar and including those for Tonk in Central India, the total strength of Rajputs under the Rajputana Agency is—

Total.	Males.	Females.
760,086	433,730	326,356

* Excluding Banswara and Partabgarh.

PROVINCIAL TABLE.

TABLE VI.—Statement showing the Sub-division of Rajputs.

Names of States.	Total of Rajputs.			I.—Gehlote or Sesodia.																	
				Gehlote.			Sesodia.			Aharya or Ada.			Mangulia.			Nadoria.			Chundawat.		
	Total.	Males.	Females.	Total.	Males.	Females.	Total.	Males.	Females.	Total.	Males.	Females.	Total.	Males.	Females.	Total.	Males.	Females.	Total.	Males.	Females.
1	2	3	4	5	6	7	8	9	10	11	12	13	14	15	16	17	18	19	20	21	22
Meywar	136,949	77,099	59,850	...	...	...	52,172	30,979	21,193	...	...	...	...	...	...	...	...	...	...	...	...
Banswara	Details not furnished by the Durbar																				
Dungarpur	11,031	5,847	5,184	170	82	88	822	441	381	234	125	109	...	...	...	...	...	...	360	198	162
Partabgarh	Details not furnished by the Durbar																				
Marwar	244,700	138,439	106,261	...	...	...	13,622	4,866	8,756	...	...	...	...	...	...	...	...	...	...	...	...
Sirohi	16,429	8,740	7,689	...	...	...	103	67	36	...	...	...	...	...	...	...	...	...	...	...	...
Jesalmir	28,329	15,899	12,430	...	...	...	428	176	252	...	...	...	...	...	...	...	...	...	...	...	...
Bikanir	66,273	38,761	27,512	...	...	...	1,313	690	623	...	...	...	...	...	...	...	...	...	...	...	...
Jeypore	127,050	76,232	50,818	...	...	...	1,300	654	646	...	...	...	...	...	...	...	...	...	...	...	...
Kishengarh	6,614	3,655	2,959	3	2	1	148	51	97	...	...	...	4	2	2	...	...	...	...	...	...
Lawa	107	51	56	...	...	...	...	...	...	...	...	...	...	...	...	...	...	...	...	...	...
Bharatpur	10,088	5,863	4,225	71	28	43	1	1	...	...	...	...	...	...	...	...	...	...	...	...	...
Karauli	8,777	4,869	3,908	...	...	...	63	28	35	...	...	...	...	...	...	...	...	...	...	...	...
Dholpur	26,955	15,462	11,493	294	93	201	41	25	16	...	...	...	...	...	...	...	...	...	...	...	...
Alwar	27,552	15,737	11,815	93	47	46	82	46	36	...	...	...	...	...	...	11	11	...	...	...	...
Jhallawar	8,407	4,840	3,567	134	79	55	250	137	113	4	2	2	7	4	3	...	...	...	133	74	59
Tonk	4,501	2,565	1,936	...	...	...	608	362	246	...	...	...	...	...	...	...	...	...	...	...	...
Bundi	6,939	3,828	3,111	...	...	...	392	112	280	...	...	...	...	...	...	...	...	...	...	...	...
Shahpura	2,217	1,265	952	...	...	...	1,027	588	439	...	...	...	...	...	...	...	...	...	...	...	...
Kota	15,777	8,450	7,327	...	...	...	141	88	53	...	...	...	...	...	...	...	...	...	2	...	2
Erinpura	146	128	18	7	4	3	22	22	...	...	...	...	...	...	...	...	...	...	...	...	...
Kherwara	21	15	6	...	...	...	...	...	...	...	...	...	...	...	...	...	...	...	...	...	...
Kotra	4	4	...	...	...	...	...	...	...	...	...	...	...	...	...	...	...	...	...	...	...
Abu	2	2	...	...	...	...	...	...	...	...	...	...	...	...	...	...	...	...	...	...	...
Total	748,868	427,751	321,117	772	335	437	72,535	39,333	33,202	238	127	111	11	6	5	11	11	...	495	272	223

Table VI.—Sub-division—Rajputana Agency.

Names of States.	I.—Gehlote or Sesodia. Ranawat. Total.	Males.	Females.	Saktawat. Total.	Males.	Females.	Sakrawat. Total.	Males.	Females.	Kelwa. Total.	Males.	Females.	Chandwat. Total.	Males.	Females.	Bhakrawat. Total.	Males.	Females.	Kotecha or Karecha. Total.	Males.	Females.	Total Gehlote or Sesodia. (I) Total.	Males.	Females.
	23	24	25	26	27	28	29	30	31	32	33	34	35	36	37	38	39	40	41	42	43	44	45	46
Meywar	...	...	...	...	...	...	...	...	...	...	...	...	...	...	...	...	...	...	1,356	758	598	53,528	31,737	21,791
Banswara	Details not furnished by the Durbar																							
Dungarpur	88	50	38	123	71	52	...	...	...	...	...	...	...	...	...									
Partabgarh	Details not furnished by the Durbar															5	4	1	...	...	...	1,802	971	831
Marwar	...	...	...	...	...	...	...	...	...	...	...	...	...	...	...	...	...	...	...	...	...	13,622	4,866	8,756
Sirohi	...	...	...	...	...	...	...	...	...	...	...	...	...	...	...	...	...	...	...	...	...	103	67	36
Jesalmir	...	...	...	...	...	...	...	...	...	...	...	...	...	...	...	...	...	...	...	...	...	428	176	252
Bikanir	...	...	...	...	...	...	...	...	...	...	...	...	...	...	...	...	...	...	...	...	...	1,313	690	623
Jeypore	...	...	...	...	...	...	...	...	...	...	...	...	...	...	...	...	...	...	...	...	...	1,300	654	646
Kishengarh	...	...	...	...	...	...	...	...	...	...	...	...	...	...	...	...	...	...	...	...	...	155	55	100
Lawa	2	...	2	1	...	1	...	...	...	...	...	...	...	...	...	...	...	...	...	...	...	3	...	3
Bharatpur	5	3	2	...	...	...	...	...	...	...	...	...	...	...	...	...	...	...	...	...	...	77	32	45
Karauli	...	...	...	...	...	...	...	...	...	...	...	...	38	20	18	...	...	...	...	...	...	101	48	53
Dholpur	...	...	...	...	...	...	...	...	...	...	...	...	...	...	...	...	...	...	...	...	...	335	118	217
Alwar	...	...	...	...	...	...	...	...	...	...	...	...	...	...	...	...	...	...	...	...	...	186	104	82
Jhallawar	28	22	6	6	3	3	...	...	...	94	40	54	337	164	173	...	...	...	...	...	...	993	525	468
Tonk	...	...	...	...	...	...	...	...	...	...	...	...	...	...	...	8	8	...	...	...	...	616	370	246
Bundi	...	...	...	...	...	...	...	...	...	...	...	...	...	...	...	...	...	...	...	...	...	392	112	280
Shahpura	...	...	...	...	...	...	...	...	...	...	...	...	...	...	...	...	...	...	...	...	...	1,027	588	439
Kota	157	66	91	389	111	278	57	33	24	...	...	...	97	57	40	...	...	...	...	...	...	843	355	488
Erinpura	...	...	...	...	...	...	...	...	...	...	...	...	...	...	...	...	...	...	...	...	...			
Kherwara	...	...	...	...	...	...	...	...	...	...	...	...	...	...	...	...	...	...	...	...	...	29	26	3
Kotra	...	...	...	...	...	...	...	...	...	...	...	...	...	...	...	...	...	...	...	...	...	...	...	...
Abu	...	...	...	...	...	...	...	...	...	...	...	...	...	...	...	...	...	...	...	...	...	...	...	...
Total	280	141	189	519	185	334	57	33	24	94	40	54	472	241	231	13	12	1	1,356	758	598	76,853	41,494	35,359

TABLE VI.—Statement showing the Sub-division of Rajputs—*contd.*

Names of States.	II.—Yadu or Jadun.															Total of Yadu or Jadun. (II)			III.—Rahtore.					
	Jadun.			Bhatti.			Jarèja.			Jatu.			Tuar.						Rahtore.			Jora or Jodha.		
	Total.	Males.	Females.	Total.	Males.	Females.	Total.	Males.	Females.	Total.	Males.	Females.	Total.	Males.	Females.	Total.	Males.	Females.	Total.	Males.	Females.	Total.	Males.	Females.
	47	48	49	50	51	52	53	54	55	56	57	58	59	60	61	62	63	64	65	66	67	68	69	70
Meywar	2,371	713	1,658	1,772	1,004	768	...	...	...	...	...	...	...	...	...	4,143	1,717	2,426	21,349	12,068	9,281	...	...	...
Banswara	Details not furnished by the Durbar																							
Dungarpur	14	8	6	21	10	11	...	...	...	...	...	...	237	124	113	272	142	130	2,889	1,517	1,372	...	...	...
Partabgarh	Details not furnished by the Durbar																							
Marwar	...	...	...	27,157	15,173	11,984	...	...	...	...	...	...	2,016	1,122	894	29,173	16,295	12,878	86,858	56,654	30,204	...	...	...
Sirohi	...	...	...	...	...	...	...	...	...	...	...	...	...	...	...	...	...	...	1,430	682	748	...	...	...
Jesalmir	...	...	...	13,711	8,712	4,999	...	...	...	...	...	...	...	...	...	13,711	8,712	4,999	4,463	1,938	2,525	...	...	...
Bikanir	...	...	...	11,865	6,141	5,724	7	6	1	...	...	...	1,978	989	989	13,850	7,136	6,714	27,754	18,638	9,116	...	...	...
Jeypore	3,941	1,670	2,271	...	...	...	...	...	...	...	...	...	11,253	7,755	3,498	15,194	9,425	5,769	19,041	5,287	13,754	9	6	3
Kishengarh	2	...	2	202	120	82	...	...	...	...	...	...	63	38	25	267	158	109	3,912	2,404	1,508	7	2	5
Lawa	1	...	1	...	...	...	...	...	...	...	...	...	...	...	...	1	...	1	...	...	...	25	14	11
Bharatpur	2,715	1,578	1,137	11	7	4	...	...	...	...	...	...	152	87	65	2,878	1,672	1,206	497	269	228	...	...	...
Karauli	4,621	3,263	1,358	...	...	...	...	...	...	...	...	...	284	71	213	4,905	3,334	1,571	58	23	35	...	...	...
Dholpur	1,366	922	444	...	...	...	...	...	...	...	...	...	2,513	1,361	1,152	3,879	2,283	1,596	351	65	286	...	...	...
Alwar	1,170	443	727	271	139	132	1	...	1	267	76	191	1,217	531	686	2,926	1,189	1,737	1,268	646	622	7	1	6
Jhallawar	236	141	95	83	51	32	...	...	...	...	...	...	325	221	104	644	413	231	1,107	649	458	...	...	...
Tonk	127	72	55	...	...	...	...	...	...	...	...	...	...	...	...	127	72	55	401	276	125	...	...	...
Bundi	115	57	58	...	...	...	...	...	...	...	...	...	55	27	28	170	84	86	378	175	203	...	...	...
Shahpura	...	...	...	232	129	103	...	...	...	...	...	...	...	...	...	232	129	103	370	210	154	...	...	...
Kota	761	407	354	32	...	32	...	...	...	...	...	...	1,258	800	458	2,051	1,207	844	548	264	284	...	...	...
Erinpura	6	6	...	...	...	...	...	...	...	...	...	...	7	6	1	13	12	1	11	11	...	...	...	...
Kherwara	...	...	...	9	7	2	...	...	...	...	...	...	...	...	...	9	7	2	...	...	...	...	...	...
Kotra	...	...	...	...	...	...	...	...	...	...	...	...	...	...	...	...	...	...	...	...	...	...	...	...
Abu	...	...	...	...	...	...	...	...	...	...	...	...	...	...	...	...	...	...	...	...	...	...	...	...
Total	17,446	9,280	8,166	55,366	31,498	23,878	8	6	2	267	76	191	21,358	13,132	8,226	94,446	53,987	40,458	172,685	101,782	70,908	48	23	25

III.—RAHTORE—*continued.*

Names of States.	Mertia.			Chandawat.			Chandel.			Champawat.			Udawat.			Chamarpa.			Dalia.			Bodana.			Bamania.		
	Total.	Males.	Females.	Total.	Males.	Females.	Total.	Males.	Females.	Total.	Males.	Females.	Total.	Males.	Females.	Total.	Males.	Females.	Total.	Males.	Females.	Total.	Males.	Females.	Total.	Males.	Females.
	71	72	73	74	75	76	77	78	79	80	81	82	83	84	85	86	87	88	89	90	91	92	93	94	95	96	97
Meywar	...	...	...	...	...	...	...	...	...	...	...	...	...	...	...	...	...	...	...	...	...	...	...	...	...	...	...
Banswara	Details	not fur	nished	by the	Durbar																						
Dungarpur	34	23	11	...	...	...	...	...	...	10	8	2	...	...	...	22	10	12	81	34	47	76	42	34	88	42	46
Partabgarh	Details	not fur	nished	by the	Durbar																						
Marwar	...	...	...	...	...	...	...	...	...	...	...	...	...	...	...	...	...	...	...	...	...	...	...	...	...	...	...
Sirohi	...	...	...	...	...	...	...	...	...	...	...	...	...	...	...	...	...	...	...	...	...	...	...	...	...	...	...
Jesalmir	...	...	...	...	...	...	...	...	...	...	...	...	...	...	...	...	...	...	...	...	...	...	...	...	...	...	...
Bikanir	...	...	...	...	...	...	...	...	...	...	...	...	...	...	...	...	...	...	...	...	...	...	...	...	...	...	...
Jeypore	...	...	...	...	...	...	85	62	23	...	...	...	...	...	...	...	...	...	...	...	...	...	...	...	...	...	...
Kishengarh		...	...	...	...	...	...	...	...	...	...	...	...	...	...	...	...	...	...	...	...	...	...	...	...	...	...
Lawa	7	3	4	2	...	2	...	...	...	4	...	4	...	...	...	...	...	...	...	...	...	...	...	...	...	...	...
Bharatpur	...	...	...	...	...	...	4	4	...	...	...	...	...	...	...	...	...	...	...	...	...	...	...	...	...	...	...
Karauli	...	...	...	33	14	19	101	60	41	...	...	...	...	...	...	...	...	...	...	...	...	...	...	...	...	...	...
Dholpur	...	...	...	...	...	...	...	...	...	...	...	...	...	...	...	...	...	...	...	...	...	...	...	...	...	...	...
Alwar	16	1	15	8	3	5	8	2	6	...	...	...	...	...	...	...	...	...	...	...	...	...	...	...	...	...	...
Jhallawar	4	4	...	...	...	...	18	12	6	20	10	10	1	...	1	...	...	...	...	...	...	...	...	...	...	...	...
Tonk	...	...	...	...	...	...	132	95	37	...	...	...	...	...	...	...	...	...	...	...	...	...	...	...	...	...	...
Bundi	...	...	...	10	2	8	...	...	...	...	...	...	...	...	...	...	...	...	...	...	...	...	...	...	...	...	...
Shahpura	...	...	...	...	...	...	...	...	...	...	...	...	...	...	...	...	...	...	...	...	...	...	...	...	...	...	...
Kota	...	...	...	...	...	...	57	25	32	...	...	...	163	163	...	...	...	...	...	...	...	7	...	7	...	...	...
Erinpura	...	...	...	...	...	...	...	...	...	...	...	...	...	...	...	...	...	...	...	...	...	...	...	...	...	...	...
Kherwara	...	...	...	...	...	...	...	...	...	...	...	...	...	...	...	...	...	...	...	...	...	...	...	...	...	...	...
Kotra	...	...	...	...	...	...	...	...	...	...	...	...	...	...	...	...	...	...	...	...	...	...	...	...	...	...	...
Abu	...	...	...	...	...	...	...	...	...	...	...	...	...	...	...	...	...	...	...	...	...	...	...	...	...	...	...
Total	61	31	30	53	19	34	405	260	145	34	18	16	164	163	1	22	10	12	81	34	47	88	42	41	88	42	46

TABLE VI.—Statement showing the Sub-division of Rajputs—*contd.*

Names of States.	III.—Rahtore—*concluded.*									Total of Rahtore (III).			IV.—Kachhawaha or Cushawah.														
	Ruaba.			Vahia.			Virpoora.						Kachhawaha.			Jhamawat.			Kullianote.			Nathawat.			Balbudbhote.		
	Total.	Males.	Females.	Total.	Males.	Females.	Total.	Males.	Females.	Total.	Males.	Females.	Total.	Males.	Females.	Total.	Males.	Females.	Total.	Males.	Females.	Total.	Males.	Females.	Total.	Males.	Females.
	98	99	100	101	102	103	104	105	106	107	108	109	110	111	112	113	114	115	116	117	118	119	120	121	122	123	124
Meywar	...	...	...	...	...	...	...	...	...	21,349	12,068	9,281	8	6	2	...	...	...	...	...	...	...	...	...	...	...	...
Banswara	Details not furnished by the Durbar								...	...	...	...	...	...	...	...	...	...	...	...	...	...	...	...	...	...	...
Dungarpur	99	58	41	18	9	9	68	43	25	3,385	1,786	1,599	52	28	24	...	...	...	...	...	...	...	...	...	...	...	...
Partabgarh	Details not furnished by the Durbar								...	...	...	...	...	...	...	...	...	...	...	...	...	...	...	...	...	...	...
Marwar	...	...	...	...	...	...	...	...	...	86,858	56,654	30,204	13,944	5,501	8,443	...	...	...	...	...	...	...	...	...	...	...	...
Sirohi	...	...	...	...	...	...	...	...	...	1,430	682	748	...	...	...	...	...	...	...	...	...	...	...	...	...	...	...
Jesalmir	...	...	...	...	...	...	...	...	...	4,463	1,938	2,525	7	7	...	...	...	...	...	...	...	...	...	...	...	...	...
Bikanir	...	...	...	...	...	...	...	...	...	27,754	18,638	9,116	7,479	4,155	3,324	...	...	...	...	...	...	...	...	...	...	...	...
Jeypore	...	...	...	...	...	...	...	...	...	19,135	5,355	13,780	66,873	48,590	18,283	...	...	...	...	...	...	...	...	...	...	...	...
Kishengarh	...	...	...	...	...	...	...	...	...	3,919	2,406	1,513	1,393	553	840	...	...	...	...	...	...	...	...	...	...	...	...
Lawa	...	...	...	...	...	...	...	...	...	38	17	21	8	6	2	...	...	...	...	...	...	...	...	...	...	...	...
Bharatpur	...	...	...	...	...	...	...	...	...	501	273	228	1,479	863	616	...	...	...	...	...	...	...	...	...	...	...	...
Karauli	...	...	...	...	...	...	...	...	...	192	97	95	779	216	563	...	...	...	...	...	...	...	...	...	...	...	...
Dholpur	...	...	...	...	...	...	...	...	...	351	65	286	299	110	189	...	...	...	...	...	...	...	...	...	...	...	...
Alwar	...	...	...	...	...	...	...	...	...	1,307	653	654	799	441	358	55	36	19	551	262	289	61	48	13	40	22	18
Jhallawar	...	...	...	...	...	...	...	...	...	1,150	675	475	201	121	80	...	...	...	...	...	...	34	17	17	...	...	...
Tonk	...	...	...	...	...	...	...	...	...	533	371	162	228	130	98	...	...	...	...	...	...	...	...	...	...	...	...
Bundi	...	...	...	...	...	...	...	...	...	388	177	211	739	271	468	...	...	...	...	...	...	...	...	...	...	...	...
Shahpura	...	...	...	...	...	...	...	...	...	370	216	154	240	131	109	...	...	...	...	...	...	...	...	...	...	...	
Kota	...	...	...	...	...	...	...	...	...	775	452	323	362	218	144	...	...	...	...	...	...	167	75	92	...	...	...
Erinpura	...	...	...	...	...	...	...	...	...	11	11	...	14	14	...	...	...	...	...	...	...	...	...	...	...	...	...
Kherwara	...	...	...	...	...	...	...	...	...	...	...	...	...	...	...	...	...	...	...	...	...	...	...	...	...	...	...
Kotra	...	...	...	...	...	...	...	...	...	...	...	...	...	...	...	...	...	...	...	...	...	...	...	...	...	...	...
Abu	...	...	...	...	...	...	...	...	...	...	...	...	...	...	...	...	...	...	...	...	...	...	...	...	...	...	...
Total	**99**	**58**	**41**	**18**	**9**	**9**	**68**	**48**	**25**	**178,909**	**102,584**	**71,875**	**94,904**	**61,361**	**33,543**	**55**	**36**	**19**	**551**	**262**	**289**	**262**	**140**	**122**	**40**	**22**	**18**

IV.—KACHHAWAHA OR CUSHWAHA—*continued.*

Names of States.	Sooltanote.			Pichanote.			Khoombhavat.			Rajawat.			Hamirdekha.			Naruka.			Jogikachhava.			Radarka.			Shekhawat.		
	Total.	Males.	Females.	Total.	Males.	Females.	Total.	Males.	Females.	Total.	Males.	Females.	Total.	Males.	Females.	Total.	Males.	Females.	Total.	Males.	Females.	Total.	Males.	Females.	Total.	Males.	Females.
	125	126	127	128	129	130	131	132	133	134	135	136	137	138	139	140	141	142	143	144	145	146	147	148	149	150	151
Meywar	...	...	...	...	...	...	...	...	...	...	...	...	...	...	...	...	...	...	...	...	...	...	...	...	...	...	...
Banswara	...	...	...	...	...	...	...	...	...	...	...	...	...	...	...	...	...	...	...	...	...	...	...	...	...	...	...
Dungarpur	...	...	...	...	...	...	...	...	...	...	...	...	...	...	...	...	...	...	...	...	...	...	...	...	...	...	...
Partabgarh	...	...	...	...	...	...	...	...	...	...	...	...	...	...	...	1	1	...	...	...	...	...	...	...	...	...	...
Marwar	...	...	...	...	...	...	...	...	...	...	...	...	...	...	...	...	...	...	...	...	...	...	...	...	...	...	...
Sirohi	...	...	...	...	...	...	...	...	...	...	...	...	...	...	...	...	...	...	...	...	...	...	...	...	...	...	...
Jesalmir	...	...	...	...	...	...	...	...	...	...	...	...	...	...	...	...	...	...	...	...	...	...	...	...	...	...	...
Bikanir	...	...	...	...	...	...	...	...	...	...	...	...	...	...	...	...	...	...	...	...	...	...	...	...	...	...	...
Jeypore	...	...	...	...	...	...	...	...	...	...	...	...	...	...	...	...	...	...	...	...	...	...	...	...	...	...	...
Kishengarh	...	...	...	...	...	...	...	...	...	...	...	...	...	...	...	...	...	...	...	...	...	...	...	...	...	...	...
Lawa	3	3	...	4	1	3	...	...	...	3	...	3	...	...	...	35	20	15	...	...	...	...	...	...	1	1	...
Bharatpur	...	...	...	...	...	...	...	...	...	...	...	...	...	...	...	33	25	8	...	...	...	...	...	...	...	...	...
Karauli	...	...	...	...	...	...	...	...	...	...	...	...	...	...	...	...	...	...	...	...	...	...	...	...	...	...	...
Dholpur	...	...	...	...	...	...	...	...	...	...	...	...	...	...	...	4	...	4	...	...	...	...	...	...	...	...	...
Alwar	...	...	...	278	176	102	184	91	93	454	303	151	271	144	127	4,466	2,848	1,618	108	92	16	277	156	121	2,448	1,812	636
Jhallawar	...	...	...	...	...	...	...	...	...	116	70	46	...	...	...	11	5	6	...	...	...	...	...	...	225	154	71
Tonk	...	...	...	...	...	...	...	...	...	...	...	...	...	...	...	63	50	13	...	...	...	...	...	...	...	...	...
Bundi	...	...	...	...	...	...	...	...	...	...	...	...	...	...	...	...	...	...	...	...	...	...	...	...	...	...	...
Shahpura	...	...	...	...	...	...	...	...	...	...	...	...	...	...	...	...	...	...	...	...	...	...	...	...	...	...	...
Kota	...	...	...	...	...	...	...	...	...	507	135	372	...	...	...	...	...	...	...	...	...	...	...	...	206	123	83
Erinpura	...	...	...	...	...	...	...	...	...	...	...	...	...	...	...	...	...	...	...	...	...	...	...	...	...	...	...
Kherwara	...	...	...	...	...	...	...	...	...	...	...	...	...	...	...	...	...	...	...	...	...	...	...	...	...	...	...
Kotra	...	...	...	...	...	...	...	...	...	...	...	...	...	...	...	...	...	...	...	...	...	...	...	...	...	...	...
Abu	...	...	...	...	...	...	...	...	...	...	...	...	...	...	...	...	...	...	...	...	...	...	...	...	...	...	...
Total	3	3	...	282	177	105	184	91	93	1,080	508	572	271	144	127	4,618	2,949	1,664	108	92	16	277	156	121	2,883	2,092	791

TABLE VI.—Statement showing the Sub-division of Rajputs—*contd.*

Names of States.	IV.—Kachhawaha or Cushwaha—*concluded.* Dherawat. Total.	Males.	Females.	Raghubansi. Total.	Males.	Females.	Dudawat. Total.	Males.	Females.	Bankawat. Total.	Males.	Females.	Total of Kachhawaha (IV). Total.	Males.	Females.	V.—Parmar or Panwar. Parmar. Total.	Males.	Females.	Sorutrah. Total.	Males.	Females.	Mori. Total.	Males.	Females.	Hankla or Sankla. Total.	Males.	Females.
	152	153	154	155	156	157	158	159	160	161	162	163	164	165	166	167	168	169	170	171	172	173	174	175	176	177	178
Mewar	...	...	...	...	...	...	...	...	...	...	...	...	11	*8*	3	7,317	*4,212*	3,105	...	...	...	402	*134*	68	1,323	*784*	539
Banswara	...	...	...	...	...	...	...	...	...	...	...	...	...	...	...	...	...	...	...	...	...	...	...	...	...	...	...
Dungarpur	...	...	...	...	...	...	...	...	...	...	...	...	53	*29*	24	615	*313*	302	...	...	...	...	...	...	16	*5*	11
Partabgarh	...	...	...	...	...	...	...	...	...	...	...	...	...	...	...	...	...	...	...	...	...	...	...	...	...	...	...
Marwar	...	...	...	...	...	...	...	...	...	...	...	...	13,944	*5,501*	8,443	11,128	*5,906*	5,222	...	...	...	...	...	...	...	...	...
Sirohi	...	...	...	...	...	...	...	...	...	...	...	...	...	...	...	...	...	...	...	...	...	...	...	...	...	...	...
Jesalmir	...	...	...	...	...	...	...	...	...	...	...	...	7	*7*	...	...	...	...	...	...	...	...	...	...	...	...	...
Bikanir	...	...	...	...	...	...	...	...	...	...	...	...	7,479	*4,155*	3,324	4,741	*2,286*	2,455	...	...	...	...	...	...	...	...	...
Jeypore	...	...	...	...	...	...	...	...	...	...	...	...	66,873	*48,590*	18,283	1,771	*687*	1,084	...	...	...	...	...	...	102	*57*	45
Kishengarh	...	...	...	...	...	...	...	...	...	...	...	...	1,393	*553*	840	76	*46*	30	...	...	...	...	...	...	25	*19*	6
Lawa	...	...	...	...	...	...	...	...	...	...	...	...	54	*31*	23	...	...	...	...	...	...	...	...	...	...	...	...
Bharatpur	...	...	...	...	...	...	...	...	...	81	*67*	14	1,593	*955*	638	1,836	*1,138*	698	...	...	...	...	...	...	...	...	...
Karauli	30	*16*	14	...	...	...	...	...	...	...	...	...	809	*232*	577	580	*141*	439	...	...	...	...	...	...	...	...	...
Dholpur	...	...	...	...	...	...	...	...	...	...	...	...	303	*110*	193	9,955	*7,048*	2,907	...	...	...	418	*170*	248	...	...	...
Alwar	60	*35*	25	...	...	...	125	*79*	46	282	*146*	136	10,459	*6,691*	3,768	799	*265*	534	...	...	...	...	...	...	61	*29*	32
Jhallawar	...	...	...	...	...	...	...	...	...	...	...	...	587	*367*	220	378	*228*	150	4	*2*	2	...	...	...	3	*2*	1
Tonk	...	...	...	614	*301*	313	...	...	...	...	...	...	905	*481*	424	409	*203*	206	...	...	...	...	...	...	...	...	...
Bundi	...	...	...	...	...	...	...	...	...	...	...	...	739	*271*	468	170	*93*	77	...	...	...	...	...	...	3	*3*	...
Shahpura	...	...	...	...	...	...	...	...	...	...	...	...	240	*131*	109	60	*35*	25	...	...	...	...	...	...	...	...	...
Kota	...	...	...	...	...	...	...	...	...	...	...	...	1,242	*551*	691	383	*112*	271	...	...	...	...	...	...	...	...	...
Erinpura	...	...	...	...	...	...	...	...	...		...	...		*14*	...	7	*7*	...	...	...	...	...	...	...	...	...	...
Kherwara	...	...	...	...	...	...	...	...	...		...	...	...	...	...	...	...	...	...	...	...	...	...	...	...	...	...
Kotra	...	...	...	...	...	...	...	...	...	...	...	...	...	...	...	...	...	...	...	...	...	...	...	...	...	...	...
Abu	...	...	...	...	...	...	...	...	...	...	...	...	...	...	...	2	*2*	...	...	...	...	...	...	...	...	...	...
Total	**90**	**51**	**39**	**614**	**301**	**313**	**125**	**79**	**46**	**363**	**213**	**150**	**106,705**	**68,677**	**38,028**	**40,227**	**22,722**	**17,505**	**4**	**2**	**2**	**620**	**304**	**316**	**1,533**	**899**	**634**

Table VI.—Sub-division—Rajputana Agency.

NAMES OF STATES.	V.—PARMAR OR PANWAR—*contd.* Khyr (Khyjar) Total.	Males.	Females.	Barasia. Total.	Males.	Females.	Barod. Total.	Males.	Females.	TOTAL OF PARMAR (V.) Total.	Males.	Females.	VI.—CHOHAN OR HARA. Chohan. Total.	Males.	Females.	Hara. Total.	Males.	Females.	Kheechee. Total.	Males.	Females.	Sonigurra. Total.	Males.	Females.	Deora. Total.	Males.	Females.
	179	180	181	182	183	184	185	186	187	188	189	190	191	192	193	194	195	196	197	198	199	200	201	202	203	204	205
Meywar	...	...	...	...	...	...	...	...	...	8,842	5,130	3,712	13,109	7,606	5,503	...	...	...	372	124	248	...	...	...	5,298	2,451	2,847
Banswara	...	...	...	...	...	...	...	...	...	...	...	...	...	...	...	...	...	...	...	...	...	...	...	...	...	...	...
Dungarpur	...	...	...	44	23	21	122	70	52	797	411	386	2,995	1,658	1,337	...	...	...	...	...	...	...	...	...	418	210	208
Partabgarh	...	...	...	...	...	...	...	...	...	...	...	...	...	...	...	...	...	...	...	...	...	...	...	...	...	...	...
Marwar	...	...	...	...	...	...	...	...	...	11,128	5,906	5,222	25,803	13,866	11,937	...	...	...	...	...	...	...	...	...	...	...	...
Sirohi	...	...	...	...	...	...	...	...	...	...	...	...	...	...	...	...	...	...	...	...	...	...	...	...	3,316	2,264	1,052
Jesalmir	...	...	...	...	...	...	...	...	...	...	...	...	1,010	490	520	...	...	...	...	...	...	...	...	...	...	...	...
Bikanir	...	...	...	...	...	...	...	...	...	4,741	2,286	2,455	5,851	3,104	2,747	...	...	...	...	...	...	...	...	...	...	...	...
Jeypore	...	...	...	...	...	...	...	...	...	1,873	744	1,129	16,147	7,852	8,295	250	113	137	...	...	...	...	...	...	163	120	43
Kishengarh	...	...	...	...	...	...	...	...	...	101	65	36	193	114	79	16	9	7	...	...	...	...	...	...	7	3	4
Lawa	...	...	...	...	...	...	...	...	...	...	...	...	...	...	...	...	...	...	1	...	1	...	...	...	...	...	...
Bharatpur	...	...	...	...	...	...	...	...	...	1,836	1,138	698	1,823	985	838	...	...	...	...	...	...	...	...	...	...	...	...
Karauli	...	...	...	...	...	...	...	...	...	580	141	439	513	212	301	...	...	...	...	...	...	...	...	...	...	...	...
Dholpur	...	...	...	...	...	...	...	...	...	10,373	7,218	3,155	1,704	378	1,326	...	...	...	...	...	...	...	...	...	...	...	...
Alwar	...	...	...	...	...	...	...	...	...	860	294	566	8,202	4,930	3,272	103	68	35	29	19	10	...	...	...	...	...	...
Jhallawar	3	1	2	...	...	...	...	...	...	388	233	155	435	227	208	459	241	218	219	100	119	323	95	228	328	174	154
Tonk	...	...	...	...	...	...	...	...	...	409	203	206	524	308	216	...	...	...	98	54	44	...	...	...	...	...	...
Bundi	...	...	...	...	...	...	...	...	...	173	96	77	150	78	72	2,904	1,908	996	...	...	...	...	...	...	...	...	...
Shahpura	...	...	...	...	...	...	...	...	...	60	35	25	73	39	34	...	...	...	...	...	...	...	...	...	...	...	...
Kota	...	...	...	...	...	...	...	...	...	383	112	271	1,070	667	403	6,819	3,839	2,980	82	17	65	...	...	...	...	...	...
Erinpura	...	...	...	...	...	...	...	...	...	7	7	...	29	24	5	...	...	...	...	...	...	...	...	...	6	5	1
Kherwara	...	...	...	...	...	...	...	...	...	...	...	...	...	...	...	...	...	...	...	...	...	...	...	...	...	...	...
Kotra	...	...	...	...	...	...	...	...	...	...	...	...	...	...	...	...	...	...	...	...	...	...	...	...	...	...	...
Abu	...	...	...	...	...	...	...	...	...	2	2	...	...	...	...	...	...	...	...	...	...	...	...	...	...	...	...
Total	3	1	2	44	23	21	122	70	52	42,553	24,021	18,532	79,631	42,538	37,093	10,551	6,178	4,373	801	314	487	323	95	228	9,536	5,227	4,309

TABLE VI.—Statement showing the Sub-division of Rajputs—*contd.*

Names of States.	VI.—Chohan or Hara—*contd.*												Total Choman or Hara. (VI).			VII.—Chalook or Solanki.									Total Chalook (VII).		
	Bahadooria.			Noorbhan.			Poorbya.			Picha.						Solanki.			Baghella.			Katara.					
	Total.	Males.	Females.	Total.	Males.	Females.	Total.	Males.	Females.	Total.	Males.	Females.	Total.	Males.	Females.	Total.	Males.	Females.	Total.	Males.	Females.	Total.	Males.	Females.	Total.	Males.	Females.
	206	207	208	209	210	211	212	213	214	215	216	217	218	219	220	221	222	223	224	225	226	227	228	229	230	231	232
Meywar	14	14	...	...	...	...	...	...	...	...	...	...	18,793	10,195	8,598	...	...	...	...	...	...	...	...	...	...	...	...
Banswara	...	...	...	...	...	...	...	...	...	...	...	...	...	...	...	...	...	...	...	...	...	...	...	...	...	...	...
Dungarpur	...	...	...	...	...	...	94	44	50	...	...	...	3,507	1,912	1,595	223	119	104	148	86	62	...	...	...	371	205	166
Partabgarh	...	...	...	...	...	...	...	...	...	...	...	...	...	...	...	...	...	...	...	...	...	...	...	...	...	...	...
Marwar	...	...	...	...	...	...	...	...	...	...	...	...	25,803	13,866	11,937	7,026	3,792	3,234	...	...	...	...	...	...	7,026	3,792	3,234
Sirohi	...	...	...	...	...	...	...	...	...	...	...	...	3,316	2,264	1,052	...	...	...	...	...	...	...	...	...	...	...	...
Jesalmir	...	...	...	...	...	...	...	...	...	...	...	...	1,010	490	520	...	...	...	...	...	...	...	...	...	...	...	...
Bikanir	...	...	...	...	...	...	...	...	...	...	...	...	5,851	3,104	2,747	423	218	205	...	...	...	...	...	...	423	218	205
Jeypore	23	13	10	...	...	...	...	...	...	...	...	...	16,583	8,098	8,485	1,488	774	714	38	19	19	...	...	...	1,526	793	738
Kishengarh	...	...	...	...	...	...	...	...	...	...	...	...	216	126	90	58	30	28	...	...	...	...	...	...	58	30	28
Lawa	...	...	...	...	...	...	...	...	...	...	...	...	1	...	1	2	...	2	...	...	...	...	...	...	2	...	2
Bharatpur	...	...	...	9	8	1	...	...	...	...	...	...	1,832	993	839	17	5	12	...	...	...	...	...	...	17	5	12
Karauli	...	...	...	...	...	...	...	...	...	...	...	...	513	212	301	83	43	40	20	15	5	...	...	...	103	58	45
Dholpur	213	84	146	...	...	...	...	...	...	...	...	...	1,934	462	1,472	192	112	80	2	...	2	...	...	...	194	112	82
Alwar	9	7	2	375	176	199	...	...	...	...	...	...	8,718	5,200	3,518	132	55	77	...	...	...	13	8	5	145	63	82
Jhallawar	68	38	30	8	7	1	8	4	4	...	...	...	1,848	886	962	412	216	196	34	16	18	...	...	...	446	232	214
Tonk	29	14	15	...	...	...	...	...	...	...	...	...	651	376	275	265	132	133	...	...	...	128	69	59	393	201	192
Bundi	...	...	...	...	...	...	19	10	9	...	...	...	3,073	1,996	1,077	1,623	935	688	...	...	...	...	...	...	1,623	935	688
Shahpura	...	...	...	...	...	...	...	...	...	...	...	...	73	39	34	89	51	38	...	...	...	...	...	...	89	51	38
Kota	1	...	1	...	...	...	...	...	...	91	46	45	8,063	4,569	3,494	973	487	486	166	166	...	...	...	...	1,139	653	486
Erinpura	...	...	...	...	...	...	...	...	...	...	...	...	35	29	6	...	...	...	...	...	...	...	...	...	...	...	...
Kherwara	...	...	...	...	...	...	...	...	...	...	...	...	...	...	...	...	...	...	...	...	...	...	...	...	...	...	...
Kotra	...	...	...	...	...	...	...	...	...	...	...	...	...	...	...	...	...	...	...	...	...	...	...	...	...	...	...
Abu	...	...	...	...	...	...	...	...	...	...	...	...	...	...	...	...	...	...	...	...	...	...	...	...	...	...	...
Total	374	170	204	392	191	201	121	58	63	91	46	45	101,820	54,817	47,008	13,006	6,969	6,037	408	302	106	141	77	64	18,555	7,848	6,207

Table VI.—Sub-Division—Rajputana Agency.

Names of States.	VIII. Prithiara or Parihara or Padyar. Total.	Males.	Females.	IX. Chaora. Total.	Males.	Females.	X. Takshac or Tak. Total.	Males.	Females.	XI. Katti. Total.	Males.	Females.	XII. Jhallá. Total.	Males.	Females.	XII. Macwaña. Total.	Males.	Females.	XIII. Gohell. Total.	Males.	Females.	XIV. Dabi. Total.	Males.	Females.	XV. Gor. Total.	Males.	Females.
	233	234	235	236	237	238	239	240	241	242	243	244	245	246	247	248	249	250	251	252	253	254	255	256	257	258	259
Meywar	1,616	613	1,003	...	...	...	75	22	53	...	...	...	2,861	1,684	1,177	...	...	...	...	...	...	...	...	...	1,407	719	688
Banswara	...	...	...	...	...	...	...	...	...	...	...	...	...	...	...	...	...	...	...	...	...	...	...	...	...	...	...
Dungarpur	21	8	13	41	27	14	...	...	...	...	...	...	15	7	8	12	6	6	...	...	...	182	100	82	...	...	...
Partabgarh	...	...	...	...	...	...	...	...	...	...	...	...	...	...	...	...	...	...	...	...	...	...	...	...	...	...	...
Marwar	6,406	3,387	3,019	...	...	...	...	...	...	...	...	...	207	118	89	...	...	...	...	...	...	...	...	...	...	...	...
Sirohi	...	...	...	...	...	...	...	...	...	...	...	...	...	...	...	...	...	...	...	...	...	...	...	...	...	...	...
Jesalmir	...	...	...	...	...	...	...	...	...	...	...	...	...	...	...	...	...	...	...	...	...	...	...	...	...	...	...
Bikanir	2,690	1,358	1,332	30	10	20	...	...	...	...	...	...	37	23	14	...	...	...	...	...	...	...	...	...	...	...	...
Jeypore	124	79	45	...	...	...	...	...	...	...	...	...	...	...	...	...	...	...	...	...	...	...	...	...	2,057	1,189	868
Kishengarh	74	39	35	...	...	...	...	...	...	...	...	...	...	...	...	...	...	...	...	...	...	...	...	...	94	47	47
Lawa	...	...	...	...	...	...	...	...	...	...	...	...	...	...	...	...	...	...	...	...	...	...	...	...	3	1	2
Bharatpur	...	...	...	...	...	...	...	...	...	...	...	...	...	...	...	...	...	...	...	...	...	...	...	...	493	307	186
Karauli	...	...	...	...	...	...	...	...	...	94	63	31	...	...	...	...	...	...	134	67	67	...	...	...	189	83	106
Dholpur	291	176	115	...	...	...	22	7	15	...	...	...	...	...	...	...	...	...	...	...	...	...	...	...	663	391	272
Alwar	...	...	...	...	...	...	...	...	...	...	...	...	...	...	...	...	...	...	...	...	...	...	...	...	352	205	147
Jhallawar	94	54	40	3	2	1	4	2	2	...	...	...	1,385	970	415	...	...	...	16	10	6	44	22	22	141	75	66
Tonk	201	157	44	...	...	...	...	...	...	...	...	...	...	...	...	...	...	...	...	...	...	...	...	...	...	...	...
Bundi	33	12	21	...	...	...	...	...	...	...	...	...	50	6	44	27	3	24	...	...	...	...	...	...	158	73	85
Shahpura	1	...	1	...	...	...	...	...	...	...	...	...	1	...	...	...	...	...	...	...	...	...	...	...	112	68	44
Kota	140	40	100	...	...	...	...	...	...	...	...	...	204	97	107	1	1	...	...	...	...	...	...	...	590	353	237
Erinpura[1]	3	3	...	...	...	...	...	...	...	...	...	...	...	...	...	...	...	...	...	...	...	...	...	...	...	...	...
Kherwara	...	...	...	...	...	...	...	...	...	...	...	...	...	...	...	...	...	...	...	...	...	...	...	...	...	...	...
Kotra	...	...	...	...	...	...	...	...	...	...	...	...	...	...	...	...	...	...	...	...	...	...	...	...	...	...	...
Abu	...	...	...	...	...	...	...	...	...	...	...	...	...	...	...	...	...	...	...	...	...	...	...	...	...	...	...
Total	11,694	5,926	5,768	74	39	35	101	31	70	94	63	31	4,760	2,905	1,855	40	10	30	150	77	73	226	122	104	6,259	3,511	2,748

TABLE VI.—Statement showing the Sub-division of Rajputs—*contd.*

Names of States.	XVI. Dor or Doda. Total.	Males.	Females.	XVII. Gherwal Bundella. Total.	Males.	Females.	XVIII. Bir Goojar. Total.	Males.	Females.	XIX. Sengar. Total.	Males.	Females.	XX. Sikarwal. Total.	Males.	Females.	XXI. Byce, Beis or Bans. Total.	Males.	Females.	XXII. Dahia. Total.	Males.	Females.	XXIII. Dahima. Total.	Males.	Females.
	260	261	262	263	264	265	266	267	268	269	270	271	272	273	274	275	276	277	278	279	280	281	282	283
Meywar	700	289	411	...	...	...	66	13	53	...	...	...	...	...	...	...	...	...	...	...	...	...	...	...
Banswara	...	...	...	...	...	...	...	...	...	...	...	...	...	...	...	...	...	...	...	...	...	...	...	...
Dungarpur	30	19	11	...	...	...	...	...	...	...	...	...	...	...	...	...	...	...	...	...	...	...	...	...
Partabgarh	...	...	...	...	...	...	...	...	...	...	...	...	...	...	...	...	...	...	...	...	...	...	...	...
Marwar	...	...	...	...	...	...	...	...	...	...	...	...	...	...	...	...	...	...	...	...	...	...	...	...
Sirohi	...	...	...	...	...	...	...	...	...	...	...	...	...	...	...	...	...	...	...	...	...	...	...	...
Jesalmir	...	...	...	...	...	...	...	...	...	...	...	...	...	...	...	...	...	...	...	...	...	...	...	...
Bikanir	...	...	...	...	...	...	...	...	...	...	...	...	...	...	...	...	...	...	...	...	...	...	...	...
Jeypore	...	...	...	29	14	15	1,555	832	723	...	...	...	405	214	191	309	184	125	...	...	...	...	...	...
Kishengarh	...	...	...	...	...	...	308	162	146	...	...	...	...	...	...	...	...	...	5	3	2	...	...	...
Lawa	...	...	...	...	...	...	1	...	1	...	...	...	...	...	...	...	...	...	...	...	...	...	...	...
Bharatpur	...	...	...	56	43	13	146	78	68	...	...	...	386	218	168	3	3	...	...	...	...	...	...	...
Karauli	...	...	...	78	34	44	277	117	160	426	209	217	...	...	...	164	76	88	...	...	...	22	15	7
Dholpur	...	...	...	2	2	...	104	59	45	19	70	12	2,660	1,284	1,376	31	9	22	...	...	...	...	...	...
Alwar	...	...	...	...	...	...	1,702	900	802	...	...	...	180	54	126	105	65	40	72	26	46	...	...	...
Jhallawar	...	...	...	4	2	2	95	45	50	17	10	7	166	102	64	150	109	41	22	10	12	...	...	...
Tonk	...	...	...	67	40	27	...	...	...	300	147	153	34	20	14	25	16	9	...	...	...	...	...	...
Bundi	...	...	...	...	...	...	2	...	2	...	...	...	61	38	23	15	9	6	...	...	...	8	4	4
Shahpura	...	...	...	...	...	...	...	...	...	...	...	...	...	...	...	...	...	...	...	...	...	...	...	...
Kota	...	...	...	...	...	...	11	8	3	6	...	6	153	...	153	...	...	...	84	30	54	...	...	...
Erinpura	...	...	...	...	...	...	...	...	...	...	...	...	...	...	...	3	3	...	...	...	...	...	...	...
Kherwara	...	...	...	...	...	...	...	...	...	...	...	...	...	...	...	...	...	...	...	...	...	...	...	...
Kotra	...	...	...	...	...	...	...	...	...	...	...	...	...	...	...	...	...	...	...	...	...	...	...	...
Abu	...	...	...	...	...	...	...	...	...	...	...	...	...	...	...	...	...	...	...	...	...	...	...	...
Total	**730**	**808**	**422**	**236**	**185**	**101**	**4,267**	**2,214**	**2,058**	**768**	**873**	**395**	**4,045**	**1,980**	**2,115**	**805**	**474**	**381**	**183**	**69**	**114**	**30**	**19**	**11**

Names of States.	XXIV.—Miscellaneous. 1.—Kharwal. Total.	1.—Kharwal. Males.	1.—Kharwal. Females.	2.—Unter. Total.	2.—Unter. Males.	2.—Unter. Females.	3.—Marahtta. Total.	3.—Marahtta. Males.	3.—Marahtta. Females.	4.—Pachoria. Total.	4.—Pachoria. Males.	4.—Pachoria. Females.	5.—Tarwarya. Total.	5.—Tarwarya. Males.	5.—Tarwarya. Females.	6.—Royzada. Total.	6.—Royzada. Males.	6.—Royzada. Females.	7.—Bharwas. Total.	7.—Bharwas. Males.	7.—Bharwas. Females.	8.—Bhoomia. Total.	8.—Bhoomia. Males.	8.—Bhoomia. Females.
	284	285	286	287	288	289	290	291	292	293	294	295	296	297	298	299	300	301	302	303	304	305	306	307
Meywar	19,605	10,873	8,732	2,487	1,422	1,065	737	204	533	...	...	...	...	...	...	...	...	...	...	...	...	...	...	...
Banswara	...	...	...	...	...	...	...	...	...	...	...	...	...	...	...	...	...	...	...	...	...	...	...	...
Dungarpur	2	1	1	[illegible]	...	...	...	...	...	...	...	...	...	...	...	...	...	...	...	...	...	...	...	...
Partabgarh	...	...	...	...	...	...	...	...	...	...	...	...	...	...	...	...	...	...	...	...	...	261	117	144
Marwar	...	...	...	...	...	...	...	...	...	...	...	...	...	...	...	...	...	...	...	...	...	...	...	...
Sirohi	...	...	...	...	...	...	...	...	...	...	...	...	...	...	...	...	...	...	...	...	...	...	...	...
Jesalmir	...	...	...	...	...	...	...	...	...	...	...	...	...	...	...	...	...	...	...	...	...	...	...	...
Bikanir	...	...	...	...	...	...	...	...	...	...	...	...	...	...	...	...	...	...	...	...	...	...	...	...
Jeypore	...	...	...	...	...	...	...	...	...	...	...	...	...	...	...	...	...	...	...	...	...	...	...	...
Kishengarh	...	...	...	...	...	...	...	...	...	...	...	...	...	...	...	...	...	...	...	...	...	...	...	...
Lawa	...	...	...	...	...	...	...	...	...	...	...	...	...	...	...	...	...	...	...	...	...	...	...	...
Bharatpur	...	...	...	...	...	...	...	...	...	...	...	...	...	...	...	...	...	...	...	...	...	...	...	...
Kharauli	25	2	23	...	...	...	...	...	...	...	...	...	...	...	...	...	...	...	...	...	...	...	...	...
Dholpur	...	...	...	...	...	...	...	...	...	...	...	...	...	...	...	...	...	...	...	...	...	...	...	...
Alwar	...	...	...	...	...	...	...	...	...	...	...	...	...	...	...	...	...	...	...	...	...	...	...	...
Jhallawar	...	...	...	...	...	...	...	...	...	...	...	...	...	...	...	...	...	...	...	...	...	...	...	...
Tonk	...	...	...	...	...	...	...	...	...	94	45	49	39	16	23	40	9	31	75	49	26	...	...	...
Bundi	...	...	...	...	...	...	...	...	...	...	...	...	...	...	...	...	...	...	...	...	...	...	...	...
Shahpura	...	...	...	...	...	...	12	8	4	...	...	...	...	...	...	...	...	...	...	...	...	...	...	...
Kota	...	...	...	...	...	...	...	...	...	...	...	...	...	...	...	...	...	...	...	...	...	...	...	...
Erinpura	...	...	...	...	...	...	...	...	...	...	...	...	...	...	...	...	...	...	...	...	...	...	...	...
Kherwara	...	...	...	...	...	...	...	...	...	...	...	...	...	...	...	...	...	...	...	...	...	...	...	...
Kotra	...	...	...	...	...	...	...	...	...	...	...	...	...	...	...	...	...	...	...	...	...	...	...	...
Abu	...	...	...	...	...	...	...	...	...	...	...	...	...	...	...	...	...	...	...	...	...	...	...	...
Total	19,632	10,876	8,756	2,487	1,422	1,065	749	212	537	94	45	49	39	16	23	40	9	31	75	49	26	261	117	144

TABLE VI.—Statement showing the Sub-division of Rajputs—*contd.*

Names of States.	XXIV.—MISCELLANEOUS—*continued.*																										
	9.—Lumawat.			10.—Khawaswal.			11.—Kanni.			12.—Dekit or Dikhiet.			13.—Godawat.			14.—Janwar.			15.—Parwal.			16.—Bagor.			17.—Dhankra.		
	Total.	Males.	Females.	Total.	Males.	Females.	Total.	Males.	Females.	Total.	Males.	Females.	Total.	Males.	Females.	Total.	Males.	Females.	Total.	Males.	Females.	Total.	Males.	Females.	Total.	Males.	Females.
	308	309	310	311	312	313	314	315	316	317	318	319	320	321	322	323	324	325	326	327	328	329	330	331	332	333	334
Meywar	...	...	...	...	...	...	...	...	...	...	...	...	...	...	...	...	...	...	...	...	...	...	...	...	...	...	...
Banswara	Details not furnished by the Durbar																										
Dungarpur	280	*106*	174	...	...	...	...	...	...	...	...	...	...	...	...	...	...	...	...	...	...	...	...	...	...	...	...
Partabgarh	Details not furnished by the Durbar																										
Marwar	...	...	...	...	...	...	...	...	...	...	...	...	...	...	...	...	...	...	...	...	...	...	...	...	...	...	...
Sirohi	...	...	...	...	...	...	...	...	...	...	...	...	...	...	...	...	...	...	...	...	...	...	...	...	...	...	...
Jesalmir	...	...	...	...	...	...	...	...	...	...	...	...	...	...	...	...	...	...	...	...	...	...	...	...	...	...	...
Bikanir	...	...	...	38	*17*	21	...	...	...	...	...	...	...	...	...	...	...	...	...	...	...	...	...	...	...	...	...
Jeypore	...	...	...	...	...	...	...	...	...	...	...	...	...	...	...	...	...	...	...	...	...	...	...	...	...	...	...
Kishengarh	...	...	...	...	...	...	...	...	...	...	...	...	...	...	...	...	...	...	...	...	...	...	...	...	9	...	9
Lawa	...	...	...	...	...	...	...	...	...	...	...	...	...	...	...	...	...	...	...	...	...	...	...	...	...	...	...
Bharatpur	...	...	...	...	...	...	124	*65*	59	...	...	...	...	...	...	...	...	...	...	...	...	...	...	...	31	*26*	5
Karauli	...	...	...	...	...	...	...	...	...	35	*15*	20	22	*10*	12	24	*7*	17	54	*35*	19	...	...	...	...	...	...
Dholpur	...	...	...	...	...	...	...	...	...	...	...	...	...	...	...	...	...	...	...	...	...	129	*26*	103	318	*93*	225
Alwar	...	...	...	38	*23*	15	...	...	...	6	*4*	2	...	...	...	...	...	...	...	...	...	...	...	...	...	...	...
Jhallawar	...	...	...	...	...	...	...	...	...	19	*17*	2	...	...	...	5	*5*	...	...	...	...	...	...	...	15	*7*	8
Tonk	...	...	...	...	...	...	...	...	...	...	...	...	...	...	...	...	...	...	...	...	...	...	...	...	...	...	...
Bundi	...	...	...	...	...	...	...	...	...	...	...	...	...	...	...	...	...	...	...	...	...	...	...	...	...	...	...
Shahpura	...	...	...	...	...	...	...	...	...	...	...	...	...	...	...	...	...	...	...	...	...	...	...	...	...	...	...
Kota	...	...	...	...	...	...	...	...	...	...	...	...	...	...	...	...	...	...	...	...	...	...	...	...	...	...	...
Erinpura	...	...	...	...	...	...	...	...	...	...	...	...	...	...	...	...	...	...	...	...	...	...	...	...	...	...	...
Kherwara	...	...	...	...	...	...	...	...	...	...	...	...	...	...	...	...	...	...	...	...	...	...	...	...	...	...	...
Kotra	...	...	...	...	...	...	...	...	...	...	...	...	...	...	...	...	...	...	...	...	...	...	...	...	...	...	...
Abu	...	...	...	...	...	...	...	...	...	...	...	...	...	...	...	...	...	...	...	...	...	...	...	...	...	...	...
Total	**280**	**106**	**174**	**76**	**40**	**36**	**124**	**65**	**59**	**60**	**36**	**24**	**22**	**10**	**12**	**29**	**12**	**17**	**54**	**35**	**19**	**129**	**26**	**103**	**378**	**126**	**247**

Names of States.	XXIV.—MISCELLANEOUS—*concluded.* 18.—Jhújhara. Total.	Males.	Females.	19.—Kirar. Total.	Males.	Females.	20.—Umat. Total.	Males.	Females.	21.—Goutam. Total.	Males.	Females.	22.—Ranghar. Total.	Males.	Females.	23.—Bandori. Total.	Males.	Females.	24.—Singrote. Total.	Males.	Females.	TOTAL MISCELLANEOUS. (1 to 24) XXIV. Total.	Males.	Females.	XXV.—OTHERS AND UNSPECIFIED. Total.	Males.	Females.
	335	336	337	338	339	340	341	342	343	344	345	346	347	348	349	350	351	352	353	354	355	356	357	358	359	360	361
Meywar	...	...	...	...	...	...	...	...	...	...	...	...	...	...	...	...	...	...	...	...	...	22,829	*12,499*	10,330	729	*405*	324
Banswara	...	...	...	...	...	...	...	...	...	...	...	...	...	...	...	...	...	...	...	...	...	...	...	...	...	...	...
Dungarpur	...	...	...	...	...	...	...	...	...	...	...	...	...	...	...	...	...	...	...	...	...	543	*224*	319	...	...	...
Partabgarh	...	...	...	...	...	...	...	...	...	...	...	...	...	...	...	...	...	...	...	...	...	...	...	...	...	...	...
Marwar	...	...	...	...	...	...	...	...	...	...	...	...	...	...	...	...	...	...	...	...	...	...	...	...	50,533	*28,054*	22,479
Sirohi	...	...	...	...	...	...	...	...	...	...	...	...	...	...	...	...	...	...	...	...	...	...	...	...	11,580	*5,727*	5,853
Jesalmir	...	...	...	...	...	...	...	...	...	...	...	...	...	...	...	...	...	...	...	...	...	...	...	...	8,710	*4,576*	4,134
Bikanir	...	...	...	...	...	...	...	...	...	...	...	...	...	...	...	...	...	...	...	...	...	38	*17*	21	2,067	*1,126*	941
Jeypore	...	...	...	...	...	...	...	...	...	...	...	...	...	...	...	...	...	...	...	...	...	...	...	...	87	*61*	26
Kishengarh	...	...	...	...	...	...	...	...	...	...	...	...	...	...	...	...	...	...	...	...	...	9	...	9	15	*11*	4
Lawa	...	...	...	...	...	...	...	...	...	...	...	...	...	...	...	...	...	...	...	...	...	...	...	...	4	*2*	2
Bharatpur	...	...	...	...	...	...	...	...	...	...	...	...	...	...	...	...	...	...	...	...	...	155	*91*	64	115	*55*	60
Karauli	...	...	...	...	...	...	...	...	...	...	...	...	...	...	...	...	...	...	...	...	...	160	*69*	91	30	*14*	16
Dholpur	54	*3*	51	639	*276*	363	...	...	...	...	...	...	...	...	...	...	...	...	...	...	...	1,140	*398*	742	4,654	*2,761*	1,893
Alwar	...	...	...	...	...	...	...	...	...	...	...	...	...	...	...	31	*11*	20	22	*18*	4	97	*56*	41	435	*229*	206
Jhallawar	...	...	...	...	...	...	27	*3*	24	27	*23*	4	31	*5*	26	...	...	...	...	...	...	124	*60*	64	86	*36*	50
Tonk	...	...	...	...	...	...	...	...	...	...	...	...	...	...	...	...	...	...	...	...	...	248	*119*	129	...	...	...
Bundi	...	...	...	...	...	...	...	...	...	...	...	...	...	...	...	...	...	...	...	...	...	...	...	...	27	*12*	15
Shahpura	...	...	...	...	...	...	...	...	...	...	...	...	...	...	...	...	...	...	...	...	...	12	*8*	4	...	...	...
Kota	...	...	...	...	...	...	...	...	...	...	...	...	...	...	...	...	...	...	...	...	...	...	...	...	92	*22*	70
Erinpura	...	...	...	...	...	...	...	...	...	...	...	...	...	...	...	...	...	...	...	...	...	...	...	...	31	*23*	8
Kherwara	...	...	...	...	...	...	...	...	...	...	...	...	...	...	...	...	...	...	...	...	...	...	...	...	12	*8*	4
Kotra	...	...	...	...	...	...	...	...	...	...	...	...	...	...	...	...	...	...	...	...	...	...	...	...	4	*4*	...
Abu	...	...	...	...	...	...	...	...	...	...	...	...	...	...	...	...	...	...	...	...	...	...	...	...	...	...	...
Total	**54**	**3**	**51**	**639**	**276**	**363**	**27**	**3**	**24**	**27**	**23**	**4**	**31**	**5**	**26**	**31**	**11**	**20**	**22**	**18**	**4**	**25,855**	**13,541**	**11,814**	**79,211**	**43,126**	**36,085**

RAJPUTANA AGENCY.

CENSUS OF 1891.

PROVINCIAL TABLE VII.—PART I.

Statement showing the number of Eunuchs by Age.

PROVINCIAL TABLE.

TABLE VII.—Part I.—Statement showing the number of Eunuchs by Age.

NAMES OF STATES.	TOTAL.	AGE PERIOD.												
		0—4	5—9	10—14	15—19	20—24	25—29	30—34	35—39	40—44	45—49	50—54	55—59	60 and over.
1	2	3	4	5	6	7	8	9	10	11	12	13	14	15
1. METWAR	22	1	...	2	...	2	3	4	3	2	1	3	...	1
2. BANSWARA	4	...	...	...	...	...	1	...	...	1	...	...	...	2
3. DUNGARPUR	6	...	...	...	...	2	2	...	...	...	...	...	1	1
4. PARTABGARH	4	...	...	...	...	1	...	1	1	1	...	...	...	...
5. MARWAR	125	...	2	2	1	4	11	27	10	19	8	11	7	23
6. SIROHI	...	...	...	...	...	...	...	...	...	...	...	...	...	...
7. JESALMIR	1	...	1	...	...	...	...	...	...	...	...	...	...	...
8. BIKANIR	11	...	...	...	1	2	1	2	...	...	2	1	1	1
9. JEYPORE	68	1	1	2	3	4	7	8	4	7	2	7	3	19
10. KISHENGARH	13	2	1	...	1	2	1	...	...	...	1	2	...	3
11. LAWA	...	...	...	...	...	...	...	...	...	...	...	...	...	...
12. BHARATPUR	20	...	1	...	...	...	1	2	1	4	1	3	...	7
13. KARAULI	4	...	...	...	1	...	1	...	...	1	...	...	...	1
14. DHOLPUR	12	...	...	...	...	...	1	...	1	1	...	2	2	5
15. ALWAR	12	...	...	...	...	...	1	1	...	1	...	1	1	7
16. JHALLAWAR	1	...	...	...	...	...	...	...	1	...	...	...	...	...
17. TONK	16	1	...	...	...	...	1	6	...	4	...	3	...	1
18. BUNDI	7	...	1	1	...	3	...	...	1	...	...	1	...	...
19. SHAHPURA	...	...	...	...	...	...	...	...	...	...	...	...	...	...
20. KOTA	30	...	...	...	2	4	7	6	1	3	2	1	2	2
Total	356	5	7	7	9	24	38	57	23	44	17	35	17	73

RAJPUTANA AGENCY.

CENSUS OF 1891.

PROVINCIAL TABLE VII.—PART II.

Statement showing the number of Eunuchs by Caste.

PROVINCIAL TABLE.

TABLE VII.—Part II.—Statement showing the number of Eunuchs by Caste.

Caste, etc.	Total Number of Eunuchs.	Meywar.	Banswara.	Dungarpur.	Partabgarh.	Marwar.	Sirohi.	Jesalmir.	Bikanir.	Jeypore.	Kishengarh.	Lawa.	Bharatpur.	Karauli.	Dholpur.	Alwar.	Jhallawar.	Tonk.	Bundi.	Shahpura.	Kotah.
	Males.	Males.	Males.	Males.	Males.	Males.	Males.	Males.	Males.	Males.	Males.	Males.	Males.	Males.	Males.	Males.	Males.	Males.	Males.	Males.	Males.
1	2	3	4	5	6	7	8	9	10	11	12	13	14	15	16	17	18	19	20	21	22
1. Rajput (Hindu)	20	...	1	...	...	13	...	...	1	4	...	...	...	...	...	1	...	...	...	...	...
2. Mahajan (Jain and Hindu)	9	...	...	...	...	1	...	...	1	5	...	...	...	2	...	...	...	...	...	...	...
3. Brahmin (Hindu)	20	...	1	...	...	6	...	...	...	4	...	...	...	1	...	2	...	1	2	...	3
4. Jat "	13	...	...	...	...	7	...	...	2	1	2	...	...	...	...	...	...	...	...	...	1
5. Kumhar "	8	...	...	...	...	5	...	...	...	1	...	...	...	...	1	...	...	...	...	...	1
6. Mali "	14	...	...	...	...	3	...	...	...	3	...	...	...	...	...	...	...	...	...	...	8
7. Kayasth "	1	...	...	...	...	1	...	...	...	...	...	...	...	...	...	...	...	...	...	...	...
8. Sadh "	2	...	...	...	...	2	...	...	...	...	...	...	...	...	...	...	...	...	...	...	...
9. Bhil (Animistic)	3	...	...	...	...	3	...	...	...	...	...	...	...	...	...	...	...	...	...	...	...
10. Chakar (Hindu)	2	...	...	...	...	2	...	...	...	...	...	...	...	...	...	...	...	...	...	...	...
11. Mina "	5	...	...	...	...	2	...	...	...	2	...	...	...	...	...	1	...	...	...	...	...
12. Bambhi "	1	...	...	...	...	1	...	...	...	...	...	...	...	...	...	...	...	...	...	...	...
13. Jogi "	2	...	...	...	...	1	...	...	...	...	...	...	...	...	...	...	...	...	...	...	1
14. Bishnoi "	3	...	...	...	...	2	...	1	...	...	...	...	...	...	...	...	...	...	...	...	...
15. Chamar "	2	...	...	...	...	...	...	...	...	1	...	...	...	1	...	...	...	...	...	...	...
16. Balai "	3	...	...	...	...	...	...	...	...	1	...	...	...	...	...	...	...	...	1	...	1
17. Daroga "	2	...	...	...	...	...	...	...	...	2	...	...	...	...	...	...	...	...	...	...	...
18. Darzi "	1	...	...	...	...	...	...	...	...	1	...	...	...	...	...	...	...	...	...	...	...
19. Gatrara "	1	...	...	...	...	...	...	...	...	1	...	...	...	...	...	...	...	...	...	...	...
20. Gujar "	4	...	...	...	...	...	...	...	...	2	...	...	...	...	...	...	...	2	...	...	...
21. Khati "	1	...	...	...	...	...	...	...	...	1	...	...	...	...	...	...	...	...	...	...	...
22. Khatic "	1	...	...	...	...	...	...	...	...	1	...	...	...	...	...	...	...	...	...	...	...
23. Koli "	3	...	...	...	...	...	...	...	...	2	...	...	...	...	...	...	...	...	1	...	...
24. Bhand "	1	...	...	...	...	...	...	...	...	...	...	...	...	...	...	...	...	...	1	...	...
25. Swami "	1	...	...	...	...	...	...	...	...	1	...	...	...	...	...	...	...	...	...	...	...
26. Kachi "	1	...	...	...	...	...	...	...	...	...	...	...	...	...	...	...	...	...	1	...	...
27. Bagri "	1	...	...	...	...	...	...	...	...	...	1	...	...	...	...	...	...	...	...	...	...
28. Dakot "	1	...	...	...	...	...	...	...	...	...	1	...	...	...	...	...	...	...	...	...	...
29. Goosain "	1	...	...	...	...	...	...	...	...	...	1	...	...	...	...	...	...	...	...	...	...
30. Khatri "	1	...	...	...	...	...	...	...	1	...	...	...	...	...	...	...	...	...	...	...	...
31. Sunar "	1	...	...	...	...	...	...	...	1	...	...	...	...	...	...	...	...	...	...	...	...
32. Chipa "	6	...	...	...	...	...	...	...	...	...	...	...	...	...	...	...	...	...	...	...	6
33. Khanzad "	2	...	...	...	...	...	...	...	...	...	...	...	...	...	...	...	...	...	...	...	2
34. Nai "	1	...	...	...	...	...	...	...	...	...	...	...	...	...	...	...	...	...	...	...	1
35. Teli "	2	...	...	...	...	...	...	...	...	...	...	...	...	...	...	...	...	...	...	...	2
36. Tamboli "	1	...	...	...	...	...	...	...	...	...	...	...	...	...	...	...	...	...	...	...	1
37. Others "	48	...	2	...	...	46	...	...	...	...	...	...	...	...	...	...	...	...	...	...	...
38. Sheikh (Musalman)	103	...	...	6	...	...	...	...	5	35	8	...	20	...	10	2	...	13	1	...	3
39. Pathan "	5	...	...	...	...	...	...	...	...	...	...	...	...	...	...	5	...	...	...	...	...
40. Sayad "	2	...	...	...	...	...	...	...	...	...	...	...	...	...	1	1	...	...	...	...	...
41. Musalman "	56	22	...	...	4	30	...	...	...	...	...	...	...	...	...	...	...	...	...	...	...
42. Pinjara "	1	...	...	...	...	...	...	...	...	...	...	...	...	...	...	...	1	...	...	...	...
GRAND TOTAL	356	22	4	6	4	125	...	1	11	68	13	...	20	4	12	12	1	16	7	...	30

RAJPUTANA AGENCY.

CENSUS OF 1891.

PROVINCIAL TABLE VIII.

Statement showing the distribution of Christians in Rajputana by Race, and for territorial units.

PROVINCIAL TABLE.

TABLE VIII.—Statement showing the distribution of Christians in Rajputana by Race.

Names of States.	FOREIGNERS.																										
	Total.			English.			Irish.			Scotch.			German.			French.			Russian.			Spanish.			Swiss.		
	Total.	Males.	Females.	Total.	Males.	Females.	Total.	Males.	Females.	Total.	Males.	Females.	Total.	Males.	Females.	Total.	Males.	Females.	Total.	Males.	Females.	Total.	Males.	Females.	Total.	Males.	Females.
1	2	3	4	5	6	7	8	9	10	11	12	13	14	15	16	17	18	19	20	21	22	23	24	25	26	27	28
Meywar	115	70	45	24	11	13	2	2	...	6	4	2	...	...	...	...	...	...	...	...	...	...	...	...	...	...	...
Banswara	...	...	...	...	...	...	...	...	...	...	...	...	...	...	...	...	...	...	...	...	...	...	...	...	...	...	...
Partabgarh	1	1	...	...	...	...	...	...	...	...	...	...	...	...	...	...	...	...	...	...	...	...	...	...	...	...	...
Dungarpur	...	...	...	...	...	...	...	...	...	...	...	...	...	...	...	...	...	...	...	...	...	...	...	...	...	...	...
Marwar	186	105	81	58	28	30	31	16	15	8	5	3	...	...	...	...	...	...	...	...	...	...	...	...	...	...	...
Sirohi and Abu	459	271	188	170	102	68	22	15	7	21	10	11	1	1	...	2	...	2	...	...	...	...	...	...	...	...	...
Jesalmir	...	...	...	...	...	...	...	...	...	...	...	...	...	...	...	...	...	...	...	...	...	...	...	...	...	...	...
Bikanir	21	13	8	5	4	1	2	1	1	1	...	1	...	...	...	...	...	...	...	...	...	...	...	...	...	...	...
Jeypore	706	375	331	163	89	74	50	25	25	43	22	21	10	2	8	4	4	...	3	1	2	1	1	...	...	...	...
Kishengarh	21	11	10	...	...	...	...	...	...	...	...	...	...	...	...	...	...	...	...	...	...	...	...	...	...	...	...
Lawa	...	...	...	...	...	...	...	...	...	...	...	...	...	...	...	...	...	...	...	...	...	...	...	...	...	...	...
Bharatpur	6	4	2	4	2	2	...	...	...	...	...	...	...	...	...	...	...	...	...	...	...	...	...	...	...	...	...
Karauli	13	7	6	5	3	2	1	1	...	...	...	...	...	...	...	...	...	...	...	...	...	...	...	...	...	...	...
Dholpur	6	5	1	2	2	...	4	3	1	...	...	...	...	...	...	...	...	...	...	...	...	...	...	...	...	...	...
Alwar	166	93	73	17	10	7	3	1	2	11	4	7	...	...	...	...	...	...	...	...	...	...	...	...	1	...	1
Tonk*	13	8	5	3	2	1	...	...	...	...	...	...	...	...	...	...	...	...	...	...	...	...	...	...	...	...	...
Bundi	...	...	...	...	...	...	...	...	...	...	...	...	...	...	...	...	...	...	...	...	...	...	...	...	...	...	...
Shahpura	2	2	...	...	...	...	...	...	...	...	...	...	...	...	...	1	1	...	...	...	...	...	...	...	...	...	...
Jhallawar	18	6	12	8	2	6	1	1	...	1	...	1	...	...	...	...	...	...	...	...	...	...	...	...	...	...	...
Kota	55	26	29	...	...	...	...	...	...	4	2	2	...	...	...	...	...	...	...	...	...	...	...	...	...	...	...
Erinpura	20	13	7	11	6	5	...	...	...	4	2	2	...	...	...	...	...	...	...	...	...	...	...	...	...	...	...
Kherwara	16	9	7	11	5	6	...	...	...	...	...	...	...	...	...	...	...	...	...	...	...	...	...	...	...	...	...
Kotra	6	3	3	3	1	2	...	...	...	...	...	...	...	...	...	...	...	...	...	...	...	...	...	...	...	...	...
Abu	25	16	9	20	14	6	5	2	3	...	...	...	...	...	...	...	...	...	...	...	...	...	...	...	...	...	...
TOTAL RAJPUTANA	1,855	1,088	817	504	281	223	121	67	54	99	49	50	11	8	8	7	5	2	3	1	2	1	1	...	1	...	1

* Excluding Tonk in Central India T. 7, M. 5, F. 2 Native Christians.

Table VIII.—Christians—Rajputana Agency.

Names of States.	FOREIGNERS—contd. Greek. Total.	Males.	Females.	American. Total.	Males.	Females.	Australian. Total.	Males.	Females.	African. Total.	Males.	Females.	Total Foreigners. Total.	Males.	Females.	EURASIANS. Armenian. Total.	Males.	Females.	Eurasians. Total.	Males.	Females.	Indo-Portuguese. Total.	Males.	Females.	Total Eurasians. Total.	Males.	Females.	NATIVES. Convert. Total.	Males.	Females.
	29	30	31	32	33	34	35	36	37	38	39	40	41	42	43	44	45	46	47	48	49	50	51	52	53	54	55	56	57	58
Mewar	...	...	...	...	...	...	...	...	...	...	...	...	32	17	15	...	...	...	6	3	3	2	1	1	8	4	4	75	49	26
Banswara	...	...	...	...	...	...	...	...	...	...	...	...	...	...	...	...	...	...	...	...	...	...	...	...	...	...	...	...	...	...
Partabgarh	...	...	...	...	...	...	...	...	...	...	...	...	...	...	...	...	...	...	...	...	...	...	...	...	...	...	...	1	1	...
Dungarpur	...	...	...	...	...	...	...	...	...	...	...	...	...	...	...	...	...	...	...	...	...	...	...	...	...	...	...	...	...	...
Marwar	...	...	...	4	1	3	...	...	...	...	...	...	101	50	51	...	...	...	13	5	8	1	1	...	14	6	8	71	49	22
Sirohi and Abu	...	...	...	6	2	4	...	...	...	...	...	...	222	130	92	...	...	...	103	53	50	19	15	4	122	68	54	115	73	42
Jesalmir	...	...	...	...	...	...	...	...	...	...	...	...	...	...	...	...	...	...	...	...	...	...	...	...	...	...	...	...	...	...
Bikanir	...	...	...	...	...	...	...	...	...	...	...	...	8	5	3	...	...	...	4	2	2	...	...	...	4	2	2	9	6	3
Jeypore	2	1	1	4	2	2	1	...	1	1	1	...	282	148	134	3	2	1	224	116	108	16	7	9	243	125	118	181	102	79
Kishengarh	...	...	...	...	...	...	...	...	...	...	...	...	...	...	...	...	...	...	...	...	...	...	...	...	...	...	...	21	11	10
Lawa	...	...	...	...	...	...	...	...	...	...	...	...	...	...	...	...	...	...	...	...	...	...	...	...	...	...	...	...	...	...
Bharatpur	...	...	...	...	...	...	...	...	...	...	...	...	4	2	2	...	...	...	...	...	...	...	...	...	...	...	...	2	2	...
Karauli	...	...	...	...	...	...	...	...	...	...	...	...	6	4	2	...	...	...	7	3	4	...	...	...	7	3	4	...	...	...
Dholpur	...	...	...	...	...	...	...	...	...	...	...	...	6	5	1	...	...	...	...	...	...	...	...	...	...	...	...	...	...	...
Alwar	...	...	...	...	...	...	...	...	...	...	...	...	32	15	17	...	...	...	17	11	6	8	4	4	25	15	10	109	63	46
Tonk*	...	...	...	...	...	...	...	...	...	...	...	...	3	2	1	...	...	...	...	...	...	...	...	...	...	...	...	10	6	4
Bundi	...	...	...	...	...	...	...	...	...	...	...	...	...	...	...	...	...	...	...	...	...	...	...	...	...	...	...	...	...	...
Shahpura	...	...	...	...	...	...	...	...	...	...	...	...	1	1	...	...	...	...	...	...	...	...	...	...	...	...	...	1	1	...
Jhallawar	...	...	...	...	...	...	...	...	...	...	...	...	10	3	7	...	...	...	7	2	5	1	1	...	8	3	5	...	...	...
Kota	...	...	...	...	...	...	...	...	...	...	...	...	4	2	2	...	...	...	...	...	...	...	...	...	...	...	...	51	24	27
Erinpura	...	...	...	...	...	...	...	...	...	...	...	...	15	8	7	...	...	...	5	5	...	...	...	...	5	5	...	...	...	...
Kherwara	...	...	...	...	...	...	...	...	...	...	...	...	11	5	6	...	...	...	5	4	1	...	...	...	5	4	1	...	...	...
Kotra	...	...	...	...	...	...	...	...	...	...	...	...	3	1	2	...	...	...	...	...	...	3	2	1	3	2	1	...	...	...
Abu	...	...	...	...	...	...	...	...	...	...	...	...	25	16	9	...	...	...	...	...	...	...	...	...	...	...	...	...	...	...
TOTAL RAJPUTANA	2	1	1	14	5	9	1	...	1	1	1	...	765	414	351	3	2	1	391	204	187	50	31	19	444	237	207	646	387	259

* Excluding Tonk in Central India T. M. F. 7 5 2 Native Christians.